Justifying Legal Punishment

Studies in Applied Philosophy
Series Editors: Brenda Almond and Anthony O'Hear

Forthcoming

Geoffrey Brown
*The Information Game: Ethical Issues
in a Microchip World*

Justifying Legal Punishment

Igor Primoratz

HUMANITIES PRESS INTERNATIONAL, INC.
New Jersey ◇ London

First published in 1989 by Humanities Press International, Inc.
Atlantic Highlands, NJ 07716

©Igor Primoratz, 1989

Library of Congress Cataloging-in-Publication Data
Primorac, Igor
    Justifying legal punishment / Igor Primoratz.
    p.   cm.   —— (Studies in applied philosophy)
    Bibliography: p.
    Includes index.
    ISBN 0–391–03574–6
    1. Punishment — Philosophy. 2. Punishment — Moral and
    ethical
aspects.   I. Title.
HV8675.P75 1989
364.6 — dc19   88–9198
                                          CIP

British Cataloguing in Publication Data
A CIP record for this book is available from the British Library.

Printed in the United States of America

For Edna

Contents

ACKNOWLEDGMENTS

I would like to thank very warmly Professor Bernard Gert of Dartmouth College and Dr. Miri Gur-Arye of the Hebrew University, who read the manuscript with great care and were generous with their time in discussing many deficiencies that plagued it. Their comments and criticisms were of great help in the final revision of the book; they saved me from several bad arguments and many unsatisfactory formulations. Even in cases where I eventually did not follow their suggestions I learned much from them.

Professor Richard M. Hare and Professor Herbert L.A. Hart kindly read the sections devoted to their respective theories of punishment; their comments helped me toward better understanding their views. I am very grateful to them.

I have also learned much from those who have criticized in print the views on punishment I advanced in some earlier publications: Professor Mario A. Cattaneo of the University of Ferrara, who discussed critically my account of Beccaria (*Beccaria e Kant. Il valore dell 'uomo nel diritto penale* [Sassari: Università di Sassari, 1981], pp. 20–30); Justice Haim H. Cohn (ret.) of the Supreme Court of Israel, who reviewed my study of Hegel's theory of punishment and criticized the retributive views propounded in it ("Ghosts of Punishment," *Israel Law Review* 22 [1987]); Professor Michael H. Mitias of Millsaps College, who subjected to detailed critical scrutiny my defense of the *lex talionis* ("Is Retributivism Inconsistent without *Lex Talionis?*," *Rivista Internazionale di Filosofia del Diritto* 60 [1983]); Professor Thomas Morawetz of the University of Connecticut, who commented on my analysis of several middle-of-the-road theories of punishment ("Comment," in R. Gavison [ed.], *Issues in Contemporary Legal Philosophy: The Influence of H.L.A. Hart* [Oxford: Oxford University Press, 1987]); Professor Don E. Scheid of the University of Utah, who responded to my critique of his interpretation of Kant's theory of punishment ("Kant's Retributivism Again," *Archiv für Rechts- und Sozialphilosophie* 72 [1986]); and Dr. Leslie Sebba of the Hebrew University, who argued against my defense of capital punishment ("On Capital Punishment — A Comment," *Israel Law Review* 17 [1982]). Although a measure of disagreement persists, their comments and objections have been very helpful.

In writing the book I made use of the material in some of my earlier publications on punishment. I am grateful for kind permission to do so to the editors and publishers of *Analysis, Archiv für Rechts- und Sozialphilosophie, Hegel–Studien, International Philosophical Quarterly, Israel Law Review, Philosophy, Rivista Internazionale di Filosofia del Diritto*, and the collection *Issues in Contemporary Legal Philosophy*.

Part of the work on the book was done in the academic year 1981/2, which I spent as a post-doctoral fellow in the Department of Philosophy of the Hebrew University. I would like to acknowledge with gratitude a grant from the Muriel and Philip Berman Scholarship and Fellowship Program, which made that possible.

1. Introduction

1. What Is Punishment?

The word "punishment" is used in various contexts. We say that a parent has punished a child, or that a teacher has punished a pupil; that a referee has punished a football player; that a party committee has punished a member of the party; that a judge has punished an offender; that God has punished a sinner. A systematic discussion of punishment in general would have to start with an investigation of basic characteristics of the use of the word "punishment" in the contexts of talking about family or school education, sporting games, voluntary associations, criminal law, or religious beliefs. Such an investigation should enable us to establish whether the use of the word in all these different contexts exhibits a common core, a set of characteristics which is the necessary and sufficient condition for applying the word "punishment," which defines "punishment" in general — or perhaps it is not at all proper to talk about "punishment in general," because God's punishment, punishment as a means of education, as an element of a game, as a disciplinary measure in a voluntary association and legal punishment are connected only by family resemblances.[1]

But I am not going to discuss this question. For this book does not deal with punishment in general (if there is such a thing), but with a specific kind of punishment only — *legal punishment*. When taken in this specific sense, "punishment" can be defined as an *evil* deliberately inflicted *qua* evil on an *offender* by a *human agency* which is *authorized* by the legal order whose laws the offender has violated. Let me say a few words about each of these components of the definition.

(1) Punishment is sometimes defined as a pain or suffering inflicted on an offender. Such a definition would be too narrow. When we mention suffering in this context, and when we mention pain even more so, we tend to think of physical suffering, physical pain. In earlier centuries punishments very frequently consisted of infliction of physical pain, physical suffering; in more recent times, however, there are hardly any punishments which would inflict this kind of pain or suffering on the convict, at least in civilized countries. But even if we were to emphasize

1

that the words "pain" or "suffering" are taken in a wider sense, so as to include mental pain and suffering, the definition would still be too narrow. For in our own time, the criminal-law systems of civilized countries as a rule provide for punishments which do not inflict pain or suffering of any kind on the convict — neither physical nor mental — but deprive him of a good he would want to keep: a fine deprives him of a certain sum of money, a prison term deprives him of liberty for a certain period of time, capital punishment deprives him of life. The conditions in which a convict is going to spend time in prison by no means have to be such as to cause him pain or suffering; even the most severe of all penalties, the penalty of death, is today generally carried out in such a way as to make it as painless as possible for the convict. Therefore it is better to define punishment as an *evil* inflicted on an offender. "Evil" is taken here in a formal sense, meaning "anything that people do not want to be inflicted on them."

It is a fact, though, that there are people who deliberately commit an offense in order to end up in jail and spend some time there, and even those who murder in order to be executed (so that their misdeed is, basically, an indirect suicide of sorts). If we define punishment as an evil, shall we have to say that such offenders in fact are not punished at all? Alternatively, if we are not ready to embrace this implication, do we have to give up the definition of punishment in terms of evil? We need not accept either alternative. For when we define punishment as an evil inflicted on an offender, and when, in the role of a lawgiver, we compile a code of criminal law and determine the punishments which will be inflicted for various offenses, we do not think of each and every individual case of punishing an individual offender; we make use of some experiential conclusions about what people *as a rule* do not want to be inflicted on them. People as a rule do not want their money to be taken away from them, or to be put in jail and made to stay there for a period of time, or to be electrocuted, or hanged; therefore, to inflict any of these things on someone means, as a rule, to inflict an evil on them. For this reason we have fines, prison terms, and executions as punishments. These are *punishments* in spite of the fact that in certain exceptional cases they are not evil for the convict — precisely because such cases are exceptional. If some day people change so much as to come to like, as a rule, to have their money taken away from them, to live in prisons, and to be executed rather than to wait for their natural deaths, or if they come to be quite indifferent to such possibilities, then to sentence a person to any of these will, in general, no longer mean to punish. In such a case we would have to introduce some new punishments, quite different from those we know — punishments which in those changed circumstances would amount to things people as a rule do not want to be inflicted on them, that is, which would amount to instances of evil.

(2) An *offender* is a person who has committed an offense. By "offense" we sometimes mean a violation of a moral norm; but the primary meaning of the word, the meaning we most frequently have in mind, is "a violation of the criminal law." This is the meaning the word has when used to define legal punishment.[2] I should emphasize that, when I define punishment as an evil inflicted on an offender, by "offender" I mean a person who has offended against *any* positive criminal law, no matter whether that law is just or unjust, whether it is an expression of a condition of universal freedom or of a tyrant's arbitrary will, whether it is morally legitimate or not.

But does "punishment" as a matter of fact always mean "an evil inflicted on an *offender*"? Does it not happen that a person who is not an offender, who has not offended against the law, gets punished? Judges are no more infallible than the rest of us; thus it can happen, and sometimes it does happen, that a judge sentences a defendant who actually has not committed the offense he is charged with. Now, when a person who has been sentenced by mistake spends time in jail or gets executed, is this not punishment in the same sense and to the same degree as if he were really guilty as charged? No doubt we would be willing to apply the word "punishment" in such cases as well; but it does not follow that we have to give up the definition of "punishment" as an evil inflicted on an offender. The only thing we have to do is to refine it: punishment is the infliction of an evil on a person *believed to be* an offender by those who decide on it. This belief on the part of the judges is (one hopes) true; still, sometimes it can be false. But even if it were more often false than true, that would not mean that we could no longer speak of punishments; for it is the belief mentioned, and not the fact that makes the belief true, which is a logical presupposition of punishment.

(3) The definition of punishment as an evil *deliberately* inflicted *qua* evil on an offender by *human agency* excludes, first, evil which might befall him as a natural consequence of his offense. The taking of narcotics, for instance, may be prohibited by the criminal law, and when mental disturbances result, that is no doubt an evil; although the evil is a consequence of the offense, it is not a punishment for it. Punishment presupposes a *punishing subject*. The latter is never the same person that

is being punished, but *someone else*. To be sure, some psychologists and some writers speak of "self-punishment." But even if that is really punishment in a literal, and not in a secondary, parasitic sense of the word (I shall leave this question aside), legal punishment cannot be self-punishment. Even if an offender happened to be a judge, he could not try his own case and convict and sentence himself. Finally, the definition excludes the evil which someone might inflict on an offender altogether unintentionally, or without an intention to inflict an *evil*. The case in point with regard to the latter possibility is compensation, which is liable to be considered an evil by the person made to extend it, but is not *meant* to be considered as such by him. He might as well be indifferent to the fact that he is made to compensate his victim, or even welcome the opportunity to do so. In this respect, punishment differs from compensation: it is meant to be an evil, and to be seen as such by the person at the receiving end.

(4) When someone deliberately inflicts an evil *qua* evil on another person, who is an offender, that still may not be punishment. The victim of the offense, or a relative or a friend, can take revenge on the offender; the mob can lynch him; but neither will be punishment. One can be punished only by a judge, or a jailer, or an executioner; for only these are *authorized* to so do by the legal order against which he has offended.

The definition of punishment which I have expounded contains four out of the five components of a definition widely used in recent philosophical literature, which is known as the "Flew-Benn-Hart definition."[3] In the opinion of these philosophers, in addition to the four components I have listed, punishment is also characterized as being inflicted *for an offense* (this is the second characteristic of punishment on their list). Ted Honderich has excluded this from the definition of punishment, for two reasons. First, to exclude it would mean to prejudge the issue of the moral justification of punishment. To say that punishment is by definition an evil inflicted for an offense, he writes,

> may be taken to imply that the moral justification of punishing a man is that he deserves it for what he has done. If we were to use this description, it might appear that we had so described punishment that the question . . . "What, if anything, justifies it morally?", was already answered by the description. The answer might appear to be built in and anyone who disputes it, or anyone else for that matter, might protest that the outcome of the inquiry could hardly be in doubt.

Second, such a definition would be too narrow: it would entail that punishment be only such evil which a judge metes out to an offender in the belief that it is morally justified because the latter has committed an offense and thereby has deserved it.[4] In my view, however, neither of the two arguments is convincing. The definition of punishment as an evil inflicted for an offense implies nothing with respect to its moral justification. To say that punishment is inflicted *for* an offense is to say that the offense is a reason for punishing; but this does not mean that it is its *moral* reason, that it is what gives us the *moral* justification to punish. The offense can be a reason of some other kind, so that the issue of moral justification of punishment remains open. Neither does the definition of punishment as an evil inflicted for an offense imply that a judge, when punishing, believes that the offense is the *moral* reason, the *moral* justification of inflicting an evil on the offender; it implies merely that for her the offense is a reason of an unspecified kind for punishing, so that the question of her belief about the moral reason, or moral justification of punishment, remains open as well. She can see the moral reason for punishment, the moral justification of it, in something else, and the evil she inflicts on the offender will still be punishment.

Nevertheless, punishment ought not to be defined as an evil inflicted for an offense. Such a definition would not imply that we have punishment only when the evil a judge inflicts on someone is her moral reason for doing so. But it would imply that the judge sees the offense as *some kind* of reason; and that would make it too narrow. If a judge says that she is punishing an offender, but not because the latter has committed an offense, for that, in her eyes, is no reason at all — neither a moral reason nor any other kind of reason — but because of the consequences the punishment is going to have, that would not mean that the evil she is inflicting on the offender is not punishment, but something else. And the definition of punishment as an evil inflicted for an offense would imply precisely this.

The most natural interpretation of the assertion that punishment is inflicted *for* an offense is to say that an offense is a reason for punishment. Could we, perhaps, interpret this assertion in another way, as an assertion that an offense is a *logical presupposition* of punishment? Thus construed, the contention would imply nothing about *reasons* for punishment; it would only state one of its logical conditions. But if we take *this* to be the meaning of the assertion, there is no need to introduce it into the definition of punishment. That an offense or, to be more precise, a belief that an offense has been committed, is a logical condition of punishment — this is already contained in the definition of punishment as an evil inflicted on an offender, or a person believed to be one.

Some authors include in the definition of punishment the idea of justice and proportion between offense and the evil inflicted by way of punishment. Sidney Gendin, for instance, writes that it could be claimed that "for punishment *to be* punishment it must be just — the suffering or deprivation must fit the crime." But if so, how shall we account for the fact that one can say without contradiction of a punishment that it is unjust, too severe, cruel? In his opinion, this can be explained

> by the fact that what the party imposing the suffering thinks constitutes a just punishment may be radically at odds with what an observer thinks is just. It would be queer if the one imposing the punishment considered it cruel and unjust. But if the observer believes that the party is not concerning himself with the matter of justice then he will withhold the appellation "punishment" altogether, rather than merely regard what he sees as a cruel and unjust punishment. Thus "cruel and unjust punishment" is not self-contradictory even though it is true that punishment to be punishment involves a consideration of justice. The expression is used by those passing judgment on those doing the punishing. It presupposes that those doing the punishing are trying to do what is right and, in the opinion of the observer, are failing to do so.[5]

Now, we might find it queer if a judge holds that she ought not to pay any attention to considerations of justice and may mete out punishments out of any proportion to the gravity of offenses committed; but I cannot see that this would be reason enough to claim that what is being inflicted is not punishment at all. It is a fact that sometimes punishments are meted out deliberately, without any thought of desert and justice, according to quite different criteria. In such cases, we do not say that these are no punishments at all — we say that these are unjust and morally unacceptable *punishments*. To define punishment in such a way as to imply that punishing people without regard to the gravity of their offenses and without thinking of desert and justice actually is no punishing at all would mean, first, to depart in an important aspect from the meaning that the word "punishment" has in ordinary language; second, to confuse the concepts of "punishment" and "deserved punishment," or "just punishment"; and third, to prejudge, in a logically inadmissible way, the *ethical* issue of the moral justification of punishment by an assertion about the meaning of the word "punishment."

2. The Philosophical Problem of Punishment

Legal punishment is a topic dealt with by several social sciences. Psychology explores the psychological mechanisms which characterize the behavior of those who get punished. Sociologists deal with the social nature and functions of punishment and the relationships between punishment and the various components of its social context. Penology studies the various types of punishment and their efficiency as means of securing socially accepted objectives of punishment. The theory of the criminal law treats punishment as an institution of the positive law, analyzing and commenting upon those rules of the system that have to do with punishment.

The philosophical approach to punishment is different from all these mentioned. To punish means to inflict an evil. But to inflict evil on someone is something that, at least *prima facie*, ought not to be done. So the question arises: What is the *moral justification* of inflicting the evil of punishment on people? What are the moral reasons which provide a justification and consecration of the evil we inflict on others when punishing them, setting it apart from the evil which we might inflict outside the framework of the institution of punishment and which would be morally unjustified and illegitimate? This is the question about punishment which is being discussed in philosophy — in moral philosophy, because we ask about the *moral* justification, and in legal philosophy as well, because what we seek to justify is a *legal* institution.

Who does the punishing? Whose actions do we attempt to justify here? To punish might mean two things: to sentence someone to be punished, and to execute the sentence, to actually inflict the punishment. The first is done by a judge, the second, say, by an executioner. Now this distinction is of no importance when we discuss the definition of punishment; for the evil of which punishment consists is inflicted by both of them deliberately and with authorization. So it can be said of both that they do the punishing. But when we turn to the question of justification, these two roles are no longer equally important. The executioner, to be sure, inflicts the punishment, while the judge merely sentences the offender; thus it might be said that the former punishes directly, and the latter only in an indirect way. Yet it is precisely the part of the judge that is in the forefront of the discussion of the justification of punishment, while the part of the executioner (or the jailer) can be set aside. For the latter merely executes a decision of the former, without having taken part in its passing and without being responsible for its being made. So the question of the moral justification of punishment does not refer to his part in punishing. What he does, when inflicting a punishment, is justified by the very same considerations which justify the judge in condemning an offender to it.

But the judge does not mete out punishments according to personal criteria, but according to the law and on the basis of it. If her authority were not based on the law she would not be a judge and could not mete out punishments. Therefore, the question regarding the moral justification of punishment refers not only to the part of the judge in punishing people, but also to what the legislator does when legislating the criminal law, constituting the role of a judge and giving her the authority to punish, and determining the rules she is to apply in punishing — the rules as to who is going to be punished, how, and for what. The legislator, on his part, does not set up laws in his own name, but in the name of the state or society. So the question of the justification of punishment turns out to be, in the final analysis, the question of the moral right of the state or society to punish. This question refers, first, to *individual punishments*, that is, to what the judge does, and second, to the criminal laws which make up the *institution of punishment*, that is, to what the state or society does through the lawgiver.

This is not all. When we talk about punishment from the moral point of view, we talk not only about the moral right but about the moral duty to punish as well, and also about the kind and amount of punishment morally appropriate for a certain offense, or for a certain kind of offense. We say, for example, that a judge has the moral duty to punish an offender, or that the state has the moral duty to punish offenses. We say that a certain punishment is more (or less) severe than the one which would be morally appropriate. So the problem of the morality of punishment includes the questions of the moral grounds of the *right* to punish and of the moral *duty* to punish, and also what ought to be the *measure* of punishment. These are different, but interconnected questions a philosopher wants to ask about punishment.

The problem of the justification of punishment is a traditional topic in moral and legal philosophy. During the last few decades it has been at the center of discussions in these branches of philosophy. This is one of those philosophical issues which has an obvious and very great practical importance. When we discuss punishment philosophically on the level of individual cases of punishing, we are striving to understand philosophically certain issues which are faced daily and in a very serious way by countless judges and jurymen, prosecutors and defense lawyers, jailers and executioners, offenders and their victims, and finally, all of us who at some time or another, directly or indirectly, have something to do with an offense, a trial, or the carrying out of a punishment. On the level of the institution of punishment, legal and moral philosophy deal with certain issues faced by every state and every society. Punishment is one of the basic institutions of every political society; what it will be like, how it will function, depends a great deal on its moral rationale.

Another reason for the great interest of philosophers in the problem of punishment is more theoretical: this problem can be used very conveniently and fruitfully as a test case for exploring the implications of the two opposed viewpoints in moral philosophy — utilitarianism and deontological ethics. The distinction between the two is a fundamental one in ethics, and their confrontation has been the most conspicuous feature of modern moral philosophy.

3. Philosophical Theories of Punishment

Attempts to answer the question of the moral justification of punishment have been numerous and varied. But most of them can be classified into one of two groups: as utilitarian or retributive theories of punishment.

The utilitarian point of view rests on the belief that human acts — individual acts, and also types of acts, rules for action, and systems of such rules which make up institutions — are to be judged by their consequences. "Utilitarianism" in a wider, generic sense, denotes any theory according to which consequences of our actions are the sole criterion of their morality. (Taken in this sense, the word is synonymous with "consequentialism" and "teleological ethics.") In another sense the term denotes doctrines such as those propounded by Bentham and Mill, according to which the degree to which our actions produce pleasure or happiness, or contribute to the elimination of pain or misery, is the sole criterion of their morality. Utilitarianism in this second, more narrow sense, is but a variety of utilitarianism in the first, generic sense of the word: the variety which determines "good" and "bad" in terms of pleasure and pain, happiness and misery. Historically, this eudaemonistic and hedonistic variety of utilitarianism has been most influential, but it is by no means the only one, for good and bad can be conceived in a more comprehensive way, so as to include values which are not eudaemonic and hedonic (then we have "ideal utilitarianism"). However, these differences between varieties of utilitarianism in the generic sense,

which reflect different conceptions of good and bad, have no implications for the issue of the justification of punishment. When it comes to
punishment, an adherent of hedonistic or eudaemonistic utilitarianism,
and an adherent of ideal utilitarianism as well, will for obvious reasons
refer to the same type of consequences. Therefore, I shall leave these
differences aside, and throughout the book use the word "utilitarianism" in its wider meaning.

The utilitarian theory of punishment is but an application of utilitarianism as a general philosophical theory to the problem of the justification of punishment. According to this theory, punishment is morally
justified by its good consequences. The evil inflicted on the person
punished is morally justified because punishment has consequences
which are good to such a degree that they outweigh both it and the good
consequences of any alternative reaction to law-breaking behavior.

What are these good consequences? Some punishments could be
made to serve as compensation. Punishment can also provide an outlet
for retaliatory feelings which the offense induces in the victim and
others. Satisfaction of these feelings could be seen as a good; but even if
we are not willing to see it this way, punishment would still be valuable
in an indirect way. For if these feelings get no satisfaction by way of
having the offender punished, they are likely to come out in a way
which would endanger the very foundations of the social order. But all
these consequences are of secondary importance. The most important
consequences of punishment are its preventive effects: its contribution
to the prevention of offenses, to the reduction of the rate of law-breaking
behavior. It is in such consequences that a utilitarian sees the real
significance of punishment and its sole, or at least its main, justification.
The basic characteristic of the utilitarian theory of punishment is its
orientatation toward the future; its basic principle is, *punitur ut ne pec-
cetur*.

Preventive effects of punishment have to do, on the one hand, with
the person who has already committed an offense (so-called particular
prevention) and, on the other hand, with those who might do that in the
future (so-called general prevention). Punishment can exert a reformatory influence on a person and thus make him more likely to abide by the
law, or it can deter him from offending against it. In addition to this, it
can disable the offender from repeating his offense, either temporarily or
for good. This last kind of prevention is of secondary importance; it is
possible in some cases only, and frequently has attendant effects
which are so bad that they override its desirable results. Leaving this

method of prevention aside, we can distinguish three varieties of the utilitarian view of punishment:

(1) The theory of *deterrence*: the most important effects of punishment are its deterrent effects, through which, on the one hand, it sways the offender not to repeat the offense and, on the other hand, serves as a frightening example which checks the inclination of potential offenders in the public to violate the law.

(2) The theory of *reformation*: punishment is, above all, a means of reforming the offender; it acts as a vehicle of moral betterment, liberating him from his asocial and criminal habits and inclinations and making him fit to return among honest, law-abiding citizens and to a normal, constructive social life.

(3) The *educative* theory: punishment demonstrates the moral wrongness and unacceptability of offenses, stimulates and strengthens moral beliefs which curb criminal inclinations, and thus acts as a means of moral education of the community.

However important these differences may be from the practical point of view, when we discuss punishment as a philosophical topic we can safely set them aside. For a utilitarian sees the moral justification of punishment in its good consequences; accordingly, in each individual case of punishment, as well as when it comes to the institution of punishment, she will have to take into account *all* its desirable consequences: the contribution to particular prevention and that to general prevention; its reformatory, educative, and deterrent effects. Any kind of preference within this range of types of consequences would be reasonable only if prevention were possible through various methods. Then a utilitarian could claim, say, that it is better to reform people than to frighten them out of violating the law, that punishment ought to prevent law-breaking behavior by its reformatory, not by its deterrent, effects, and that, consequently, it is the reformatory results of punishment that provide its justification. But this preference could not be an absolute one: it would be legitimate only when prevention of offenses could be effected equally well by reformatory and deterrent effects of punishment. But there are cases when by deterring people we achieve much more than by trying to reform them by punishment, and even cases when punishment has no reformatory effects whatsoever, so that it is only by way of deterrence that it can help prevent offenses in the future. In such cases a utilitarian would have to refer to the deterrent results of punishment as to its justification. For no utilitarian reservations about using deterrence as a means of influencing people could serve as reason enough for the conclusion that in such circumstances punishment would be morally unjustified and illegitimate — that we ought to desist from trying to prevent future offenses rather than try to prevent them by deterring their potential perpetrators.

As opposed to the utilitarian theory, which seeks to justify punishment by its consequences and thus looks to the future, we have the retributive theory, which looks to the past. It sees the moral basis of punishment in the offense committed; its basic principle is, *punitur quia peccatum est*. According to this theory, when it comes to punishment, *the* moral criterion is the criterion of justice; punishment is morally justified because it is just, because we execute justice when we punish. The standard of justice in punishment is to be found in the idea of desert: punishment is just because it is deserved by the offense. This means that it is justified because it is retribution — it is an evil the offender has deserved by his offense, an evil by which the state or society, so to say, pays him back for what he has done. This backward-looking character of the retributive theory, this contention that the offense committed is the sole moral basis of punishment, does not imply that consequences are of no importance whatsoever. But it does entail that, however great their importance might be, it is exclusively of a practical nature. When we talk about its *moral* justification, they are irrelevant; they have no *moral* weight whatsoever. When a punishment is deserved, when it is a retribution and execution of justice, it is thereby morally justified; it is irrelevant whether, at the same time, it does or does not have those consequences in which utilitarians claim to have found its moral justification. In terms of the basic division within moral philosophy, the retributive theory is a *deontological* one.

In its most complete form the theory contains the following five tenets:

(1) The moral *right* to punish is based solely on the offense committed.
(2) The moral *duty* to punish is also grounded exclusively on the offense committed.
(3) Punishment ought to be *proportionate* to the offense (the *lex talionis*).
(4) Punishment is the *"annulment"* of the offense.
(5) Punishment is a *right* of the offender.

In all these theses but the last, the term "offense" is used; in the last one the concept is present as well, only in an implicit way. I ought to point out that in this context I do not take the term in its widest sense, as

I did when discussing the concept of punishment, in the sense of a violation of *any* criminal law, no matter whether it is just and morally legitimate or not. The retributive theory of punishment is not a theory of the meaning of the word "punishment," but a philosophical theory about the *justification* of what the word denotes. When adherents of the theory refer to the offense committed as the moral basis for punishment, they do not mean any act which could be *described* as an offense without violating the rules of ordinary language — that is, any act of breaking a criminal law, whatever the contents, nature, and moral status of the law might be. There are laws and there are laws; some are morally legitimate, some are illegitimate, for one reason or another. When retributivists claim that the moral justification of punishment is in the offense committed, by "offense" they mean only a violation of a *morally legitimate* criminal law. There is a good reason for this narrowing of the concept, for if the word "offense" were to be taken in its widest sense, the theory would imply that punishment is sometimes *morally legitimate* precisely because it is retribution for the violation of a *morally illegitimate* law.

The history of the retributive view of punishment begins with the biblical and talmudic ethical and legal ideas, and can be followed all the way up to contemporary retributivists such as H.J. McCloskey, C.W.K. Mundle, or J.G. Murphy. The most important and influential among classical retributivists are Kant and Hegel. Hegel's formulation of the retributive view is more interesting than that of Kant: it is elaborated in greater detail, and it is also richer in content, Hegel having systematically developed all the five main tenets of retributivism, whereas Kant had explicitly advanced and argued for the first three of them, and only hinted at the fifth. The utilitarian theory also has had a long history, from Plato to contemporary philosophers such as T.L.S. Sprigge, S.I. Benn, or J.J.C. Smart. But the most comprehensive and thoroughly developed formulation of the theory in philosophical literature is still to be found in the writings of Bentham. Since this book is not a historical study, I shall not trace the history of the philosophy of punishment. Instead, I shall give some account of the doctrines of Bentham and Hegel, and then examine critically and in detail the arguments that have been used in the debates between the two camps. Next I shall discuss the various attempts at a middle-of-the-road theory of punishment that would avoid the difficulties of both utilitarianism and retributivism, while appropriating what is seen as true in each of them. Finally, I shall take up the ever-topical issue of capital punishment, and consider it both from utilitarian and retributive points of view.

2. The Utility of Punishment: Bentham

1. The Principle of Utility

The utilitarian theory of punishment is but the result of applying utilitarianism as a general ethical theory to the issue of the morality of punishment. It is therefore to be expected that whatever is seen as an advantage of the latter should be thought to accrue to the former as well. Utilitarianism certainly has a number of features that, at least on the face of it, present it in a very attractive light. First, there is a certain immediate plausibility to the view that human actions ought to be evaluated in the light of their consequences, together with the accompanying belief that only this consequentialist approach will enable us to deal with moral issues in a rational, objective, clear, and precise manner, while any other approach would be plagued by dogmatism, subjectivism, and sentimentalism, and would only lead to confusion. "Whether happiness be or be not the end to which morality should be referred," wrote Mill, "that it be referred to an *end* of some sort, and not left in the dominion of vague feeling or inexplicable internal conviction, that it be made a matter of reason and calculation, and not merely of sentiment, is essential to the very idea of moral philosophy; is, in fact, what renders argument or discussion on moral questions possible."[1] This consequentialist outlook seems to open up the possibility of constructing a theory that is comprehensive yet has a very simple structure: a theory which encompasses the whole realm of moral experience within a system based on a single fundamental principle, makes no concessions to other ethical views, and submits all moral concepts, rules, values, to a uniform interpretation, nothwithstanding their *prima facie* diversity and incommensurability. A universal moral currency seems to have been found in the consequences of our actions, and the possibility of cashing all moral considerations in this currency seems to clear the way for applying a single approach to all moral issues. If all such issues come down to questions of the consequences of alternative courses of action, that is, questions of fact, such issues may and ought to be approached empirically; those among them that are of public concern will be be best dealt with by social science. Thus the old dream of many a philosopher, of making ethics a science, finally seems to be coming true. Last but not least, since the utilitarian calculus of consequences takes into account the interests of all those concerned, including the agent, on an equal footing, it has been claimed that utilitarianism secures a reasonable and morally proper balance between the agent's good and that of others. This theory thus transcends the conflict between egoism and altruism, individualism and collectivism, and provides a solid foundation for social ethics and political and legal philosophy.

These, then, are the main reasons for the wide influence utilitarianism has exerted; they also seem to strongly recommend a utilitarian view of punishment. The most thoroughgoing and elaborate formulation of that view is still the theory of punishment expounded in the writings of Bentham. In his teachings on the purpose and justification of punishment, Bentham took into account and systematized all the desirable effects of punishment, and then went on to consider in great detail more specific, but no less important, questions posed by the practice of punishing: What are its proper limits? What should be the criteria for determining the severity of punishment? What are its desirable traits? Greatly impressed both by the system and the details, Mill wrote that Bentham had brought the theory of punishment almost to perfection;[2] with regard to the utilitarian theory of punishment, I think, this is not too much of an overstatement.

This theory of punishment, together with the rest of Bentham's moral, legal, and political philosophy, is based on the principle of utility. Bentham opens his *Introduction to the Principles of Morals and Legislation* by announcing this principle and pointing to its psychological foundations:

> Nature has placed mankind under the governance of two sovereign masters, *pain* and *pleasure*. It is for them alone to point out what we ought to do, as well as to determine what we shall do. On the one hand the standard of right and wrong, on the other the chain of causes and effects, are fastened to their throne. They govern us in all we do, in all we say, in all we think: every effort we can make to throw off our subjection, will serve but to demonstrate and confirm it. . . . The *principle of utility* recognizes this subjection, and assumes it for the foundation of that system, the object of which is to rear the fabric of felicity by the hands of reason and of law.[3]

Utility is "that property in any object, whereby it tends to produce benefit, advantage, pleasure, good, or happiness (all this in the present case comes to the same thing) or (what comes again to the same thing) to prevent the happening of mischief, pain, evil, or unhappiness to the party whose interest is considered." Thus the principle of utility is "that principle which approves or disapproves of every action whatsoever, according to the tendency which it appears to have to augment or diminish the happiness of the party whose interest is in question . . . to promote or to oppose that happiness."[4] Since the concept of utility is defined in terms of happiness, this principle is also called "the greatest happiness principle." Happiness, in turn, is defined in terms of pleasure, as nothing but "enjoyment of pleasures, security from pains."[5]

Two clarifications are in order at this point. First, the utility, happiness, and pleasure referred to are those of all persons affected by the consequences of the act being judged; sometimes it is just one person, at other times several, or even the whole community. Second, the phrase "every action whatsoever" is meant to include not only actions of individuals pure and simple, but also measures undertaken by governments, laws passed by legislators, and in general any social rule and institution. (A methodological individualist, Bentham believes that all these can be analyzed in terms of actions of individuals.) Thus the principle of utility is the supreme law of morality and at the same time the fundamental principle of legal and political philosophy.

The principle of utility being the only basic principle of ethics, all ethical concepts are to be interpreted in terms of utility; whatever is being judged morally is to be judged from the point of view of its utility: "Strictly speaking, nothing can be said to be good or bad, but either in itself; which is the case only with pain or pleasure: or on account of its effects; which is the case only with things that are the causes or preventatives of pain and pleasure."[6] No actions are intrinsically right or wrong, obligatory or prohibited; no motives or dispositions are good or bad in themselves — it is only their consequences with regard to pleasure and pain, happiness and misery, that give them their moral status. "When thus interpreted, the words *ought*, and *right* and *wrong*, and others of that stamp, have a meaning: when otherwise, they have none."[7]

As for various nonutilitarian approaches in ethics and social philosophy, Bentham has an extremely low opinion. He believes that they are but variations of one of the three "principles": the theological principle, the principle of asceticism, or that of sympathy and antipathy. The will of God is not an independent principle, for whenever we refer to it, we actually refer to what we presume to be his will; and such presumptions are always made in accordance with some other principle.

The principle of asceticism, according to Bentham, is but a perversion of the utility principle. It cannot possibly be be taken as a guide in moral matters in any consistent way; in particular, it cannot be applied in politics or legislation: "Let but one tenth part of the inhabitants of this earth pursue it consistently, and in a day's time they will have turned it into a hell."[8] There is, finally, the principle of sympathy and antipathy, which

> approves or disapproves of certain actions, not on account of their tending to augment the happiness, nor yet on account of their tending to diminish the happiness of the party whose interest is in question, but merely because a man finds himself disposed to approve or disapprove of them: holding up that approbation or disapprobation as a sufficient reason for itself, and disclaiming the necessity of looking out for any extrinsic ground.[9]

It is Bentham's view that a large part of traditional moral and social philosophy can be reduced to this principle — that theories as diverse as those of natural law, moral sense, or rational intuition are "so many contrivances for avoiding the obligation of appealing to any external standard, and for prevailing upon the reader to accept of the author's sentiment or opinion as a reason for itself. The phrases different, but the principle the same."[10] Or rather, since a principle is by definition a standard external to our feelings and attitudes, which enables us to justify, criticize, revise them, not a principle, but a negation of all principle.

2. The Aims of Punishment

Bentham believes that the "principle" of sympathy and antipathy is the real source of the retributive theory of punishment: "It is the principle of antipathy which leads us to speak of offences as *deserving* punishment. It is the corresponding principle of sympathy which leads us to speak of certain actions as *meriting* reward. This word *merit* can only lead to passion and to error. It is *effects*, good or bad, which we ought alone to consider."[11]

The effects of punishment on the person punished are painful, harmful, undesirable. Accordingly, "upon the principle of utility, if it ought at all to be admitted, it ought only to be admitted in as far as it promises to exclude some greater evil."[12] A punishment well chosen and appropriately measured carries such a promise with it.

If we could consider an offence which has been committed as an isolated fact, the like of which would never recur, punishment would be useless. It would only be adding one evil to another. But when we consider that an unpunished crime leaves the path of crime open, not only to the same delinquent, but also to all those who may have the same motives and opportunities for entering upon it, we perceive that the punishment inflicted on the individual becomes a source of security to all. That punishment which, considered in itself, appeared base and repugnant to all generous sentiments, is elevated to the first rank of benefits, when it is regarded not as an act of wrath or of vengeance against a guilty or unfortunate individual who has given way to mischievous inclinations, but as an indispensable sacrifice to the common safety.[13]

Various desirable consequences of punishment — of a particular punishment and of the whole institution — outweigh by far the evil it consists of, and therefore provide its justification. They can be listed systematically in the following way:

    (I)   prevention
        (1) particular
            (a) disablement
            (b) reformation
            (c) deterrence
        (2) general
   (II) satisfaction
        (1) material compensation
        (2) vindictive satisfaction

(I) The offense committed is but an act of the past, while the future is endless; the offense has affected (directly) only the victim, while similar misdeeds in the future can affect anyone; the evil inflicted by the offense often cannot be rectified, while future offenses, in Bentham's view, can always be prevented. For these reasons the *prevention* of future offenses is the principal end of punishment and its main justification.

(1) The prevention of future offenses is achieved, on the one hand, by influencing the behavior of the actual offender, so as to get her to desist from repeating her misdeed. This is *particular prevention*. We can prevent her from offending against the law again in three ways: by disabling her from doing that, by eliminating her desire to do that, and by deterring her through fear from doing that.

(a) With many offenses, to *disable* the offender from repeating the offense means to deprive her of the physical ability of doing that. This can be done temporarily, by a prison term, or for good, by a conviction for life, mutilation, or execution. With other offenses, e.g. embezzlement, disablement is secured by less severe measures: by dismissal or debarring from holding public office. Of all the objectives of punishment, disablement is the most easily achieved; its drawback is that by disabling the offender from doing evil, we often at the same time disable her from doing good, both for herself and for others.

(b) The *reformation* of the offender is a result more difficult to achieve, but also more worthy of effort. To "reform" or "amend" the offender means to effect a change of her inclinations, motives, habits, character. If an offender wanted to repeat the offense, but desisted under the influence of fear of punishment, we should not say that she has been successfully reformed; we should say that she is no better than before, but has been efficiently deterred by fear. An offender truly reformed is one who does not desist from breaking the law again out of fear, but one who no longer wants to do that, who is free from criminal inclinations and habits. She will not break the law even when she has reason to believe that she will not be discovered and need not fear punishment.

(c) The third method of particular prevention is *deterrence*. In contrast to the bad example of the offense committed, which, if it goes unpunished, induces the offender to repeat the misdeed, and encourages potential offenders in the public to do the same, the punishment offers a frightening example of an evil inflicted for the offense committed, both to the actual offender and to those others who might be tempted to do what she has done, and thereby induces them to desist. Thus the method of deterrence is common to particular and general prevention.

(2) Bentham sees *general prevention* almost exclusively as the method of deterring potential offenders from violating the law by displaying to them the frightening example of the evil of punishment. He believes that such prevention is always feasible, for "how great soever the advantage of the offence may be, the evil of the punishment may be made to surpass it."[14]

In describing this mechanism of prevention, Bentham applies his hedonistic account of motivation. "Pain and pleasure are the great springs of human action," he says. "When a man perceives or supposes pain to be the consequence of an act, he is acted upon in such a manner as tends, with a certain force, to withdraw him, as it were, from the commission of that act. If the apparent magnitude, or rather value of that pain be greater than the apparent magnitude or value of the pleasure or good he expects to be the consequence of the act, he will be absolutely prevented from performing it."[15]

This analysis of the motivation of a potential offender is not only hedonistic, it is also extremely rationalistic. Is this not its weak point? Is it not a onesided, exaggerated, and hence implausible view to hold that every offender, before committing his misdeed, performs a sober and detailed calculation of harm and benefit to be brought about by it, carefully and accurately calculating its hedonic value and then deciding exclusively on the basis of the result of this calculation? What of the role of irrational factors in criminal behavior, of affects and passions? Bentham is aware of this objection but finds it unconvincing. The claim that passion does not calculate, he says,

> like most of these very general and oracular propositions, is not true. When matters of such importance as pain and pleasure are at stake, and these in the highest degree (the only matters, in short, that can be of importance) who is there that does not calculate? Men calculate, some with less exactness, indeed, some with more: but all men calculate. I would not say, that even a madman does not calculate. Passion calculates, more or less, in every man . . .[16]

The prevention of offenses, in Bentham's view, is the immediate and most important end of punishment. The offender punished is but one, while there are many of those who have not committed such an offense but might do so in the future; accordingly, general prevention is much more important than particular: "General prevention ought to be the chief end of punishment, as it is its real justification."[17]

(II) In addition to the prevention of future offenses, which is its chief objective, punishment can also have a consequence unrelated to possible violations of the law in the future: it can give *satisfaction*. Satisfaction through punishment can be of two kinds: material compensation and vindictive satisfaction.

(1) Punishment can be made to serve as *material compensation* to the victim, and thus do away with the bad consequences of the offense which have affected him. This, of course, is not always possible; still, Bentham emphasizes that it can be done in many cases: "the means of procuring almost all pleasures, money is an efficacious compensation for many evils."[18] This is especially appropriate and called-for in cases when the harm done to the victim and the benefit the offender secured for herself by her misdeed are material, such as theft or embezzlement.

(2) Another kind of satisfaction attainable by punishment is *vindictive*.

Any pain, any evil inflicted on the offender can be a source of such satisfaction, first for the victim, and then for all those who, for whatever reason, feel indignation at the offense committed and want its perpetrator punished. Taken by itself, such pleasure is as good as any other. Certain moralists, deluded by mere words and given to prejudice, do not understand that "it is not vengeance which is to be regarded as the most malignant and dangerous passion of the human heart; it is antipathy, it is intolerance — the hatreds of pride, of prejudice, of religion, of politics. The enmity which is dangerous is not that which is well founded, but that which springs up without any substantial cause." Moreover,

> useful to the individual, this motive is also useful to the public; indeed, it is necessary. It is this vindictive satisfaction which sets the tongues of witnesses in motion; it is this which animates the accuser and engages him in the public service, in spite of the embarrassments, the expenses, the enmities to which it exposes him; it is this, too, which surmounts the public pity in the punishment of criminals. Take away this resource, and the power of the laws will be very limited; or, at all events, the tribunals will not obtain assistance, except for money — a means not only burdensome to society, but exposed to other very serious objections.[19]

Therefore, when determining punishments, we should not only think of the aims of prevention and, wherever possible, those of material compensation, but should take into account the vindictive satisfaction attainable by punishment as well. But this refers only to such modifications of punishment which do not aggravate it, over and above what is needed for reasons of prevention, general and particular; no penalty is to be meted out or made more severe for the purpose of satisfying the pleasure of vengefulness. Such pleasure, however great in itself, is always outweighed by the suffering which causes it.[20] Therefore, punishments determined primarily with this end in view would be very uneconomical: they would make us pay for the good secured by a disproportionately high amount of evil.

3. The Limits

The ends of punishment enumerated in the preceding section are at the same time its justification: punishment is justified because it secures those ends, and in so far as it does so. The same ends determine the limits of punishment: punishment is undesirable and unjustified whenever those ends cannot be attained by punishing, or cannot be attained in a rational, economical manner, or can be attained by some other method, without inflicting the evil of which punishment consists. In the first case, punishment will be (1) groundless or (2) inefficacious, in the second it will be (3) unprofitable, in the third it will be (4) needless.

(1) Punishment is *groundless* where there is no mischief, harm, or evil to be prevented, that is, where there are no good utilitarian reasons for prohibiting by law the act committed. It is no less groundless when a real offense has been committed, that is, an act which as a rule causes harm, pain, or mischief, but has caused none in the particular case at hand because those whose interests are concerned consented to it (*volenti non fit injuria*). Finally, punishment is groundless when a harmful action was necessary for preventing an even greater evil, or for securing an overriding good.

(2) We ought not to punish in cases when punishment is going to be *inefficacious*. Such are punishments meted out on the basis of retroactive laws, or for misdeeds committed unconsciously, unintentionally, without the knowledge of their being prohibited by the law, or under duress; finally, punishments of irresponsible persons — minors, drunkards, insane offenders. In none of these cases could punishment influence the will of the person punished, nor of others, so as to prevent them from offending in the future.

(3) Punishment is *unprofitable* and therefore unjustified if the evil it consists of is greater than the evil it prevents. This would be the case, for instance, if punishing an offender would (for whatever reason) cause great displeasure to the public or to a foreign power. Another characteristic example is the case of an offender who could render an important service to the community, if she were not made to undergo punishment.

(4) Finally, we ought not to punish if punishment is *needless* because its aims can be achieved by other, non-punitive means, such as various measures of social policy and education.

The limits of punishment is one of those specific issues which are directly related to the main issue of the justification of punishment. The way we deal with the latter will commit us to a corresponding solution of the former. Therefore, this issue helps bring into sharp relief some basic features of the opposing theories of punishment — the retributive and the utilitarian. For instance, retributivists would not agree with the utilitarian thesis that punishment is unjustified whenever it is unprofitable; in their view, punishment is justified insofar as it is deserved, whatever its profitability might be. Another example: retributivists would agree with Bentham that we should not punish on the basis of retroactive laws, and that children and insane persons ought not to be punished. But they would not go along with the utilitarian rationale of these restrictions — the argument that such punishments are unjustified because they cannot efficiently prevent future offenses; they would insist that such punishments would be undeserved, and therefore unjust and unjustified. Precisely on account of this basic tenet of the retributive theory, that the offense committed and the consequent ill desert is the sole justification of punishment, which entails the view that the limits of desert are also the limits of justifiable punishment,[21] the difference between the two theories regarding the limits of punishment comes out in a most striking manner over the issue of punishment of the innocent.

For a retributivist, the line between guilt and innocence is the line between justified and unjustified punishment. For a utilitarian, on the other hand, the matter is not so simple.

When discussing the definition of legal punishment, Bentham emphasizes that it is (logically) possible to punish an innocent man:

> But so it be on account of some act that has been done, it matters not by whom the act was done. The most common case is for the act to have been done by the same person by whom the evil is suffered. But the evil may light upon a different person, and still bear the name of punishment. In such case it may be styled punishment *in alienam personam*, in contradistinction to the more common case in which it may be styled punishment *in propriam personam*.[22]

Thus Bentham holds that it (logically) *can* be done.[23] *May* it be done, morally speaking? Bentham holds that the retributivist insistence on the illegitimacy of punishment of the innocent is untenable, and that it is only the utilitarian approach that can provide a rational and convincing solution. In his analysis of various types of such punishment, which he designates as "mis-seated," "misapplied," or "mistaken" punishment, the crucial role belongs to the distinction between the cases in which such punishment can be avoided and those in which it is unavoidable. The word "unavoidable," however, is not taken in its usual, literal sense — for in that sense no punishment is unavoidable — but with an important qualification: "without preponderant inconvenience." On account of this qualification, his distinction is actually a distinction between cases in which punishment of the innocent cannot be avoided, except at the price of mischief, harm, pain, or evil greater than that which would affect the innocent person punished, and cases in which we can desist from such punishment without thereby opting for such an inconvenient result. In a word, the distinction comes down to the one between profitable and unprofitable punishment of the innocent.

Punishment of the innocent which can be avoided without preponderant inconvenience, that is, unprofitable punishment of the innocent, is unjustified and inadmissible precisely on account of its being unprofitable:

> In so far as it is mis-seated, and is not unavoidably so, punishment, it is almost needless to observe, is, with reference to the person on whom it is thrown, *groundless*: as such it is thrown away; it is so much evil expended in waste: — reformation, determent, disablement — it contributes not anything to any one of the proper ends of punishment — not so much as to vindictive satisfaction for injury . . .[24]

On the other hand, when it comes to "unavoidable," profitable punishment of the innocent, such punishment, in Bentham's view, "not only may, but ought to be introduced." Those who accept the principle of utility commit themselves, among other things, to punishing the innocent whenever that is the alternative with the best consequences attainable: "to say . . . of punishment so circumstanced that it ought not to be introduced, would be equivalent to a contradiction in terms."[25]

Bentham is well aware that many a critic will object at this point, claiming that to punish an innocent person would mean to "violate one of the most important, and fundamental, and universally recognised principles of justice." But he does not find this objection damaging; he sees it as but an invocation of one of those principles which are frequently referred to, but never clearly formulated and convincingly argued for, and which, therefore, cannot maintain themselves when they conflict with the clear, thoroughly thought-out, and solidly established principle upon which his theory of punishment is based — the principle of utility. Accordingly, he defines his stand on punishment of the innocent in the following way:

> To inflict punishment when, without introducing preponderant inconvenience, the infliction of such punishment is avoidable, is, in the case of the innocent, contrary to the principle of utility. Admitted: — and so is it in the case of the guilty likewise. To punish where, without

introducing preponderant inconvenience, such punishment is unavoidable, is not in either case contrary to the principle of utility; —
not in the case of the guilty: no, nor yet in the case of the innocent.[26]

This is entirely in line with Bentham's repudiation of the retributivist
criterion of desert as a mere expression of sympathy and antipathy of
the philosopher, the lawgiver, the judge. When one rejects the idea of
desert, neither guilt nor innocence *in itself* can retain any real weight for
one's decisions about punishment. Punishment is justified, and ought
to be inflicted, when it is useful, whether the person punished be guilty
or innocent; it is unjustified and inadmissible when it is not useful,
whether we are dealing with an innocent or a guilty person.

When is punishment of the innocent useful? Bentham finds the
criterion in the possibility of distinguishing between those guilty and
those that are innocent of an offense committed. When the person guilty
of an offense is known, so that the penalty required by the aims of
punishment can be inflicted on her, there is no need to punish the
innocent; to do so would be unprofitable. Sometimes, however, it
cannot be established who is guilty and who is innocent. Then the aims
of punishment cannot be attained by inflicting it exclusively upon the
guilty, and therefore punishment of the innocent cannot be avoided
"without preponderant inconvenience." In such cases the course of
action with the best consequences attainable will not be to desist from
punishing the innocent, but to punish them.

An example of punishment of the innocent which, in Bentham's view,
can sometimes be useful, and thus also justified, is collective punishment. When it cannot be established who is the perpetrator of an
offense, and therefore the guilty cannot be punished without the innocent being punished at the same time, and when the suffering thereby
inflicted on the latter, together with the suffering that is inflicted on the
former, is not greater than the good secured by such punishment, it will
be useful, and therefore also justified, to punish the whole group which
is known to include the unidentifiable offender or offenders.

4. The Measure

The answer to the question of the appropriate measure of punishment
depends on the answer given to the fundamental question: What is it
that justifies punishment? For a utilitarian, who sees the justification of
punishment in its good consequences, those consequences will at the

same time provide the standard for meting out punishments. He will hold that for each and every offense, the appropriate punishment is the one measured out so as to bring about those consequences which make up the purpose of punishment and its justification in the greatest degree possible. On the other hand, every punishment is an evil; therefore a utilitarian will also insist on the principle of economy, requiring that those effects be secured at the lowest price possible, that is, by the least amount of evil of which punishment consists.

This is Bentham's view on the subject. He develops it in great detail, and gives a long list of rules to be applied when measuring out punishments. I shall touch upon three of them only.

(1) A punishment must not be less severe than what is needed to outweigh the benefit secured by the offense. Otherwise the price to be paid for breaking the law in the form of punishment would be acceptable to the offender, and punishment could not prevent anyone from doing so. This is one of the two most important rules on the whole list, for it determines the lower limit of the severity of punishment, which cannot be crossed without making punishment inefficient. The benefit of an offense, of course, includes not only material profit, but "the pleasure or advantage, of whatever kind it be, which a man reaps, or expects to reap, from the gratification of the desire which prompted him to engage in the offence."[27]

In order not to be inefficient, punishment must also be the more severe, the greater the temptation to commit the offense. For temptation (in the wide sense of the word) is the factor making for the perpetration of the offense; if punishment is to prevent it, it has to be harsh enough to outweigh the temptation. Those who do not approach the question of the measure of punishment along utilitarian lines will not accept this; they will point out that, with regard to some types of temptation at least, the greater the temptation, the lesser the guilt, so that the punishment ought to be less severe as well. Accordingly, they will view punishments meted out in accordance with Bentham's thesis on the relation between punishment and temptation as too severe. Bentham, however, does not want to speak of punishments as intrinsically "mild" or "severe" at all; in his view, such assessments only evince prejudices toward certain penalties and contribute nothing to rational discussion of their appropriateness. To discuss this question in a rational and objective way means to talk of punishments exclusively as being efficient or inefficient, economical or uneconomical. As for the sympathy or benevolence to the offender, which tends to reduce punishment below the line determined by the first of Bentham's rules as its lower limit, it

> would counteract as well those purposes which such a motive would actually have in view, as those more extensive purposes which benevolence ought to have in view: it would be cruelty not only to the public, but to the very person in whose behalf it pleads: in its effects, I mean, however opposite in its intention. Cruelty to the public, that is cruelty to the innocent, by suffering them, for want of an adequate protection [through efficient punishment], to lie exposed to the mischief of the offence: cruelty even to the offender himself, by punishing him to no purpose, and without the chance of compassing that beneficial end, by which alone the introduction of the evil of punishment is to be justified.[28]

(2) The more mischievous an offense is, the more evil it inflicts, the more severe the punishment meted out for it ought to be. This rule, says Bentham, "is so obvious in itself, that to say any thing in proof of it would be needless"[29]; still, it is often disregarded. The most drastic example of this is the death penalty, which, in Bentham's times, was prescribed for numerous offenses of all kinds, some of which were not at all very serious.

(3) The first of Bentham's rules determines the lower limit of the severity of punishment; as to its upper limit, the rule is to punish in an economical manner. Punishment must not be more severe than what is necessary for the attainment of its purposes.

5. The Properties

Another subject discussed in Bentham's writings in great detail is that of the desirable properties of punishment. Out of a long list of such properties, I shall mention only three, which are particularly significant for a critical understanding of his theory. They are exemplarity, popularity, and remissibility.

(1) Each punishment has a *real value* — the amount of pain, suffering, evil which is in fact inflicted on the person punished, and an *apparent value* — the idea of its real value in the minds of others, the value it appears to have to them. Punishment accomplishes its main task, which is the deterrence of potential offenders, by its apparent value. With regard to this function of punishment, which is the main one, all that is good comes from its apparent facet; real punishment, taken by itself, produces only the evil that affects the convict. Thus real punishment is,

as a rule, needed and justified in order to produce the apparent effect of punishment. A punishment really inflicted but without any apparent effect would be useless, and therefore unjustified and inadmissible, at least from the point of view of the most important function of punishment and its basic justification:

> Ought any real punishment to be inflicted? most certainly. Why? for the sake of producing the *appearance* of it. Upon the principle of utility, except as to so much as is necessary for reformation and compensation, for this reason, and for no other whatever. Every particle of real punishment that is produced, more than what is necessary for the production of the requisite quantity of apparent punishment, is just so much misery run to waste. . . . If delinquents were constantly punished for their offences, and nobody else knew of it, it is evident that, excepting the inconsiderable benefit which might result in the way of disablement, or reformation, there would be a great deal of mischief done, and not the least particle of good. The *real* punishment would be as great as ever, and the *apparent* would be nothing. The punishment would befall every offender as an unforeseen evil. It would never have been present to his mind to deter him from the commission of crime. It would serve as an example to no one.[30]

In view of this, when punishing, we should always strive to make the apparent value of punishment as great as possible, that is, to make the punishment as *exemplary* as it can be. How is this to be accomplished? The simplest way is to increase the real punishment; by increasing the latter, we automatically increase the former. But the same aim can be achieved by other methods: by careful choice of the type of punishment, without increasing its severity; or by carrying out punishments in a dignified, solemn way, with a ritual calculated to impress the spectators and to frighten them as much as possible. In this respect, in Bentham's opinion, there is much to be learned from the Inquisition; for instance, "the *auto-da-fé* would be one of the most useful inventions of jurisprudence, if instead of being an act of faith it were an act of justice."[31] In general, we ought to strive to make the proportion between the real and apparent punishment as much in favor of the latter as possible: "the real punishment ought to be as small, and the apparent punishment as great as possible. If hanging a man *in effigy* would produce the same salutary impression of terror upon the minds of the people, it would be folly or cruelty ever to hang a man *in person*."[32]

(2) Punishment ought to be *popular*, or, rather, it should not be unpopular: it should not cause the aversion, revulsion, or opposition of

the public. The consequences of an unpopular punishment are analogous to those of an uneconomical one, with the difference that the latter causes unnecessary suffering of the offender, while the former causes equally unnecessary suffering of innocent people, whose moral and religious beliefs, feelings, or traditions cannot be reconciled to the infliction of certain penalties. A further consequence of unpopular punishment is the weakening of the legal order; instead of giving assistance to the law, people turn into its passive, or even active opponents; they help the guilty escape the hand of the law, will not prosecute and give testimony, and even obstruct inquiry and the carrying out of sentences.

To be sure, the requirement that punishment should not be unpopular is necessitated by the fact that people are prone to prejudice, that is, to nonutilitarian views, feelings and habits:

This property . . . necessarily supposes, on the part of the people, some prejudice or other, which it is the business of the legislator to endeavour to correct. For if the aversion to the punishment in question were grounded on the principle of utility, the punishment would be such as, on other accounts, ought not to be employed: in which case its popularity or unpopularity would never be worth drawing into question. It is properly therefore a property not so much of the punishment as of the people: a disposition to entertain an unreasonable dislike against an object which merits their approbation. . . . Be this as it may, so long as any such dissatisfaction subsists, it behoves the legislator to have an eye to it, as much as if it were ever so well grounded. Every nation is liable to have its prejudices and its caprices, which it is the business of the legislator to look out for, to study, and to cure.[33]

(3) Since judges and jurors are no more infallible than anyone else, it occasionally happens that a person who should not be punished does get punished. Accordingly, the evil inflicted by punishment ought not to be completely irreparable. Punishment ought to be *remissible*, so that, in cases when it turns out that it has been meted out by mistake, it can be remitted or, if that is impossible, at least the person mistakenly punished can be somehow compensated. One of the greatest disadvantages of capital punishment is its absolute irremissibility and irreparability.

Discussions of judicial errors usually concern, first and foremost, the possibility of punishment of the innocent. Bentham also points out the possibility, and adduces it as a reason for punishments to be remissible.

We have seen, however, that he does not take innocence in itself to be a limit to legitimate punishment. For him it is only the ground for a utilitarian presumption against punishing: punishment of the innocent is *generally* unprofitable, and therefore *generally* unjustified.[34] Thus his demand that punishment be remissible is not based simply on the fact that an innocent person can be punished by mistake; it is based on the fact that an innocent person can be punished by mistake *and* without a good utilitarian justification for punishing her, her innocence notwithstanding. More generally, remissibility of punishments is required in view of the possibility that any kind of punishment which is not the one with the best consequences attainable under the circumstances might be meted out as a result of mistaken beliefs about the facts of the case.

3. Arguments Against the Utilitarian Theory

1. Ends and Means in Punishing

Seen from a utilitarian point of view, punishment, like any other social practice, is a means to an end: society has to defend itself against crime. It can never realistically hope to eradicate it completely, but it has to keep on doing its best to keep it under control, to reduce it as much as possible. Punishment is a means to this end; for a utilitarian, this is its main purpose and its true justification. An evil in itself, it is justified because it helps achieve a socially vital objective.

Or does it? In the face of the high rates of criminality in most modern societies, the tendency of these rates to go up, or at least not to go down, despite all attempts at improvement of punitive practices and institutions, and the phenomenon of widespread recidivism, many have come to doubt both the deterrent and reformatory effectiveness of punishment as we know it. Many have come to the conclusion that it simply does not work, or at least not in a reasonably efficient and economical way. This belief has motivated various proposals for dismantling the institution of punishment and replacing it by a completely different social response to crime — by restitution of the victim, or by therapy provided for the offender. This is the first and most obvious objection to the utilitarian theory of punishment: that it is predicated on an empirically false belief. Punishment cannot be justified in terms of its utility, for, as a matter of fact, it is not useful.

It is true that, whatever their doubts and reservations regarding various specific punishments or the practice of punishment in general at certain times or in certain jurisdictions, adherents of the utilitarian theory normally believe that punishment is basically sound: that it does, or can be made to, work efficiently and economically, and that it is a socially necessary institution. They normally believe, as Bentham has it, that

we should never be able to subjugate, however imperfectly, the vast empire of evil, had we not learned the method of combating one evil by another. It has been necessary to enlist auxiliaries among pains, to oppose other pains which attack us on every side. So, in the art of curing pains of another sort, poisons well applied have proved to be remedies.[1]

Still, the empirical objection to the utilitarian view of punishment is not very weighty. For the utilitarian can retort that even if it were shown, to the satisfaction of all concerned, that punishment does not work, that would not mean that his theory has been refuted. This conclusion would follow only if it were assumed that punishment *is* justified, and that the only question is, just what is it that justifies it? But he can refuse to make this assumption. The utilitarian claim is that only utility can justify punishment. Even if it turns out that, contrary to what people have thought for centuries or even millennia, punishment is not useful, or not useful enough, the theory will stand; the conclusion will be that punishment is *not* justified, and that we should replace it by whatever seems to be the most promising alternative.

There is another, non-empirical objection that can be brought forward against the view that punishment is to be morally justified as a means to an end. This view is a corollary of a view of humanity characteristic of utilitarianism in general. The confrontation between the utilitarian and retributive views of punishment is rooted in a confrontation at a deeper level, between two very different, even irreconcilable views of human beings. As we shall see in the following chapter in some detail, the retributive theory insists on justice and desert as *the* moral criteria of punishment. Talk of justice and desert makes sense when we relate to a being who decides and acts freely, and therefore carries responsibility for its decisions and actions; when dealing with animals, or with the insane, or with children, we normally go by other standards. Retributivism approaches the problem of punishment from the standpoint of a conception of humans as free, mature, responsible, self-determining beings. It sees and respects the offender as such a being, and relates to his act as to an act of such a being. The punishment is then viewed as a reaction that is fully determined — with regard to the right to punish, the duty to punish, and the proper measure of punishment — by the free action of the offender, an action for which he is responsible and by which he has accordingly deserved to be punished. By viewing both offense and punishment in these terms, retributivism affirms the conception of human beings as persons; for we relate to another as a person when the way *we* treat him is determined by *his own* decisions and actions.

From the utilitarian point of view, on the other hand, the offense as such is not essential for the justification of punishment; what counts are the objectives secured through punishment. Punishment, and *ipso facto* the person punished, is but a means for attaining the aims of society. If the objective of punishment is reformation of the offender, he is being treated as an unfree, immature being, whose behavior may legitimately be reshaped by others in accordance with their notions of what is good, desirable, and socially acceptable. If the punishment aims at exerting an educative influence on the public at large, that public is treated as a collectivity of such beings. If the aim of punishment is to intimidate the offender or potential offenders in the public at large, both the offender and everyone else whom punishment is meant to deter are treated in a way that ignores their basic human dignity. As Hegel puts it, "to base a justification of punishment on threat is to liken it to the act of a man who lifts his stick to a dog. It is to treat a man like a dog instead of with freedom and respect due to him as a man."[2] In the view of humanity that is the basis of the utilitarian theory of punishment and utilitarianism in general, there is no room for the idea of the dignity of every human being *as human being*, and the individual is not seen first and foremost as a person, that is a being whose freedom and responsibility are to be respected and who, to a considerable extent, shapes his own fate. He is rather seen as a being who may legitimately be used for attaining the objectives of others, and whose destiny is not crucially determined by his own free decisions and actions, but by the aims for which he will be used as a means; this, again, is determined by circumstances which he cannot control and very often cannot even predict.

All this is rather general. What it amounts to will become clearer in the next section, where I take up various types of punishment that might turn out to be useful, and therefore also justified from the utilitarian point of view.

2. Utilitarianism and Justice

In addition to the general point about the view of man which is the basis of the utilitarian theory of punishment, there are a number of more specific arguments against this theory. All of them have to do with the distinctively utilitarian view of justice.

For a utilitarian, justice — as all other moral concepts, ideals, principles — is but a particular facet of utility, a particular way of promoting the common good. To be sure, a utilitarian, no less than anyone else, accepts a concept of justice which could be termed legal justice pure and simple, and which means the application of law in an impartial, objective manner, with no regard to individual or group interest. In this sense, a judge who enforces an unjust law will be acting justly as long as she enforces it without any regard to either personal interest or the interest of a particular social group, in a consistent and impartial way. But this notion of justice is of no great philosophical interest; philosophical questions about justice are for the most part posed and discussed at another, higher level, at which it makes sense to inquire about the justice or injustice of a particular law, or even of a whole system of law, as well as other social rules and institutions. At this level the utilitarian will view justice as "an imaginary personage, feigned for the convenience of discourse, whose dictates are the dictates of utility, applied to certain particular cases . . . nothing more than an imaginary instrument, employed to forward on certain occasions, and by certain means, the purposes of benevolence. The dictates of justice are nothing more than a part of the dictates of benevolence."[3] Consequently, within a utilitarian theory of punishment there is no need, and no room, for the idea of desert, which is logically connected with that of justice, so that, as J. Plamenatz has neatly put it, from a utilitarian perspective "no one can deserve punishment; it can merely be right that he should be punished."[4] This is the root of a whole series of difficulties that plague the utilitarian view of punishment.

One of them has to do with mercy and pardon. It may be claimed that every theory of punishment should be able to allow for the application of the ideal of mercy in certain cases, and make some room for the institution of pardon as the legal embodiment of this ideal. The utilitarian theory is unable to do this. It makes sense to say that we have shown mercy to the offender only if we have reduced, or completely repealed, the punishment which he has *deserved* by his act and which is consequently *just*. Acts of mercy shown to offenders are logically possible only against the background of a conflict of two considerations: the principle of just, deserved punishment, and the ideal of mercy.[5] But within utilitarianism such a conflict cannot take place, for "desert" and "justice" have no standing of their own, independent of utility; the latter is the sole criterion of our choices. Therefore, if a punishment

served no good purpose, then the question of imposing it wouldn't come up at all; nor consequently would the question of mercy. The utilitarian has no choice; he must recommend the course of action that produces most good, and if this means a certain penalty he cannot act mercifully and impose less than that penalty. Real mercy is never a possibility for him because he must always impose what is, according to his ethic, the fully justifiable penalty. Even where there is a serious conflict of interests, and punishment is suspended because the harm it would do to others is greater than the good it will do, this cannot properly be called mercy, because there is no significant sense in which the utilitarian can say "I *ought* to do such and such, but special considerations persuade me to act differently on this occasion." For him, the statement "I shall act mercifully" can *only* mean "I shall impose a penalty less than the one which will produce most good," which in turn can *only* mean "I shall impose a penalty less than the one which will produce most good because this action is the one which will produce most good."[6]

Bentham's account of punishment bears this out: it allows for pardon only when that is the way to correct a law or a sentence that is not fully justified in utilitarian terms — that is, as a way of ensuring that the option most desirable from the utilitarian point of view is taken after all. This, of course, is not mercy properly speaking; mercy proper remains beyond the scope of the utilitarian theory. Bentham explicitly states this: "In a Penal Code, having for its first principle the greatest-happiness principle, — no such word would have place."[7]

Further difficulties in the utilitarian theory arise in connection with the question of the proper measure of punishment. It has been claimed that the utilitarian is committed to draconian penalties: "Why stop at the minimum, why not be on the safe side and penalise [the offender] in some pretty spectacular way — wouldn't that be more likely to deter others? Let him be whipped to death, publicly of course, for a parking offence; that would certainly deter *me* from parking on the spot reserved for the Vice-Chancellor!"[8] This objection, as it stands, is obviously misguided, for preventing parking offenses in such a spectacular manner would mean preventing an evil by inflicting an incomparably greater one. Utilitarians would want punishments to be effective, but at a reasonable price. Still, the argument points in the right direction: utilitarianism *would* justify disproportionately harsh punishments, as long as they satisfied the condition of economy at the same time. For instance, if a certain not particularly grave offense such as shoplifting became extremely widespread, and the usual, comparatively short prison term was no longer efficient in preventing it, it might be useful to prescribe very stiff prison sentences for it. If we managed to prevent shoplifting almost completely for a very long period of time by giving, say, two-year terms to a few offenders, these punishments would be effective but economical, and accordingly justified from the utilitarian point of view. But they would be out of all proportion to the gravity of the offenses committed, and thereby clearly undeserved and unjust.

On the other hand, the utilitarian would also be committed to injustice in punishment in the opposite direction. If it turned out, for example, that six months in prison were deterrent enough for rape, or that a year's term were enough with regard to murder, these would be punishments she would consider right and proper for the crimes of rape and murder, respectively. Depending on the circumstances, the utilitarian would be meting out punishments that are way beyond, or below, what is proportionate to the gravity of the offenses committed, and consequently deserved and just.

Another kind of injustice the utilitarian would be committing when measuring out punishments has to do with offenses committed under provocation or in a passion. A retributivist would say that in such cases the guilt is reduced, and consequently the punishment should be less severe than otherwise. This is also the view accepted in criminal court practice. As we have seen in the preceding chapter, however, a utilitarian sees things quite differently: for her, punishments for offenses committed in a passion or under provocation should be especially severe.[9] That is, the very same factors that are normally taken for extenuating circumstances within the utilitarian theory become aggravating ones. For, if prevention of offenses is the main objective of punishment and its basic justification, then, as E. Westermarck says,

> the heaviest punishment should be threatened where the strongest motive is needed to restrain. Consequently, an injury committed under great temptation, or in a passion, should be punished with particular severity; whereas a crime like parricide might be treated with more indulgence than other kinds of homicide, owing to the restraining influence of filial affection. Could the moral consciousness approve of this?[10]

Another difficulty the utilitarian theory meets, even more compromising, arises with regard to the mentally ill. It is generally held that offenders proven to be mentally ill ought not to be punished, and that the state should respond to their offenses in some other way, most likely by compulsory therapy or hospitalization. Could a utilitarian subscribe to this view as well? Bentham thinks so. To be sure, he does not believe that such offenders must not be punished because of the lack of guilt or desert on their part, and the injustice that will consequently be involved in having them punished; from the utilitarian point of view such considerations are irrelevant. Bentham's explanation is that such punishments could not be efficient, for their deterrent efficiency — and human nature being what it is, it is mainly by deterring people that we prevent them from offending against the law — presupposes the very rationality and ability to control one's actions that the mentally ill lack.[11]

This explanation is not convincing. True, we cannot hope to influence the behavior of the mentally ill by punishment: we cannot deter the actual mentally ill offender from breaking the law again by punishing him, nor will his punishment deter those mentally ill in the public at large who might break the law. But it does not follow that such punishments have to be inefficient. For they could have a strong deterrent effect on *normal* potential offenders. If the insanity defense were abolished and the law provided for the mentally ill offenders to be punished in the same way as normal offenders, the perspective faced by a sane would-be offender would be considerably graver than the one he faces now in an important respect: he could entertain no hope of getting himself declared not responsible for his action and evading punishment for it by convincingly simulating mental illness.[12]

A utilitarian could deny that her theory commits her to punishing the mentally ill. She could claim that the final balance of consequences would go against it after all. The common moral consciousness views this matter in a completely nonutilitarian way, and could not possibly reconcile itself to what it would consider a grave violation of justice. Therefore, such punishments would bring about very unfavorable reactions from the public, which would come to think that the whole criminal law system is unjust and would accordingly deny it support and cooperation. This would undermine the system in a serious way. Such consequences, obviously, would be so bad that they would override any preventive effects that could possibly be secured by punishing mentally ill offenders along with the sane. In Bentham's terminology, such punishments would be so unpopular that they would become unprofitable.[13]

This defense, however, is not plausible. Our refusal to accept punishment of the mentally ill is not a concession to nonutilitarian prejudices of the common moral consciousness; it follows from a clear and deeply rooted moral conviction which is part of our understanding of justice.

We would consider such punishment no less morally wrong for a society in which the common moral opinion would not object to it than for a society in which it would be very unpopular.[14]

Another possible response of the utilitarian to the argument on punishment of the mentally ill would refer to the distinction presupposed by the argument, between a normal and a mentally ill offender. If it is possible to formulate the criteria for applying the distinction in practice in an adequate and reasonably precise way, normal offenders will have no reason to hope that they will manage to deceive the court into thinking that they are mentally ill and not responsible for their misdeeds, and thus get away with them; therefore there is no need for punishing the mentally ill so as to prevent the sane from counting on this. On the other hand, if such criteria cannot be established, we cannot differentiate between the two groups of offenders, and the whole issue of punishing the mentally ill cannot arise at all.[15]

This defense is no more successful than the previous one. It is a fact that courts have at their disposal certain criteria for distinguishing between offenders who are sane and responsible and those who are not. These criteria, though not perfect, are reasonably good. The dilemma posed with regard to these criteria simplieies the matter by ignoring the question of the degree to which the public is informed and enlightened and the way it relates to these criteria and the use of psychiatry in criminal courts in general. This is crucial for any good assessment of the utility of applying the criteria and desisting from punishing mentally ill offenders. H.J. McCloskey has nicely reviewed the possibilities and the corresponding implications of the utilitarian theory of punishment:

> In an ignorant community it might well be useful to punish as responsible moral agents "criminals" who in fact were not responsible for their actions but who were generally believed to be responsible agents. The experts suggest that many sex offenders and others who commit the more shocking crimes, are of this type, but even in reasonably enlightened communities the general body of citizens do not always accept the judgements of the experts. Thus, in communities in which enlightened opinion generally prevails (and these are few) punishment of mentally deranged "criminals" would have little if any deterrent value, whereas in most communities some mentally deranged people may usefully be punished, and in ignorant, backward communities very useful results may come from punishing those not responsible for their actions. Similarly, very undesirable results may come from not punishing individuals generally believed

to be fully responsible moral agents. Yet, clearly, the morality of punishing such people does not depend on the degree of the enlightenment of the community. Utilitarian theory suggests that it does, that such punishment is right and just in ignorant, prejudiced communities, unjust in enlightened communities. The utility of such punishment varies in this way, but not its justice.[16]

We have seen that from the utilitarian theory it follows that under certain circumstances it would be morally justified to mete out punishments that are considerably more, or considerably less, severe than those that would be deserved and just in view of the gravity of the offenses committed and the measure of responsibility with which they were committed, and also to punish those whose punishment is wholly undeserved and hence unjust — the mentally ill offenders. On the other hand, it also follows from the theory that sometimes the guilty should not be punished at all. From the utilitarian point of view, only consequences constitute good reason for punishing or abstaining from punishment; desert and justice do not count in their own right. Punishment is an evil which a utilitarian considers morally justified only when it is the means for securing a greater good, which is usually but not always the case. Sometimes the opposite is to be expected: punishing the offender would have worse consequences than were he to get away with his misdeed; punishment would prove unprofitable. And according to utilitarianism, every unprofitable punishment is *ipso facto* morally unjustified: as Bentham puts it, "it is cruel to expose even the guilty to useless sufferings."[17]

When would punishing an offender be unprofitable? As we have seen in the preceding chapter, Bentham has in mind cases such as the following: when the punishment would cause such a great displeasure of the public, or a foreign power, that in the final account it would have worse consequences than abstaining from punishing; or when an offender, if not punished, could render a service to the community which outweighs the utility of his punishment. In such cases punishing the guilty would "cost society too dear" and therefore would be morally unjustified.[18] From a nonutilitarian point of view, on the other hand, a criminal law system guided by calculations of this kind would thereby gravely compromise itself; and the implication of the utilitarian theory of punishment that such calculations are morally relevant and even binding goes to compromise the theory. "What then are we to think of the proposal," asks Kant, "that the life of a condemned criminal should be spared if he agrees to let dangerous experiments be carried out on him in order that the doctors may gain new information of value to the commonwealth, and is fortunate enough to survive?" His answer is that " a court of justice would dismiss with contempt any medical institution which made such a proposal; for justice ceases to be justice if it can be bought at a price."[19]

Another kind of situation in which it would be morally justified not to punish the guilty is when the desirable effects of punishment can be secured without actually punishing — by producing an illusion of punishment. In cases when the utilitarian cannot or need not count on the effects of punishment in the way of particular prevention and when, accordingly, the decision depends solely on the contribution of punishment to its most important purpose, the general prevention, a crucial role in her deliberation will have to be accorded to Bentham's distinction between real and apparent punishment — punishment which is actually inflicted on someone, and the idea of that punishment formed in the minds of others — and to the rule that the proportion between the two should be as favorable as possible to the latter. Punishment works as a means of general prevention by its apparent aspect; real infliction of punishment is needed only to produce the apparent effect. Whenever the deterrent effects of punishment on the general public can be attained by having the offender punished only apparently, without actually inflicting punishment, this will be the best option from the utilitarian point of view. Really to inflict punishment in such cases would mean to be unreasonably and unjustifiably cruel.[20]

A telling example of this kind of utilitarian economy is recounted by Bentham from a report published in *Lloyd's Evening Post* in 1776:

> At the Cape of Good Hope, the Dutch made use of a stratagem which could only succeed among Hottentots. One of their officers having killed an individual of this inoffensive tribe, the whole nation took up the matter, and became furious and implacable. It was necessary to make an example to pacify them. The delinquent was therefore brought before them in irons, as a malefactor: he was tried with great form, and was condemned to swallow a goblet of ignited brandy. The man played his part; — he feigned himself dead, and fell motionless. His friends covered him with a cloak, and bore him away. The Hottentots declared themselves satisfied. "The worst we should have done with the man," said they, "would have been to throw him into the fire; but the Dutch have done better — they have put the fire into the man."[21]

According to the utilitarian theory of punishment, whenever this would be the alternative with the best possible consequences, a feigned punishment should be staged instead of a real one, and the public should be put in a position analogous to that of the innocent Hottentots.

The arguments on non-punishment of the guilty demonstrate how the utilitarian theory of punishment would, in certain circumstances, transform the criminal law system into a market for trading in justice, or a stage on which, instead of doing justice, shows of its being done are performed. On the other hand, under different circumstances still, this theory would imply that it is morally justified to punish the innocent.

Bentham holds that whenever punishment of the innocent is the option with the best consequences, such punishment "not only may, but ought to be introduced." As an example of such punishment, he cites collective punishment in cases when it is impossible to differentiate between the innocent and the guilty.[22] But if we take the view that it is morally right to punish the innocent whenever that is the course of action with the best consequences, the situation mentioned by Bentham will by no means be the only one in which we shall decide on such punishment. Collective punishment might be the thing to do from the point of view of the consequences of alternative options, even when we know who is the offender: punishing him *and* his family, or all the inhabitants of his village, or a group of his compatriots can sometimes have a much greater deterrent effect than punishing only the offender, and at the same time satisfy the condition of economy, the evil of offenses prevented still outweighing the evil inflicted by such collective punishment.[23]

Again, punishing a single scapegoat will sometimes be the course of action with the best consequences under the circumstances. Suppose there is a country where, due to the incompetence of the police and the courts, criminal behavior has become widespread, and popular trust in the legal order has been seriously undermined. The only expeditious and efficient way out of this situation, and of preventing many offenses from being committed, as they assuredly will be if things remain the way they are, is finally to punish an offender. This punishment, with proper publicity, will have a strong preventive effect on a large number of potential offenders, and will help a great deal toward restoring popular confidence in the ability of the legal order and the police to provide the necessary protection. However, precisely because the police are so incompetent, the opportunity never arises. Once again they have got the wrong person — a person innocent of the crime he is charged with, that is. His acquittal will have good consequences as far as he is concerned, but an opportunity to ensure consequences that are far more desirable from the standpoint of the common good will be lost. On the other hand, to punish him, his innocence notwithstanding, will have bad consequences for him, but overwhelmingly good consequences for the common good. From the utilitarian point of view, it would be morally unjustified and wrong to do the former, and morally justified and even obligatory to do the latter.

I think that the case against the utilitarian theory of punishment can be strengthened at this point by adding an argument complementary to the previous one, which might be termed the argument of self-sacrifice of the innocent. From Kant, who seems to have been the first to suggest the punishment-of-the-innocent argument, onwards, critics of utilitarianism have always viewed the situation described in the argument from the point of view of the *judge*, pointing out the unacceptable implication of utilitarianism as to what the judge would be obligated to do . But the situation could profitably be examined from another angle, that of the *innocent person accused*. If the circumstances are such that punishing an innocent will have the best possible effects and is, therefore, according to utilitarianism, the morally right thing to do, this provides moral guidance not only for the judge, but for all those on whose conduct the outcome depends. The accused is, obviously, one of them: in such cases, cooperation on the part of the accused can only make the trial more convincing, and thereby render the positive effects expected from it and from the punishment which is to follow — the effects that provide the moral justification of such a course of action — much more likely than they otherwise would be. Thus the same premises which, according to the utilitarian view of punishment, make it incumbent upon the judge to pronounce an innocent person guilty and to sentence him, and imply that it would be morally wrong for her to act otherwise, also make it incumbent upon the innocent defendant to cooperate in passing and carrying out the sentence. Regardless of the fact that he is innocent, and that he knows that the judge is aware of his innocence, he ought to collaborate assiduously in his own condemnation and punishment by "confessing" to the false charge and perhaps by pretending to be repentant as well. From the utilitarian standpoint, any insistence on his innocence and any attempt to change the outcome of the trial would be morally impermissible. The only morally right thing for him to do under the circumstances is to sacrifice himself for the common good.

These are some of the implications of the utilitarian theory of punishment. Each one of them suggests as the morally right course an action which is obviously and seriously unjust and will therefore be found by most of us to be morally unacceptable. If they were to be graded in terms of their moral reprehensibility, I believe that the last two — that it is sometimes right to punish an innocent person, and that in such cases the innocent should collaborate in their own sentence and punishment — would be placed on top of the list. In the next three sections, therefore, I shall consider in detail various attempts by utilitarians to defend their theory against the punishment-of-the-innocent argument. For the sake of brevity, I shall speak about punishing the innocent, but what I have to say will also be relevant to the complementary objection about self-sacrifice of the innocent for the common good.

3. Punishment of the Innocent (a): Moral Acrobatics

The validity of the argument about punishing the innocent is sometimes questioned by pointing to the unusual, exceptional nature of the situation it assumes. It is said that ethical theory should provide a sound basis for morally judging actions and choices which may occur in real life, and not in some unusual, imaginary, even fantastic situations. If it provides satisfactory guidance to real choices, why invent unreal situations and fantastic dilemmas, and wonder whether the answers it provides would still be acceptable? In real life, punishment of the guilty produces good effects. The utilitarian theory of punishment recognizes this fact and maintains that the good effects stemming from punishment are what give those who mete out punishment the moral right and impose on them the moral duty to do so. One could argue for or against this theory in various ways. But the argument must always assume human life and the human condition as they really are, and not some fantastic situation. As T.L.S. Sprigge puts it, there is "no need for moral acrobatics relevant only to situations which in fact are quite out of the question."[24]

In response, the critic of utilitarianism can insist that in order to test the implications of an ethical theory it is not necessary that every case to which it is applied be taken from real life. It is perfectly legitimate to consider a situation which is merely *possible*. And it is not *empirical* possibility that is referred to; it is enough that the case hypothesized be *logically* possible. Consequently, "whether or not unjust punishments [such as punishment of the innocent] are in fact useful, it is logically

possible that they will at some time become useful, in which case utilitarians are committed to them."[25] In other words, "to object that the
conditions imagined in the example [of punishment of the innocent]
have never been fulfilled . . . would be beside the point. Moral theory is
a priori . . . It is, as Leibniz would say, true of all possible worlds."[26]

Opposing this view of the limits of ethical argumentation, T.L.S.
Sprigge says that moral attitudes which would be appropriate in a world
very different from our own might be entirely different from those we
have adopted while growing up and living in the world as it is.[27] In
terms of the issue at hand this means that in our world, punishment of
the guilty normally has good consequences and punishment of the
innocent bad ones. Accordingly, our moral attitudes to punishment of
the guilty are positive, while those to punishment of the innocent are
negative. But if we lived in a world in which punishment of the innocent
usually had good consequences, then perhaps it would no longer be
appropriate to take a negative stand on such punishment.

I do not find this retort convincing. When pointing out that under
certain conditions utilitarianism would imply that it is morally justified
to punish an innocent person, the critic is convinced that such an
implication is morally unacceptable. This *moral* conviction is not based
on any belief as to the *factual* frequency of cases in which these conditions are met in our world; it is felt that such punishment would be
morally wrong in a world in which these conditions were met relatively
often or even as a rule, no less than in a world where they are met only
very rarely.

In an interesting paper entitled "Against Moral Conservativism," Kai
Nielsen tries to bring into question the argument about punishing the
innocent in a way similar to that adopted by Sprigge. Commenting on
the claim which attributes an *a priori* character to moral judgments and
ethical theories, Nielsen agrees that moral judgments are indeed *a priori*,
if this means that they are not empirical statements, or that they cannot
be deduced from nonmoral judgments, or that a true moral judgment
holds for all possible worlds in which situations completely identical to
the situation characterized in the judgment obtain. He maintains, however, that moral judgments are not *a priori* in the sense relevant to the
discussion of the punishment-of-the-innocent argument: in the sense
"that rational men must or even will make them without regard for the
context, the situation, in which they are made":

> We say people ought not to drive way over the speed limit, or speed
> on icy roads, or throw knives at each other. But if human beings had a

kind of metallic exoskeleton and would not be hurt, disfigured, or seriously inconvenienced by knives sticking in them or by automobile crashes, we would not — so evidently at least — have good grounds for saying such speeding or knife throwing is wrong. It would not be so obvious that it was unreasonable and immoral to do these things if these conditions obtained. In the very way we choose to describe the situation when we make ethical remarks, it is important in making this choice that we know what the world is like and what human beings are like. Our understanding of the situation, our understanding of human nature and motivation cannot but effect our structuring of the moral case. [The utilitarian] is saying that, as the world goes, there are good grounds for holding that judicial killings are morally intolerable, though he would have to admit that if the world (including human beings) were very different, such killings could be something that ought to be done. But, in holding this, he is not committed to denying the universalizability of moral judgments, for, where he would reverse or qualify the moral judgment, the situation must be different. He is only committed to claiming that, where the situation is the same or relevantly similar and the persons are relevantly similar, they must, if they are to act morally, do the same thing. However, he is claiming both (1) that, as things stand, judicial killing of the innocent is always wrong and (2) that it is an irrational moral judgment to assert of reasonably determinate actions (e.g., killing an innocent man) that they are unjustifiable and morally unacceptable in all *possible* worlds, whatever the situation and whatever the consequences.[28]

But the example Nielsen uses to illustrate his claim, that in a different world different moral judgments would sometimes be appropriate, is in one important point dissimilar from the situation of punishing the innocent; as a result, his analogy does not work. We do indeed hold that one ought not to throw knives at people or drive a car in a way likely to cause an accident. When we affirm this we proceed, explicitly or implicitly, from the moral principle that undeserved evil ought not to be inflicted on other people. This principle, as our first premise, and the statement that in the world as it is such actions as a rule bring such evil to other people, as our second premise, lead to the conclusion that these things should not be done. The second premise in this piece of reasoning is an empirical statement; the state of affairs to which it refers is a contingent one. If this state of affairs did not obtain, the conduct in question would not fall under the ban contained in the moral principle, and there would be nothing morally questionable about it. Empirically speaking, it is quite unlikely that our physical make-up could change so much — say, in the way hypothesized by Nielsen — that throwing knives at people or causing a car crash would not result in an undeserved evil being inflicted on someone. Such a change, however, is logically possible. And it is precisely because it is *logically possible* to envision a world in which such changes have occurred, and in which, accordingly, it would be appropriate to pronounce a moral judgment on such actions that is entirely different from the judgment we pass in the world we live in, that it would be untenable to claim that such conduct is morally wrong in all possible worlds.

When we denounce punishment of the innocent, we are assuming the same moral principle on the wrongness of inflicting undeserved evil on others. But there is an important difference between this and the previous case. People are punished, for instance, by being kept in prison, because to keep them there for a number of months or years means to inflict an evil on them. If people suddenly developed a taste for living in prison, that would no longer be a form of punishment. This connection between punishment and evil is not based on an empirical generalization which would permit exceptions; it is of a conceptual, logical nature and therefore holds true *a priori* and universally, without exception. "Punishment" logically implies "an evil inflicted on someone." Therefore, between the moral principle that one ought not to inflict undeserved evil on others, on the one hand, and the moral judgment that the innocent ought not to be punished, on the other, there is no mediating empirical statement which describes a certain state of affairs and thus subsumes punishment of the innocent under the principle, and on whose truth the acceptability of the judgment depends. On the contrary, this judgment follows directly from the principle by virtue of the very definitions of "punishment" and "innocence": to punish an innocent person means precisely to inflict an undeserved evil on that person. Punishment of the innocent, irrespective of all the contingent features of the world, always falls under the category of acts which are banned by the above principle. In contrast with the empirically quite improbable, but logically possible, world in which throwing knives at other people or causing accidents do not inflict undeserved evil on others and in which, therefore, such actions are not wrong, the world in which one could punish innocent people without *ipso facto* inflicting undeserved evil on them is not logically possible. Therefore, if we subscribe to the princple that it is morally wrong to inflict undeserved evil on others, we must maintain that punishment of the innocent is morally wrong *in all possible worlds*.

Thus there is no good reason why we should have to stick to real, typical situations when critically examining ethical theories — why we should not also take into account their implications concerning various morally relevant situations which may not be real or probable, but are logically possible. If this is moral acrobatics, such acrobatics are quite legitimate. But this is only part of the answer to the objection that the situation assumed in the argument on punishment of the innocent is atypical, unrealistic, and only logically possible. The other part of the answer is: unfortunately, the argument is not a piece of moral acrobatics, for such a situation is not at all only logically possible. One need not be an expert in psychology or sociology to know that, in view of human nature and the nature of man's social life, it is indeed empirically possible; and one need not be a specialist in history to be able to cite examples showing that it is empirically possible, and in certain social and political conditions even probable. In our century — to go back no farther in time — the trials in Moscow in the thirties, or in Budapest in 1949, or in Prague in 1952 gave eloquent proof of this.

At these trials, people who had devoted their entire lives to the revolution were condemned as counter-revolutionary conspirators; people who had done nothing against their country but, on the contrary, had always been patriots, were denounced as foreign spies. Besides these standard accusations, in Budapest and Prague the accused were punished, equally without grounds, as "Titoists" and "Zionists." Of course, many of the protagonists in these trials — investigators, judges, prosecutors, and defending attorneys — did what they did not because they were guided by utilitarian (or any other) moral convictions, but for entirely different reasons. Similarly, many of the accused confessed to things they had not done simply because they could no longer stand the torture they were undergoing, because their children's lives were threatened, or because they naively believed that if they "confessed" they would save their own necks. It is reasonable to presume, however, that at least some of the leading actors in these trials, at least some of those who initiated the trials, had the main say in them, and were largely responsible for them organized the entire business because they believed that these trials were politically necessary, and acted with a perfectly clear conscience, in the conviction that what they were doing was morally justified. With respect to false confessions and repentances of the accused, one can reasonably claim, on the basis of what has been learned about these trials so far (one of the main sources being the testimony of those victims who survived), that many of the accused made these confessions because (or also because) they had come to the conclusion that, under the circumstances, it was their moral duty to do so.[29]

The ethical standpoint which led the one and the other to reach such a conclusion was a variant of utilitarianism widespread in our century, which is best described as "revolutionary Machiavellianism." This standpoint is clearly stated in the well-known words of Lenin and Trotsky:

> We reject any morality based on extra-human and extra-class concepts. We say that this is deception, dupery, stultification of the workers and peasants in the interests of the landowners and capitalists. We say that our morality is entirely subordinated to the interests of the proletariat's class struggle. Our morality stems from the interests of the class struggle of the proletariat. . . . We say: morality is what serves to destroy the old exploiting society and to unite all the working people around the proletariat, which is building up a new, a communist society.[30]

> To accomplish the overturn, the proletariat needs all its strength, all its audacity, passion, and ruthlessness. Above all it must be completely free from the fictions of religion, "democracy," and transcendental morality — the spiritual chains forged by the enemy to tame and enslave it. Only that which prepares the complete and final overthrow of imperialist bestiality is moral, and nothing else. The welfare of the revolution — that is the supreme law![31]

For those who take this point of view, all nonutilitarian moral convictions which could restrain this "revolutionary Machiavellianism" are, at best, naive "Kantian-priestly and vegetarian-Quaker prattle"[32] — or, at worst, "spiritual chains" forged by the enemy.

This was the ethical basis on which Soviet Attorneys-General N.V. Krylenko and A.Y. Vyshinsky built their theory of criminal procedure, the judiciary, and punishment. According to this theory, both the demand for proportion between guilt and punishment and the very notion of guilt are irrelevant, antiquated "bourgeois" ideas.[33] The truth which is to be determined by the court is, like every truth, essentially "relative."[34] In political trials, admission of guilt on the part of the accused is in principle more important than any evidence.[35] The court is nothing but "a political weapon," "an organ of the class struggle"; hence it must not be governed in its work by "the eternal law of truth, justice, etc.," but must always act "from the point of view of the interests of the revolution . . . having in mind the most desirable results for the masses of workers and peasants."[36]

This moral outlook and the theory of criminal law based upon it, together with the empirical assumption that the trials referred to were, under the circumstances, the most effective, or even the sole means of safeguarding the achievements of the revolution, lead to the conclusion that these trials were completely morally justified.[37]

The utilitarian might counter this by refusing to accept the empirical assumption about the instrumental value of the trials. It is well known, she might say, that the truth of the matter is quite the opposite: that those trials did immense harm to the cause they were supposed to serve. This has not only been pointed out by numerous scholars, but has also been avowed by the heirs of those who had decided that the trials should be held. So the trials were neither useful nor justified after all.

This, however, will not help much. Granted, the trials did not serve their purpose well enough, or even did not serve it at all; those who believed that they would were mistaken, and what they did lacks utilitarian moral justification. But it lacks such justification only in a particular, purely objective and retrospective sense: what *we now* know about subsequent developments enables us to say that, in terms of the "revolutionary Machiavellianism" itself to which those responsible for the trials subscribed, those trials were not justified. But we also have to grant that from *their own* perspective things looked different. Those among them who had given the matter the most serious consideration and done their best to predict and assess the consequences of options facing them, and then came to the conclusion that to hold the trials was the course of action with best consequences attainable, *were* right to think the trials morally justified. That is, the trials *were* justified in another, subjective and prospective sense. (And when we are considering a theory whose major purpose is to guide our choices and actions, and only secondarily to pass judgment on the past — as is surely the case with utilitarianism — we shall judge it first and foremost in the light of its implications regarding what is subjectively and prospectively right and wrong, justified and prohibited.)

4. Punishment of the Innocent (b): The Definitional Stop

Some utilitarians have tried to rebut the punishment-of-the-innocent argument by an appeal to the meaning of the word "punishment." This maneuver — which has been termed the "definitional stop"[38] — begins by reminding us that "punishment" is by definition "infliction of an evil on an offender." It implies that the infliction of an evil on someone who is not guilty could not be properly described as punishment; "punishment of the innocent" is logically impossible. Therefore one cannot say that the utilitarian view of punishment would justify anything of the sort: "The short answer to the critics of utilitarian theories of punishment, is that they are theories of *punishment*, not of *any* sort of technique involving suffering."[39]

Does "punishment" necessarily mean "infliction of an evil upon the guilty," so that it is logically impossible to punish the innocent? Hobbes insists that infliction of an evil on the guilty is a defining feature of punishment: "punishment is only for transgression of the law, and therefore there can be no punishment of the innocent." However, on the very same page, he also speaks about punishment of the innocent: "all punishments of the innocent subjects, be they great or small, are against the law of nature."[40] Is it not unnecesary, even pointless, to prohibit that which is logically impossible to do? Similarly, Kant stresses that one could not describe suffering inflicted on an innocent person as punishment, but in his critique of the utilitarian theory he suggests the argument about punishment of the innocent.[41] Are these philosophers more faithful to ordinary language when they speak about the meaning of the word "punishment," or when they move on to normative grounds and discuss the morality of the practice the word denotes? Is not punishment of the innocent logically possible after all?

H.J. McCloskey holds that it is. In his opinion, the analysis of punishment according to which guilt is its logical condition, and on the basis of which the argument on punishment of the innocent is declared irrelevant, testifies to a confusion between two different notions — the notion of "punishment" and that of "deserved punishment" — but is adequate to neither. Guilt is not a logical condition of punishment; we can say without contradiction "he was punished for something he did not do" or "she was punished although she was innocent." Thus, punishment of the innocent is not logically impossible, and the argument concerning such punishment cannot be pronounced irrelevant.[42]

McCloskey is unquestionably right in pointing out that one can say without contradiction "he was punished for something he did not do," or "she was punished although she was innocent." But this does not imply that guilt is not a logical prerequisite of punishment. When we say something of that sort, we presuppose that a judicial error has been committed, that the judge mistakenly believes in the guilt of the accused, whom we know to be innocent. That is why the possibility of using the word "punishment" in this way does not show that there is no logical connection between guilt and punishment. This would be shown only if *the judge* could say without contradiction to the accused, "I am punishing you for something you did not do," or "I am punishing you although you are innocent," and if we were still willing to call that "punishment." But neither the first nor the second holds true.[43] The possibility of saying without contradiction that someone has been punished although innocent has to do with the fact that judges, like everyone else, can and do make mistakes, and does not show the absence of logical connection between punishment and guilt, but only that the connection must be stated more accurately. We should not say that punishment logically presupposes that the person punished *is* guilty, but rather that the person who is punishing *believes* that the person being punished is guilty.[44]

Of course, the argument under discussion does not refer to unintentional punishment of the innocent, to judicial errors,[45] but to conscious and deliberate punishment of the innocent. We see, however, that punishment of the innocent is logically possible only in the first sense, but not in the second. Does this not finally do away with the argument?

It does not: the only thing that the utilitarian can really accomplish by appealing to this fact of ordinary language is to force the critic to make a verbal modification of the argument. Punishment of the innocent, in the relevant sense of a conscious and deliberate procedure, is indeed logically impossible, and consequently cannot be brought up against the utilitarian theory of punishment. But something dangerously similar to it *is* logically possible: "punishment" of the innocent. It can be readily conceded that, given the circumstances described in the original formulation of the argument, it does not follow from the utilitarian theory that the innocent person ought to be *punished*. For it *does* follow that he ought to be "punished" — that we should inflict on him an evil which, if he were guilty, could be correctly described as punishment; which, since he is not guilty, cannot be so described, but must be called something else (say "victimization" or "social surgery"); and which should be falsely presented to the public as punishment by falsely presenting the innocent person as guilty, because only in this way can we secure the good consequences of the whole enterprise which provide its utilitarian justification.[46]

Admittedly, the utilitarian can still insist that this will not be *punishment* and that, accordingly, it cannot be considered an implication of the utilitarian theory of *punishment*. This, however, will be poor consolation. For although this is not, strictly speaking, an implication of the utilitarian view of punishment, it is most certainly an implication of utilitarianism as a general ethical theory. The utilitarian view of punishment is but the application of this theory to the problem of the moral justification of punishment. So although the argument does not strike directly at the utilitarian doctrine of punishment, it does strike at its theoretical foundations. And it is together with these foundations that this doctrine, along with other utilitarian teachings, stands or falls.

5. Punishment of the Innocent (c): The Scope of the Argument

I hope to have shown in the preceding two sections that attempts by advocates of the utilitarian theory of punishment to refute the "punishment"-of-the-innocent argument have failed. The argument stands. It is time to take up the question, just what is its real weight?

It is by no means obvious how far the argument takes us. A utilitarian could say at this point: All right, it has really been established that my theory does imply that "punishment" of the innocent would under certain circumstances be morally justified. But this does not worry me at all; for under those circumstances such "punishment" *would indeed* be justified. This is the stand taken by one of the foremost proponents of utilitarianism in our day, J.J.C. Smart; on account of this a new term has been introduced into the philosophical slang, "to outsmart," meaning "to embrace the conclusion of one's opponent's *reductio ad absurdum* argument." The dictionary from which I quote this definition goes on to give the following illustration of the usage: "They thought they had me, but I outsmarted them. I agreed that it *was* sometimes just to hang an innocent man."[47]

After this move on the part of the utilitarian, it might seem that we have ended up in a blind alley. For on the other side of the fence we have nonutilitarians such as A. Donagan, who claims that "however much certain judicial murders may be excused or even defended, they are *not* morally right,"[48] or G.E.M. Anscombe, who says that "if someone really thinks, *in advance*, that it is an open question whether such an action as procuring the judicial execution of the innocent should be quite excluded from consideration — I do not want to argue with him; he shows a corrupt mind."[49] Does the discussion have to be brought to an end, by simply recording the opposing views?

The question to ask at this point is, just what kind of a *reductio ad absurdum* is attempted by the argument? What is it that is being contradicted by the implication that "punishment" of the innocent is sometimes morally justified? In one of the most detailed accounts of the subject, the book *Behavior Modification and "Punishment" of the Innocent* by George Schedler, we read that on this point utilitarianism comes into conflict with a "widely shared" moral intuition. The function of moral philosophy is to explain and systematize such intuitions, defined as feelings, beliefs, or judgments about moral matters voiced by "plain people." These intuitions are "touchstones" of ethical theories. They are not to be questioned; an ethical theory is to be accepted if its implications square with these intuitions, and rejected if they contradict them.[50] This is an old and well-known view of the nature of ethics, shared by philosophers such as Kant, Bradley, or Nicolai Hartmann; but its difficulties are known as well. How "widely" in space and time do these intuitions have to be shared in order to qualify as "touchstones" of philosophical theories of morality? What are we to do about those ethical issues on which there are conflicting "widely shared" intuitions — is it plausible to do away with this difficulty by claiming that such disagreements are "resolvable in principle although not in practice because of human stubbornness and dishonesty"?[51] Finally, should philosophy opt *in principle* for the *status quo* in morals, and against all those who find the current moral views wrong, irrational, and prejudiced, and undertake to criticize them and bring about change, not only against Smart, but also Socrates, Bentham, Marx, Nietzsche, Russell?

I shall not dwell here on the merits and demerits of the method of appealing to the "common moral consciousness" in dealing with problems in moral philosophy. Whatever the outcome of discussing this issue, the method does not help at all with the problem of punishment in general, nor the question of "punishing" the innocent in particular. It is a fair guess that the "plain people" are not very consistent when facing many ethical issues; it is an established fact that they are not at all consistent when they have to deal with punishment. Bradley, who was a retributivist, argued in his time in the following way: "our people" see the rationale of punishment in terms of retribution; the utilitarian view of punishment is opposed to the retributive view and incompatible with it; *therefore* "our people"do not accept the utilitarian view.[52] But empirical research has shown that when confronted with casuistic questions on punishment, "our people" tend to switch from retributive to utilitarian judgments and back again, and that the same lack of basic consistency comes to the fore when more specific questions, relating to "punishment" of the innocent, have to be answered.[53] In the opinion of the authors of the study referred to, there was a more general lesson to be learnt here, namely "that the fundamental mistake of Mr. Bradley, — in which he is very far, indeed, from being alone, — lies in the assumption that any one consistently maintained standard forms the basis of the judgments of 'our people' in the matter of punishment, or, indeed, of anything else."[54]

So we can safely forget about the "common moral consciousness" and turn to our own. What are we to do if *we* feel that "punishment" of the innocent is morally wrong, even if it is the action which would have the best consequences attainable under the circumstances? What reasons can be given to make us suppress our moral repugnance to such "punishment," in order to be able to accept wholeheartedly the utilitarian theory together with all its implications? In his monograph *An Outline of a System of Utilitarian Ethics*, J.J.C. Smart has this to offer:

> Some writers seem to think that to refute utilitarianism it is sufficient to show that it conflicts with some of our particular moral intuitions or feelings. . . . A false analogy with science seems to operate. In science we certainly must correct our general principles in the light of particular observations. But in ethics our particular statements are not observation reports but recommendations. It therefore seems to me that the matter is the other way round. Our general principle, resting on something so simple and natural as generalized benevolence, seems to me to be more securely founded than our particular feelings, which are subtly distorted by analogies with similar-looking (but in reality totally different) types of cases, and with all sorts of hangovers from traditional and uncritical ethical thinking.[55]

The first thing to which one could object here is that there does not seem to be any reason why particular moral convictions should be considered less simple or less "natural" than generalized moral feelings. Secondly, it is not obvious why that which is simpler or "natural" should carry greater moral weight than that which is complex or not "natural" (which here presumably means "acquired" or "learned"). Moreover, a careful reader of Smart's study is bound to be surprised to find the author disqualifying the method he himself used in an earlier chapter when criticizing an alternative theory.[56]

This last point is the most telling: it is not accidental that an author who, when replying to objections to his theory, explicitly rejects the method of testing ethical theories with the help of our particular moral convictions, makes use of the very same method when criticizing other theories. For what other method is at his disposal? To test an ethical theory means, first and foremost, to test what the theory puts forward as the fundamental moral principle. A fundamental moral principle, being *fundamental*, can be neither established nor refuted from the standpoint of another *moral* principle. Being a *moral* principle, it cannot be derived from a principle which is *not moral*, nor can it be criticized for not having been established in such a way. At the same time, anything proposed as a fundamental moral principle will invariably be very general. Such a principle, taken by itself, will hardly ever appear obviously unacceptable. The Golden Rule, for instance, certainly strikes us as quite reasonable and decent. So does the Categorical Imperative, both when it demands that the maxims we act on should be universalizable and when it commands that we respect the humanity of every human being and never treat a human as a mere means. Maximizing the good and minimizing the bad in the world seems no less irreproachable on the face of it. We cannot know whether we can really accept such a principle to live by and judge our own actions and those of others until we have some more specific idea of its contents. Now, the contents of a moral principle are its implications as to what would be right and wrong, what we should do and what we must not do, in various situations that come up in the life of an individual and a society. The way to assess an implication of a principle concerning a particular situation is to compare it to the personal, pretheoretical moral conviction (intuition, feeling, judgment) which would be our response to that situation.

This does not mean to say that these personal convictions of ours are sacrosanct. They are liable to be considered and reconsidered; we might be willing to discard some of them, either because they turn out to be inconsistent with some others which we feel to be more deeply ingrained, or because they contradict some moral principle or some ethical theory which we accept. But there are bound to be some which we are not willing to give up; for otherwise there will be no *terra firma* for us to stand on when deciding for or against various moral principles or ethical theories. The outcome of a quest for moral orientation in some particular field, or even in our moral experience as a whole, which would proceed along these lines, might be a state which Rawls has termed "reflective equilibrium."[57]

So the method of critically examining ethical theories by confronting their implications with our particular moral convictions is perfectly legitimate. The effectiveness of applying this method, however, will depend in each case on whether these convictions will be in keeping with what the critic expects. Consequently, the critic of utilitarianism, leaving the common morality aside, can present the argument on "punishment" of the innocent as an argument which is *ad hominem* in that it is addressed to each one of us personally. Faced with this argument, everyone can envisage the situation described to see what his or her own moral response would be. I imagine that some of us will feel that in such a situation it *would* be morally right to "punish" an innocent; what the critic of utilitarianism presents as an argument against this theory, such persons will see merely as part of its analysis. In such cases the critic will be "outsmarted," not by the utilitarian, but by the reader. But I also believe that many will evince an unshakeable conviction that "punishment" of the innocent is morally wrong even when it would have better consequences than any other possible action. To them the argument will show, in a clear and striking way, that the theory which morally consecrates such an injustice is not their theory.

In an article written after the monograph from which I qouted above, J.J.C. Smart tries to turn the argument about "punishment" of the innocent against the nonutilitarian viewpoint in ethics:

> Surely if it is shown that, in certain circumstances . . . a utilitarian ought, on his own principles, to commit a serious injustice, such as punishing an innocent man, then it seems that this *does* and *should* weaken the appeal of utilitarianism. And yet one can be made to vacillate back again. We also reflect that the serious injustice would *ex hypothesi* be the only possible alternative to an even greater total misery than would be caused by the injustice. . . . If a case really *did* arise in which injustice was the lesser of two evils (in terms of human happiness and misery, that is) the anti-utilitarian conclusion is a very unpalatable one too, namely that in some circumstances one should choose the greater total misery. . . . It seems to me that some of the implications of any ethical theory will be unsatisfactory. If the theory is a utilitarian one, then the possibility that one ought to commit injustice will be felt to be acutely unsatisfactory by someone who has had a normal civilized upbringing. If, on the other hand, it is a theory with deontological elements, then it will have the unsatisfactory implication that sometimes avoidable misery ought not to be avoided.[58]

This is very true. The argument on "punishment" of the innocent strikingly shows that, no matter how much the good and the just may frequently coincide, this is by no means inevitable; there are cases when the two come into sharp conflict, so that we cannot but run counter to one of them. Therefore we have to choose — in ethical theory, and in life as well. One choice will proceed from the view that the human good is the substance of morality and its supreme criterion and that, accordingly, the execution of justice is meaningless, morally and humanly unacceptable, if it conflicts with that. The other choice will express the conviction that justice is not merely an instrument of the common good, but is an autonomous moral principle, whose demands ought to be carried out even when this means paying a price in human well-being, in happiness and misery.

Here the utilitarian, elaborating a suggestion in the passage I quoted from Smart, could make one more objection. Would the nonutilitarian choice imply that it is *never* morally permissible to "punish" the innocent, whatever the consequences? The implausibility of such moral absolutism becomes clear when the situation described in the argument is somewhat modified. In its original version, the argument describes a judge who must choose between "punishing" an innocent person, thereby forestalling a number of offenses and restoring public confidence in the legal order, and acquitting him, after which offenses will continue to be committed and public confidence in the ability of the police and the judiciary to protect law-abiding citizens will continue to decline, with all the attendant undesirable consequences that such a process is bound to have concerning the legal order and social life in general. The consequences of doing justice in this case would, unquestionably, be very bad; but we can also imagine a case when they are much, much worse. We can suppose, for instance, that the judge has to choose between "punishing" an innocent person and the definitive ruin of an entire nation — as, according to the New Testament, Caiaphas believed he had to do.[59] Would it not be farfetched, even fantastic, to maintain that even in such a case it is not morally permissible to "punish" an innocent person, but the entire people should be allowed to perish? *Fiat justitia, pereat mundus*? On the other hand, if the critic of utilitarianism were to allow for "punishment" of the innocent in such a case, would that not render his criticism of utilitarianism meaningless? Would that not show that on the level of practical implications the critic's own view is no different from that of the utilitarian, that it is exposed to the same objection he brings up against the latter?[60]

In reply, the critic of utilitarianism can choose to stand by the unconditional prohibition of "punishment" of the innocent, whatever the consequences. He can maintain that the law of justice is absolute, so that no compromise must be made in its regard, no matter what the circumstances and the price which may have to be paid in human well-being. This is the view of Kant; he holds that the importance of justice is paramount, so that "if justice perishes, there is no further point in men living on earth."[61]

This kind of moral absolutism, embraced in our day by philosophers such as A. Donagan or G.E.M. Anscombe, is admittedly difficult to accept; but it is by no means the only alternative to the utilitarian readiness to "punish" the innocent. There is a third possibility, somewhere between the permissiveness of utilitarians and the rigorism of absolutists. It can be maintained that justice is a fundamental moral principle, but not an absolute one. There is a plurality of basic moral principles, but none is so weighty that it will *always* tip the scales over any other principle with which it might come into conflict. Certain principles usually carry greater weight than certain others, but there are cases when a principle of the first kind has to give way to a principle of the second. Thus justice usually overrides the principle of beneficence; still, there may be cases in which the latter principle will carry the day. Such was, characteristically, the case of Caiaphas, who had to choose between "punishing" an innocent person, which would be gravely unjust, and the ruin of the entire nation, which the principle of beneficence commanded him to prevent. The best known proponent of this kind of ethical pluralism in our century is W.D. Ross; having in mind, apparently, the case of the high priest, he says that "the interests of the society may sometimes be so deeply involved as to make it right to punish an innocent man 'that the whole nation perish not'."[62]

If, with philosophers such as Ross or McCloskey, we approach the issue of "punishment" of the innocent along these lines, we can allow such an action to be justified, but only when it is the sole way of preventing an evil of enormous magnitude. A utilitarian, on the other hand, will not consider the option of "punishing" the innocent only in those cases where she has to avoid some truly immense evil. According to her theory, such "punishment" will be morally justified *whenever* its consequences are even *slightly better* than those of desisting from it. She will consider it right, for example, to pass the death "sentence" on an innocent person whenever the circumstances are such that in this way, and in this way only, even two murders will be prevented. Thus there is, after all, a significant difference between the utilitarian and her critic

— certainly difference enough to make it legitimate for the latter to bring up the argument on "punishment" of the innocent against the former.

Another difference between the two concerns the guilt which the nonutilitarian will feel if he "punishes" an innocent person. Such "punishment" is a paradigmatic case of injustice, and that is what makes it intrinsically, although not absolutely, wrong. In certain exceptional cases, the principle of justice in punishment will have to give way to another principle, so that it will be morally justified to "punish" an innocent person. But even in cases in which it is *justified*, it will not thereby become *just*, nor will the *prima facie* wrongness which characterizes every injustice be obliterated. The *prima facie* wrongness of "punishment" of the innocent, the sense that a highly important moral principle was sacrificed, will be the ground of the feeling of guilt. There is something tragic in cases of this kind; as Nicolai Hartmann puts it, "it is inherent in the essence of such moral conflicts that in them value stands against value and that it is not possible to escape from them without being guilty. . . . Real moral life is not such that one can stand guiltless in it."[63]

A utilitarian is immune to this sense of the tragic and to the feeling of guilt which brings it about. From her point of view, whenever the balance of consequences favors "punishing" the innocent, that is all there is to it, morally speaking; so one should "punish" them and feel no compunction. She will be sorry for the evil inflicted on the innocent, of course, but that is something essentially different. There can be no sense of an important moral consideration being sacrificed, for there are no autonomous moral considerations, considerations which cannot be cashed out in consequences; justice is but a kind of utility, injustice a kind of disutility. There can be no feeling of guilt, for guilt presupposes that one has done something wrong.

If a judge, whose moral convictions are nonutilitarian, comes to the conclusion that it is morally justified to "punish" an innocent person — that justice ought to be sacrificed in order to prevent a tremendous evil — he will nevertheless feel guilty for doing so. I believe we should find this quite understandable and appropriate; if he did not feel this way, we should think him morally obtuse or even callous. If so, the fact that utilitarianism implies that such feeling would be predicated on a false belief and accordingly be unreasonable and uncalled for, points to an additional serious defect in the theory.

6. Some General Traits of Utilitarianism

The arguments advanced in the preceding sections show some very unattractive implications of the utilitarian view of punishment; they also point to some basic traits of utilitarianism in general, which are the source of some of the main difficulties plaguing this kind of ethics. Let me spell them out quite briefly.

When it comes to punishment, the facts of desert, of guilt of innocence, have no intrinsic moral significance for utilitarians; it is the consequences of punishment that count, and nothing else. This is but a special case of a basic attitude of utilitarianism to the past. As the consequences of our actions are to be considered the sole criterion of their morality, the moral point of view is completely forward-looking, and the past as a whole has no intrinsic moral weight. To be sure, the past can be relevant, morally speaking, but only extrinsically, *via* the future. This exlusive orientation of utilitarianism toward the future gives rise to the well-known problems with duties pertaining to relations based on facts of the past: duties of keeping promises, gratitude, loyalty to parents or friends, and the like.

The attitude of utilitarianism to the past and future is also manifest in the utilitarian view of praise and blame. If we wanted to place punishment in a wider context, we would say that it is a type of blame, reprobation, or criticism.[64] A nonutilitarian would think of this as consideration against the utilitarian theory of punishment: he would say that praise and blame are obviously connected to desert and guilt, not only logically, but from the moral point of view as well, so that the fact that punishment is a special kind of blame suggests a retributive account of its moral basis. In reply to this, a utilitarian would bring in her own theory of praise and blame, the basic tenet of which is that praise and blame are also *actions*, so that when praising and blaming, as when doing anything else, we have to look to the future and go solely by the consequences. Now *this* kind of praise and blame will very often be quite different from the praise and blame nonutilitarians are used to — and also from the praise and blame a beginner in utilitarianism might practice. Sometimes the actions that are wrong from the utilitarian point of view itself will be praised, and *vice versa*.

For example, a man near Berchtesgaden in 1938 might have jumped into a river and rescued a drowning man, only to find that it was Hitler. He did the wrong thing, for he would have saved the world a lot of trouble if he had left Hitler below the surface. On the other hand his motive, his desire to save life, was one which we approve of people having: in general, though not in this case, the desire to save life leads to acting rightly. It is worth our while to strengthen such a desire. Not only shall we praise the action (thus expressing our approval of it) but we shall perhaps even give the man a medal, thus encouraging others to emulate it. Indeed praise itself comes to have some of the social functions of medal giving: we come to like praise for its own sake, and are thus influenced by the possibility of being given it. Praising a person is thus an important action in itself — it has significant effects. A utilitarian must therefore learn to control his acts of praise and dispraise, thus perhaps concealing his approval of an action when he thinks that the expression of such approval might have bad effects, and perhaps even praising actions of which he does not really approve.[65]

When it comes to "punishing" the innocent and their having to sacrifice themselves, or to staging a show of punishment instead of actually inflicting it, it is obvious that the good consequences of so doing, which make out the justification of such actions, can be attained only by keeping the facts of the matter secret and deceiving the public about them. Such a resort to secrecy is not something that characterizes a utilitarian only when dealing with punishment: it is rather a practice she has to adopt in general. Since one and the same action often has different consequences, depending on whether it is known to others or done in secrecy, it follows — as one of the foremost proponents of utilitarianism was the first to emphasize — that for a utilitarian in general

> it may be right to do and privately recommend, under certain circumstances, what it would not be right to advocate openly; it may be right to teach openly to one set of persons what it would be wrong to teach to others; it may be conceivably right to do, if it can be done with comparative secrecy, what it would be wrong to do in the face of the world; and even, if perfect secrecy can be reasonably expected, what it would be wrong to recommend by private advice or example.[66]

In addition to this, of course, "the opinion that secrecy may render an action right which would not otherwise be so should itself be kept comparatively secret; and similarly it seems expedient that the doctrine that esoteric morality is expedient should itself be kept esoteric."[67] That is, a utilitarian is eventually committed to "the oddest and perhaps the most corrupting exercise in secrecy . . . secrecy about one's moral position: esoteric ethics."[68]

So much for secrecy; as for the lying and deception involved, I would not go so far as to maintain, as Quinton does with regard to "punishment" of the innocent, that "the peculiar outrageousness of the rejection of [the principle that only the guilty are to be punished] is a consequence, not of the brutality that such rejection might seem to permit, but of the fact that it involves a kind of lying."[69] From the moral point of view, surely, the injury comes first; still, the lying literally adds insult to injury, making a morally reprehensible action even more so. The same kind of lying and deception will be involved in self-sacrifice of the innocent. Another sort of lying and deception will be called for whenever the appearance of punishment is to be attained without actually punishing. This is not limited to the utilitarian theory of punishment either. Lying, deception and manipulation are means a utilitarian is bound to adopt whenever necessary for reaching the best possible results under the circumstances — which, all things considered, will be very often indeed.[70]

Some of the arguments against the utilitarian theory of punishment presented in the preceding sections refer to situations in which, according to the theory, innocent or irresponsible people are to be sacrificed for the common good. Here we have another feature of utilitarianism in general — the tendency to sacrifice the individual for the sake of the group, and also the group for the sake of a larger group. This takes us back to the view of humanity implicit in utilitarianism. Utilitarianism is a monistic ethical theory, a feature which, as I have said, accounts for much of its appeal. It does not leave room for any moral concepts, norms, or ideals which are really autonomous, that is, which cannot be interpreted in terms of the common good. There is no room for rights conceived in a way which does not reduce them to instruments for maximizing the good.[71] Nor for the idea of humans as beings endowed with dignity — a very special kind of value which is not comparable to other values; beings not to be treated as a means only; beings who cannot be taken as units of calculation, or as Arthur Koestler once put it, beings to whom the rules of mathematics do not apply. Utilitarians conceive of people as so many *loci* of the good, and the good (be it pleasure, happiness, satisfaction of desires or interests, or whatever) is something to be quantified, not necessarily along the lines of Bentham's notoriously unsuccessful "moral arithmetics," but in some way nevertheless. A utilitarian will normally come to moral decisions on the basis of calculations. These will not be different in any important respect when it comes to calculating the good of a single person and the good of two or more persons: "if it is rational for me to choose the pain of a visit to the dentist in order to prevent the pain of toothache, why is it not rational of me to choose a pain for Jones, similar to that of my visit to the dentist, if that is the only way in which I can prevent a pain, equal to that of my toothache, for Robinson?"[72] Now when one thinks about moral matters in this way, one is bound to end up using people in various ways, including sacrificing them. Rawls describes this aspect of utilitarianism by saying that it conflates impartiality with impersonality, and does not take seriously the distinction between persons.[73] This is something to be expected of an ethical theory which, owing to its view of human beings, does not and cannot take persons themselves seriously.

4. Punishment as Retribution: Hegel

1. Fundamentals of the Philosophy of Right

According to Hegel, right is based on the will. To claim this is to claim that right is based on freedom, for freedom "constitutes the concept or substantiality of the will."[1] Thus "freedom is both the substance of right and its goal, while the system of right is the realm of freedom made actual, the world of mind brought forth out of itself like a second nature."[2] This characterization of will as essentially free is at the same time a fundamental characterization of the nature of human beings.

By freedom of the will, two rather different things may be meant. To say that someone's will is free may mean that he can do what he wants to, that he is not prevented from doing whatever he feels like doing. This is what Hegel calls "arbitrary," "relative," "formal" freedom. When the will is free in this sense, it chooses from various natural urges and inclinations; it opens up to one of them and accepts it, while rejecting others, being able to raise itself above any of them at all times: "In this element of the will is rooted my ability to free myself from everything, abandon every aim, abstract from everything. Man alone can sacrifice everything, his life included; he can commit suicide. An animal cannot; it always remains . . . in an alien destiny to which it merely accustoms itself."[3] Since urges and inclinations from which the arbitrary will chooses, to which it opens up, which it accepts and which thus determine it, are something external and alien to it, arbitrary freedom is the freedom of humans as natural beings. Their "true" freedom is different: it is what Hegel terms "absolute" freedom. The will is free in this sense insofar as it is the "general will" that expresses the conditions in which individuals, each having an arbitrary will, can live together in a community. Like Rousseau, who emphasizes that the general will is not the same as the empirical "will of all," Hegel conceives of the general will as being basically different from any aggregation of arbitrary wills of individuals. At the same time, the difference between the arbitrary and the general will is not one between the will of the individual and a transcendent collective will. He makes the distinction — as Kant did before him — *within* the will of the individual. As with Kant, this distinction is based on a dualistic view of human beings as natural beings subject to instincts, urges, and passions, and at the same time spiritual beings, endowed with the ability to choose and act in accordance with the demands of morality and the law. As a natural being, the individual is the subject of the arbitrary will, preoccupied with himself and his individual wants and interests, different from others, sometimes in conflict with them. At the same time, as a spiritual being, he is the subject of the general will; this will is no less his very own — his ethical and therefore "true" will, and something he has in common with others.

Naturally enough, the individual's arbitrary will is not always in accord with his "true" will. When these two come into conflict, the latter ought to prevail, to subjugate the former and set limits to it. A conflict of the two wills which ends with a victory of the true, general will and subjugation of the arbitrary will is not a defeat of the individual and a triumph of a force alien and opposed to him; it is the emancipation of the individual from that which is subjective, transient, and inferior in him, and the affirmation of that which is higher, objective, and permanent in his nature. In contrast to the widely shared view that an individual is really free only when he can do whatever he happens to wish to do, and that for him to control his needs, wishes, and urges, and to subject them to the rule of morality and the law would be to restrict his freedom, Hegel — like Kant before him — sees the individual as "truly" free, free in the way appropriate to humans as spiritual beings, when he subjects his urges, desires, and interests to the rule of ethical principles and acts as he ought to.

The general will is expressed in laws, when these are in accord with reason (*Vernunft*). Laws demand "that every individual be respected and treated by others as a free being, for only thus does the free will find itself as its subject and contents in another [human being]."[4] To recognize another as a free being means to treat him as a person. Accordingly, the fundamental principle of right commands, "Do not infringe personality and what personality entails."[5] It follows that an act is right if it does not restrict the freedom of another, and wrong if it violates the freedom of another and thereby does not respect him as a person.

True, there are laws which permit human beings to be treated not as persons, but as objects; the paradigmatic example is the laws of slavery. Now such laws may be binding in the sense of being enacted and enforced within a certain jurisdiction, but they are not legitimate in a deeper, philosophical sense, for they are opposed to reason and justice and do not express the general will. Mere existence of slavery is "an outrage on the conception of man," and "it is the nature of the case that a slave has an absolute right to free himself."[6] Laws which respect the personality of one human being more than that of another on account of differences in class, nation, or religion are unjust and illegitimate for the same reason. World history is essentially the progress of the consciousness of freedom; its most momentous result, the fundamental principle of the modern age, is the knowledge that a human being is free as a human being: that "a man counts as a man in virtue of his manhood alone, not because he is a Jew, Catholic, Protestant, German, Italian etc."[7] In Hegel's view, the demand for equality of people in the eyes of the law is implied by the very basic principle of right.

2. Retribution, Revenge, Punishment

When, in a conflict of the two wills within the individual, the arbitrary will prevails and the individual breaks the law, the law strikes back and exacts retribution. From the point of view of the person on the receiving end, retribution is a kind of coercion. Coercion is the very opposite of freedom. If freedom is "the substance of right and its goal," if the system of right is nothing but "the realm of freedom made actual," how can coercion be in accordance with right, how can it be just and legitimate?

True, coercion is opposed to right, and inadmissible when it is exerted as *mere* coercion — when it comes as the first, one-sided coercion, that is, as an offense. But as a reaction to coercion already exerted, as "the second coercion," "coercion against coercion," it is just and necessary. The first act of coercion already contains a demand for the second and its justification. The second act of coercion annuls the first, and reaffirms the law which the first act violated. Such coercion "does not contradict the dignity of a free being."[8] Accordingly, the fundamental principle of right does not entail, simply and unconditionally, that nobody may be coerced; it entails that "no man may be coerced, except in order to annul the coercion he has exerted on another."[9] An offense is the first, one-sided, and therefore illegitimate coercion. Retribution is, by definition, "the second coercion," "coercion against coercion." Therefore, it is in accordance with right, just and legitimate.

The thesis that coercion is legitimate, insofar as it comes as a response to coercion already exerted, is based on a fundamental moral standpoint. This standpoint is opposed to Socrates' conviction that "we ought not to retaliate or render evil for evil to any one, whatever evil we may have suffered from him,"[10] as well as to Plato's view that "it is never right to harm anyone at any time,"[11] and to Jesus' command, "Do not resist one who is evil. But if anyone strikes you on the right cheek, turn to him the other one also; and if anyone would sue you and take your coat, let him have your cloak as well; and if anyone forces you to go one mile, go with him two miles."[12] In opposition to the ethics of turning the other cheek, Hegel opts for the view that "man ought to be bad towards badness, to take ill the evil done to him, to harm those that harm him," or, more generally, "as a man has done, so it should be requited him; he has deserved it by his act."[13]

The import of this principle, which could be taken as the reverse of the Golden Rule, is well put by Walter Moberly:

> The deep-seated sense of fairness which revolts against punishment of the innocent revolts also against any treatment of the guilty which appears to confound guilt and innocence. It is felt to be unfair that a man's grievous fault should make no difference to the treatment he receives and that he should be treated just as favourably as if he had done no wrong. It is reasonable that we should do unto others as we would wish them to do unto us. But, conversely, it is fitting and proper that, what others are to do us, should be affected for better or worse by the quality of what we have done to them.[14]

According to the view based upon this principle, in judging the morality and legality of actions, justice ought to be *the* criterion, while the crucial concepts should be those of desert and reciprocity. It is justified to requite evil with evil, for it is only just; and it is just because when doing so, we treat another person in the way he has deserved. He has deserved to be treated ill, to have evil inflicted on him, because that is no more and no less than paying him back in the same currency for what he has done to us. A person who has treated someone ill normally finds it hateful to be treated the same way in return. He can offer various reasons for not being treated that way, but he cannot seriously and convincingly claim that he has not deserved it, that an injustice is being done to him.

Retribution is an act of reciprocity, and thus something that the person on whom it is inflicted has deserved; therefore it is just, justified, legitimate. It has two forms: revenge and punishment.

Revenge is retribution executed by the person injured. Being retribution, it is justified in principle — that is, when it is proportionate to the wrong suffered. In the state of nature, in which there are no state, no legal order and no courts, revenge is the only way to satisfy the demands of justice. But it is deficient in two respects. First, very often revenge is not retribution measured out and executed in an impartial way, solely according to the seriousness of the wrong suffered; for it is determined and executed by the injured side, which takes over the role of a judge in its own case. A person who had been injured often views the wrong done to him in a subjective way and under the influence of hurt feelings, so that his revenge only "confuses the right" — it is not strictly limited to the proper, just measure, but goes too far and requites the wrong suffered with a greater wrong. Second, revenge is not institutionalized; it is executed out of subjective motives, feelings, and passions. Thus the person on whom it is taken will not see it as a legitimate act of a higher authority. He may come to see it as a wrong pure and simple, and to react to it by perpetrating still another wrong. Thus, instead of a reaffirmation of justice, which would lead to reconciliation, a chain of injuries and counterinjuries may be set in motion, a chain which can be endless. "Amongst uncivilized peoples," says Hegel, "revenge is deathless; amongst the Arabs, for instance, it can be checked only by superior force or by the impossibility of its satisfaction."[15]

In contrast to revenge, which is often not just, and even when it is, accords with justice with respect to contents only (because it is retribution) but not in form (because it is an act of a private individual), punishment is just both in its contents and in its form. It is retribution "carried out through a general will and in its name," so that it executes justice "freed from subjective interest and a subjective form and no longer contingent on might."[16] A judge who metes out punishments "must have one interest only at heart — the interest that the law should be carried out."[17] Thus punishment is retribution freed from both limitations which plague revenge; it executes justice in the proper way and in the proper measure. Therefore, where the institution of punishment has been set up, revenge is no longer necessary or admissible.

3. Punishment Justified Objectively

Hegel develops his justification of punishment along two lines: he wants to show that punishment is justified both when one takes an external, impartial standpoint and when one tries to see it from the point of view of the person punished. Thus his rationale of punishment can be divided into two main parts: the objective and the subjective justifications.

When approaching the issue from the objective point of view, Hegel concentrates on the nature of offense and the law that has been broken. Criminal offense, that is, an offense which involves malicious will (*mens rea*) on the part of the offender, is something negative and contradictory; it is a mere show, a nullity. First and foremost, it "is not something positive, not a first thing, on which punishment would supervene as a negation. It is something negative"[18] — the violation of someone's right, the breaking of a law, and thus a negation of that right and that law. Being a negation of a right and a law, it is only possible in the context of rights and the law. By negating its own presuppositions, an offense is immanently contradictory. For the same reason, it is "a show." Hegel defines show in the *Science of Logic* as "the negative which has a being, but in an Other, in its negation: Show is instability which . . . is null."[19] By being a show, offense is "null."

This does not mean to say that offense is null in the sense of being nonexistent or amounting to nothing. Offense is, on the contrary, very real, its effects are usually quite palpable. Hegel has in mind nullity in a normative sense. Offense is null, first, in the sense of giving expression to the arbitrary will of the criminal, which aims at an unlawful objective. This will is opposed to the general will, which is the will of the offender himself as well — his "true" will, which expresses the higher and better part of his nature, and is thus to be preferred to his arbitrary will and to prevail over it. An offense is, further, an act of a rational being and, as such, an exemplification and affirmation of a general rule; but the rule it exemplifies is opposed to another, generally valid rule, and cannot maintain itself in its opposition to the latter. This is another sense of its nullity. It is also null in that it is a negation of a recognized, valid right. Finally, it is null because its very notion implies its negation, that is, punishment for it.

Punishment is entailed by the concept of offense because the latter is based on the concept of law, and "the essense of law, whether this relates to external Nature or the ethical world order, consists in an inseparable unity, a necessary inner connection, of distinct determinations. Thus it is that law necessarily links punishment with crime; it is true that the criminal may regard punishment as something extraneous to him, but the Notion of crime essentially involves its opposite — punishment."[20] Punishment is but the second half of the whole whose first half is offense. It is the "negation" of offense. Offense is not something immediately given, which exists on its own; it is possible only against the background of right and the law, as their negation. So punishment is not simply a negation, but the second negation, the "negation of the negation." It demonstrates the nullity of offense by nullifying it.

How is this accomplished? The characteristics of offense cited are in fact characteristic of wrong in general — that is, both of the kind of wrong dealt with by criminal law, and of what Hegel terms non-malicious wrong, which is the subject-matter of civil law. This latter kind of wrong is also necessarily connected with its negation, and must be nullified. Since it exists only as an act and its consequences, in a "positive," "external" way, not in the malicious will of its perpetrator, it is negated or nullified when its consequences are nullified by restitution. It is otherwise with a criminal offense: in addition to the mere act and its consequences, there is also the malicious will of the offender, and it is precisely this malicious will that is essential and distinctive. Therefore, mere restitution could not effect the negation required, for it relates only to the external aspect of the act. An offense must be negated by negating what is essential to it — the malicious will of its perpetrator. This is done in the same way in which he has negated the right of the victim and the law on which that right is based: by coercion. This not only nullifies the external aspect of the offense, but displays its "inner nullity."

Further, punishment "annuls" the offense. Use of the word "annul" to translate Hegel's term *aufheben* gives rise to a terminological difficulty which ought to be noted. Neither "annul" nor other words which have been used by Hegel's English translators (such as "transcend," "sublate," or "cancel") have the dual meaning characteristic of the German word; their meaning is wholly negative, while *aufheben* has a positive meaning too. To annul, says Hegel, "has this double meaning, that it signifies to keep or to preserve and also to make to cease, to finish."[21] The negative element in the annulment of an offense by punishment is the negation or nullification of the offense, that is, of the malicious will of the offender. The positive element in this annulment is that the offense is at the same time, in a way, present and "preserved" in punishment. First, in a logical sense: the concepts of offense and punishment are logically connected, punishment is defined in terms of offense, as its negation. Second, the offense is "preserved" in punishment in a practical sense, as that which justifies it as the "second coercion" and as evil paid back for an evil inflicted.

Hegel frequently speaks of punishment as the "annulment" of offense; this is one of the basic tenets of his theory of punishment, and one of its most distinctive ones. In this context he usually also depicts punishment as the restoration of right. This is no coincidence: the thesis of the reaffirmation of right through punishment is but a further explication of the doctrine of "annulment." Punishment "annuls" the offense first and foremost by negating it. Offense is the negation of right; therefore punishment, as the negation of the offense, is not a negation of something positive, but a negation of a negation. By negating a negation one gets what was negated by the first negation. Thus punishment restores what the offense has negated — the right and the law. Of course, the double negation does not restore the identical original position, as if this were a mathematical operation. The right and the law are restored, but not in the same mode in which they had been given before the offense was committed. In their original, immediate mode they express a mere "ought," postulated but not tried in practice, an "ought" based on an authority whose strength has not been made manifest, whose superiority to those who challenge it and rebel against it has not been demonstrated. In contrast, the right and the law which have been negated by an offense, and have emerged from the conflict victorious, have been restored by punishment — theirs is a mature form, which has been tried and proven in practice.

> The show . . . is the falsity which disappears in claiming independent existence; and in the course of the show's disappearance the essence reveals itself as essence, i.e. as the authority of the show. The essence has negated that which negated it and so is corroborated. Wrong is a show of this kind, and, when it disappears, right acquires the character of something fixed and valid. What is called here the essence is just the principle of rightness, and in contrast with it the particular will annuls itself as a falsity. Hitherto the being of the right has been immediate only, but now it is actual because it returns out of its negation.[22]

A full-fledged retributive theory sees in the offense committed not only the ground of the right to punish, but the source of the duty to punish as well. In this respect, Hegel is a true retributivist: his doctrine of annulment of the offense and restoration of right through punishment is primarily an attempt to establish the second of the two claims. If an offense has been committed, then not only may we annul it and reaffirm the right and the law, but we also ought to do so; we not only have a right, but also a duty to punish: "It would be impossible for society to leave a crime unpunished, since that would be to posit it as right . . ."[23]

4. Punishment Justified Subjectively

A main tenet of Hegel's philosophy of history and the state is that "the principle of the modern world requires that what anyone is to recognize shall reveal itself to him as something entitled to recognition,"[24] that "the right of the subjective will is that whatever it is to recognize as valid shall be seen by it as good."[25] This applies to punishment no less than to anything else that is in need of justification. It is not enough to show the legitimacy of punishment from an external, objective standpoint; it must also be justified subjectively, from the point of view of the offender himself, in terms of his own will.

But punishment is by definition an evil, something undesirable, a kind of coercion, deprivation. How, then, can it be justified in this way?

In Hegel's view, punishment is justified subjectively as an expression of the general will. Laws embody the general will. This will is not external and alien to the individual, but his own "true" will, which expresses the higher and better part of his nature and enables him to participate in the world of morality and right and to attain "true" freedom. Accordingly, Hegel says that in an offense, the will is "differentiated not in the sense of . . . being contrasted with another person, but in the sense of [being] related to itself . . . as a particular will at variance with and opposed to itself as an absolute will."[26] Offense does not only injure the person whose right has been violated, the law which defines that right, the general will expressed by it, and thus, indirectly, everyone else; it also injures the general will embedded in the offender himself, the general will as his own will — that is, it injures the offender himself. Thus, when an offense is requited by punishment, the punishment ensues not only from the general will of all and the law as its embodiment, but from the general will as the will of the offender himself — it is an expression of his own will.

This does not mean to say that the offender must will his own punishment on the level of his empirical, subjective will. For "it may be the case that a man is not aware of his own general will. A man may believe that something is happening in opposition to his will, even though it comes from his own will. A criminal being punished can . . . want that punishment should pass him by; but the general will entails that crime is punished. It must be supposed, therefore, that the absolute will of the criminal itself implies that he shall be punished."[27] In this sense punishment, although a form of coercion, "also has an aspect in which it is not coercion and does not contradict the dignity of a free being, because the [general] will is the absolute will of every individual as well."[28]

But Hegel's subjective justification of punishment is not merely an appeal to the general will as the will of the offender himself. Hegel wants to show that punishment is grounded in his empirical, subjective will as well. How can this be?

According to W.H. Walsh, the answer to this question is to be found in Hegel's view of the offender as a free and responsible being, which implies that he "knows what he is doing and so commits himself to accepting the consequences of his act, including punishment if his crime is detected."[29] This interpretation is not plausible. If this were the import of what Hegel is saying, he would be advancing a variety of the deterrent theory of punishment; but, as we have seen in the preceding chapter, he rejects this theory as being incompatible with the respect due to every human being.[30] Moreover, the argument would justify too much: it would sanction any kind of oppression, provided it was announced in advance and conditioned on certain actions of citizens. If it is to be justified subjectively, punishment must be grounded in the offender's will in a different way.

Philosophers of the social contract school, such as Rousseau and Beccaria, try to do this by claiming that the contract contains the consent of every citizen to be punished in case he breaks the law.[31] Hegel, however, cannot do this; for he completely rejects the contractarian view of the state. Thus his solution is different. Beccaria was right, he says, when he set the consent of the person punished as the condition of the legitimacy of punishment, only he was looking for it in the wrong place. There is no need to assume a social contract, for the consent of the offender to be punished is involved in his own act, in the offense itself.

Every offense contains an element of generality. It is an act of a rational being, and ought to be recognized and treated as such. To relate to an act as to an act of a rational being means not to see it exclusively in its particularity, but to identify and take into consideration a rule involved in it. In the case of an offense, this rule is opposed to the principles of right, so it cannot be accepted as universally valid: "others do not recognize it in relation to themselves. But in relation to [the offender] it holds, for him it is valid, he makes it valid through his own act."[32] He has proclaimed it by his act as his own rule; therefore he may be treated in accordance with it. If he has stolen, he has thereby proclaimed the rule that the property of others may be violated; accordingly, his property may be taken away from him. If he has murdered, he has thereby laid down the rule that human life may be taken; therefore, the same may be done with his life. When we treat him this way, we do not apply to him a rule that is foreign and hostile to him; on the contrary, we merely go by his own rule, the rule involved in his own act. "There is no need for a special stipulation that the state, in case of crime, may dispose of my life," says Hegel; "rather, the right of the state lies in the very act of the criminal, by which he himself admits that he ought to be executed. As a murderer, he lays down the law that life ought not to be respected. In his act he expresses that which is general, thereby expressing his own death sentence."[33] These words refer specifically to murder and the death penalty, but the same holds of offenses and punishments in general. For "what is right to one man in relation to others, what holds as right for him, holds as right for others in relation to him." Therefore, "the wrong which he has committed, done to him, is right, because this second act, which he has recognized, reestablishes equality."[34]

Critics have questioned Hegel's view of offense as an implicitly general act. They have pointed out that the offender wants to proclaim no rule by his act; on the contrary, he wants to make an exception in his favor, while wishing that others should honor the rule he is breaking. "By his act," writes Ossip K. Flechtheim, for instance, "the criminal wants to make an exception to the rule, to secure a *privilege* for himself as against the *general* right; and a privilege obtains only as long as it has not become general! A thief who steals cannot want that the person from whom he steals, or someone else, should steal from *him* again; for then he should not have stolen in the first place."[35]

Still, I believe that Hegel is right on this point. If only showing that the very act of an offense implies the offender's wish to be punished would count as a subjective justification of punishment, then punishment could not be justified subjectively at all (except for fairly atypical kind of offenses: those which are motivated by a wish for punishment). The question to ask at this point is rather: Just what is the importance, what is the real weight of the offender's wish to secure a privilege for himself, to make an exception in his favor to a rule he requires others to follow? To keep the example given by Flechtheim, can a thief say that he did not want to affirm the rule that the institution of property is not to be respected; that he, generally speaking, has much respect for it, and only wanted to make an exception for himself, and that, accordingly, punishment which hits at his property might be justified in an objective sense, from a point of view which is completely alien to him — but that *for him*, that is, subjectively, the punishment remains something unjustified and morally unacceptable? If we came across a thief who argued along these lines, we should retort that his punishment is merely an application of the rule contained implicitly in his act, that it is *in this sense* based on his own will and *in so far* justified not only objectively, but subjectively as well. If he persisted in his refusal to universalize the rule and insisted on being privileged, on being an exception, the question would be: On whom does the *onus justificandi* rest? I think that it would rest on him, rather than on those who wanted to treat him the same way he had treated his victim. *He* would be bound to prove that he has a right to treat others in a way in which they have no right to treat him — that, for example, he can rightfully take the property of others, but others have no right to take his property. This would be a tall order indeed.

When an offender is treated in accordance with the rule he has affirmed by his own act, it turns out that having injured another, he has also injured himself; his own act becomes a force hostile to him, and returns as such upon his head. This point is made in a striking way in one of Hegel's early theological writings, *The Spirit of Christianity and Its Fate:*

> The law has been broken by the trespasser; its content no longer exists for him; he has canceled it. But the form of the law, universality, pursues him and clings to his trespass; his deed becomes universal, and the right which he has canceled is also canceled for him. . . . The illusion of trespass, its belief that it destroys the other's life and thinks itself enlarged thereby, is dissipated by the fact that the disembodied spirit of the injured life comes on the scene against the trespass, just as Banquo who came as a friend to Macbeth was not blotted out when he was murdered but immediately thereafter took his seat, not as a guest at the feast, but as an evil spirit. The trespasser intended to have to do with another's life, but he has only destroyed his own, for life is not different from life . . . In his arrogance he has destroyed indeed, but only the friendliness of life; he has perverted life into an enemy. It is the deed itself which has created a law whose domination now comes on the scene; this law is the unification, in the concept, of the equality between the injured, apparently alien, life and the trespasser's own forfeited life. It is now the first time that the injured life

appears as a hostile power against the trespasser and maltreats him as he has maltreated the other. . . . The same blows which the trespasser has dealt he experiences himself; tyrants are confronted by torturers, murderers by executioners. The torturers and executioners, who do the same as the tyrants and the murderers did, are called just, simply because they give like for like.[36]

To punish an offender because he has offended is to punish him because he deserves it; for to relate to another in accordance with his deserts is to take the way he treats others as the criterion of the way he is to be treated. To treat another according to his deserts is to relate to him as a responsible and free being. Freedom is a manifestation of rationality; thus, to recognize another's freedom is to recognize him as a rational being. Freedom and rationality pertain to persons. Accordingly, when an offender is punished because he has committed an offense, he is being recognized as a person, and respect is shown to that which is distinctively human in him, that which gives him the dignity that sets him apart from all other beings — his freedom and rationality. Consequently, not only does the state have a right to punish the offender; in Hegel's view, punishment is also a right of the offender himself.

Punishment is thus shown to be legitimate both objectively and subjectively. It is justified objectively because it is retribution, annulment of the offense and restoration of right and the law. It is also justified subjectively: first, as an expression of the general will, which is the true will of the offender himself; second, because the very act of offending against the law implies consent of the empirical, subjective will of the offender to be punished. In accordance with this, Hegel says that both objectively and subjectively, punishment effects reconciliation:

> Objectively, this is the reconciliation of the law with itself; by the annulment of the crime, the law is restored and its authority is thereby actualized. Subjectively, it is the reconciliation of the criminal with himself, i.e. with the law known by him as his own and as valid for him and his protection; when this law is executed upon him, he himself finds in this process the satisfaction of justice and nothing save his own act.[37]

5. *Lex talionis*

So far I have given an account of Hegel's reply to the questions about the grounds of the right to punish and the source of the duty to do so. These are the basic questions for any theory of punishment. The next one concerns the measure of punishment: What kind and what degree of punishment is legitimate and called for?

The answer to this question will depend on the answer given to the previous two. If punishment is justified in utilitarian terms, and the right and duty to punish are grounded in the good consequences of punishment, these consequences will provide its measure as well. In each case, the appropriate punishment will be that which secures the best consequences possible. If, on the other hand, one adheres to the retributive view of the right and duty to punish, and holds that punishment is justified by being just, and is just when it is deserved by the offense, the offense committed will also be the measure of punishment. On the question of the measure of punishment, retributivism entails the *lex talionis*: as the offender has done, so it should be done to him.

However, it has frequently been remarked that the *lex talionis* cannot always be applied, since it is often in the nature of the case that we cannot requite the offense in the same way and in the same measure. Confronted with this argument, some retributivists have given up the *lex talionis* and opted for the view that the offense committed is ground for the right and duty to punish but that, once these exist, punishment is to be measured out according to utilitarian criteria.[38]

Hegel is not willing to make this concession to utilitarianism, for he does not find the objection convincing: "It is easy enough . . . to exhibit the retributive character of punishment as an absurdity (theft for theft, robbery for robbery, an eye for an eye, a tooth for a tooth — and then you can go on to suppose that the criminal has only one eye or no teeth). But the concept [of retributive punishment] has nothing to do with this absurdity. . . ."[39] The *lex talionis* can be interpreted in two ways. It can be taken literally, as the demand for equality of punishment and offense in respect of their specific features: we should do to the offender the same thing he has done to his victim. Thus interpreted, the demand is admittedly often impracticable. But it can also be taken as the demand that punishment and offense be equal in respect of what is common to them, what makes them comparable: in respect of "value", or their "universal property of being injuries."[40] Thus "theft and a term in prison are quite different things, the thief is deprived of external freedom, something entirely different from that which he has taken away from the person injured, but in respect of value these two ought to be equal. . . ."[41] Properly understood, the *lex talionis* requires that punishment should affect the offender as much as his offense has affected the victim. This can be attained even in cases in which the principle "an eye for an eye, a tooth for a tooth" cannot be appled literally. This explains the use of fines and prison terms, which in respect of severity can be made proportionate to all kinds of offenses.

This should not be taken to imply that for every offense there is a punishment absolutely equal to it in severity, and that we ought to prescribe such punishment for each and every offense, once and for all. Were this to be required, we would soon reach the conclusion that it is impracticable and that, consequently, every or almost every punishment inflicted is unjust and unacceptable, be it one dollar more or less, or one day in prison more or less than what would be absolutely proportionate to the offense. Both the requirement and the conclusion it leads to are wrong. They testify to a mistaken conception of the nature of right and the law, and to excessive, absurd expectations of reason and legislation to entirely master the matter they deal with, to subsume it completely under *a priori* rules. It is in the nature of the matter they have to deal with, as of everything empirical, to resist such attempts; this matter can never be wholly subsumed under general rules, nor completely predicted, controlled, regulated.

> Reason cannot determine, nor can the concept provide any principle whose application could decide whether justice requires for an offence (i) a corporal punishment of forty lashes or thirty-nine, or (ii) a fine of five dollars or four dollars ninety-three, four, etc., cents, or (iii) imprisonment of a year or three-hundred and sixty-four, three, etc., days, or a year and one, two, or three days. . . . Reason itself requires us to recognize that contingency, contradiction, and show have a sphere and a right of their own, restricted though it be, and it is irrational to strive to resolve and rectify contradictions within that sphere.[42]

5. Arguments Against the Retributive Theory

1. Vengeful

One of the more popular objections to the retributive theory is the claim that it is in fact a philosophical rationalization of vengefulness. Utilitarians refer to the good consequences of punishment as its point and justification; retributivists, in contrast, are not interested in the future at all, they do not aim at any positive results, but look solely backwards, focusing on the evil done which is a fact of the past and cannot be undone, and require that another evil be added to it, even if no good whatever is to result from that. Therefore, retributivism is not really a philosophical theory, but merely an expression of a primitive craving for revenge clothed in philosophical attire.[1]

It is not difficult to show that this objection is misguided. The truth of a statement of fact is completely independent of the motive its author has for making it. If what a statement asserts is really the case, no unseemly motive of its author will make it false; if that is not the case, no worthy motive for making it can render it true. Analogously, there is no logical connection between the validity of a moral judgment and the motive its author has for expressing it. The same holds for theories. An ethical theory can be criticized for being inconsistent, psychologically unrealistic, predicated on beliefs about facts that are not true, or — most interestingly — for containing morally unacceptable implications. But it is entirely irrelevant what conscious or unconscious motives led its author to advance it and what dark urges she is supposedly rationalizing by it.

This is elementary logic of argument. But the objection can also be put in a way that is not *ad hominem* and thus obviously irrelevant. Leaving aside the motives of retributivists, it can be claimed that their theory identifies punishment with revenge, that it reduces it to revenge, that is, to something which frequently (some will even say always) stands morally condemned.

83

Revenge and vengefulness are indeed often considered morally dubious and even outright impermissible. Why is that?

One could, of course, embrace the view put forward by Socrates in the *Crito* that "we ought not to retaliate or render evil for evil to anyone, whatever evil we may have suffered from him."[2] But even if one does not accept this kind of unqualified pacifism, one might still have reservations about revenge. They would seem to concern the human limitations and deficiencies of those who resort to it. Why is it generally accepted that nobody should be the judge in his own case? Because the person wronged is more often than not incapable of relating quite coolly and impartially to his malefactor. Therefore, revenge is frequently not matched to the verdict which an impartial, just arbiter would pronounce, but rather tends to be determined by hurt feelings and to go beyond what would be proportionate to the wrong suffered. It is for this reason that the classics of retributivism themselves emphasize that revenge is generally wrong.[3]

But this tendency not to be objective when relating to those who have wronged us is something contingent, not a necessary trait of every act of revenge. We do differentiate between just and unjust acts of revenge, and there are cases of revenge almost everyone would consider proportionate, just, and morally legitimate. A good example would be the revenge executed straight after World War Two by members of the Jewish organization D.I.N. on some of the participants in the "final solution" who otherwise would have escaped justice for good.[4] For "to strike back and to strike first are two very different things, morally speaking."[5] Thus mere similarity between retributive punishment and revenge does not amount to much of an argument against retributivism.

Moreover, the retributive theory clearly differentiates between punishment and revenge. The difference is obvious in the definition of punishment on which most utilitarians *and* retributivists would agree: by definition, punishment is determined and executed by those *authorized* to do so — judges, prison officials and executioners — and not by anyone who decides to retaliate for a wrong suffered.[6] Retributivists themselves insist that punishment is not the same as revenge. "Punishment is not a function which the injured party can undertake on his private authority, but rather the function of a tribunal distinct from him, which gives effect to the law of a *supreme authority* over all those subject to him," writes Kant.[7] The committing of a crime, says Hegel, poses "a demand for a justice freed from subjective interest and a subjective form and no longer contingent on might, i.e. it is a demand for justice not as revenge but as punishment."[8]

Thus retributive punishment differs from revenge by the very fact that it is not plagued by the main limitation of revenge, the limitation which tends to make revenge disproportionate and unjust. In punishment, as opposed to revenge, those who mete out and execute retaliation — the judge, the prison official, the executioner — are not the ones who have been wronged by the offender; therefore retribution can be determined and carried out as impartially and fairly as it is humanly possible.

2. Inapplicable

Of all arguments against the retributive theory, probably the most popular is the one directed at the demand that punishment should fit the offense committed. "You shall give life for life, eye for eye, tooth for tooth, hand for hand, foot for foot, burn for burn, wound for wound, stripe for stripe," says the Bible.[9] How can this be done? almost every critic of retributivism has asked, going on to cite various cases in which, in his opinion, the *lex talionis* could not possibly be applied. Let me quote the *locus classicus* of this criticism, Blackstone's discussion of the *lex talionis* in his *Commentaries*:

> It will be evident, that what some have so highly extolled for its equity, the *lex talionis*, or law of retaliation, can never be in all cases an adequate or permanent rule of punishment. In some cases, indeed, it seems to be dictated by natural reason . . . But, in general, the difference of persons, place, time, provocation, or other circumstances, may enhance or mitigate the offence; and in such cases retaliation can never be a proper measure of justice. If a nobleman strikes a peasant, all mankind will see, that if a court of justice awards a return of the blow, it is more than a just compensation. On the other hand, retaliation may, sometimes, be too easy a sentence; as, if a man maliciously should put out the remaining eye of him who had lost one before, it is too slight a punishment for the maimer to lose only one of his: and therefore the law of the Locrians, which demanded an eye for an eye, was in this instance judiciously altered by decreeing, in imitation of Solon's laws, that, he who struck out the eye of a one-eyed man, should lose both of his own in return. Besides, there are very many crimes, that will in no shape admit of these penalties, without manifest absurdity and wickedness. Theft cannot be punished with theft, defamation by defamation, forgery by forgery, adultery by adultery, and the like.[10]

Criticism of the *lex talionis* has not stopped at this. It has also been said that, if we accept it as the correct answer to the question of the proper measure of punishment, we shall have to find practically every punishment unjust and illegitimate. There is a hint of this argument in Hegel[11] and T.H. Green;[12] it comes up in a fully developed form in A.C. Ewing's book *The Morality of Punishment*. The difficulties of applying the retributive criterion, Ewing says, show

> not only that the retributive theory cannot be applied with anything like success, but also that it is wrong even to attempt to apply it. It shows not only that the retributive principle cannot tell us the exact degree of the punishment, but that it could not justify us in inflicting any punishment whatever. The object of the retributionist is that the punishment should be just, and every excess over the just amount must be in the same ethical position as punishment of "the innocent," an injustice which seems much worse than non-punishment of the guilty. Yet it is certain that either this injustice or the opposite one of inflicting too slight a penalty will be perpetrated in nine cases out of ten, nay in 999 out of a thousand, so great are the difficulties in the way of securing the right proportion between the punishment and the guilt of the offender. If failure is likely or, rather, almost certain, ought the state to inflict punishment for the sake of retribution at all? . . . We may be certain that, if and in so far as justice consists in a retributive proportion to guilt, almost all punishments will be unjust. But to do injustice seems worse than to do nothing at all, at least in so far as injustice consists in punishment of the innocent, and, according to the view we are discussing, punishment of the guilty beyond the retributively just amount must be in the same category, ethically, as punishment of the completely innocent. Ought the State to aim at retributive justice, if the overwhelming probability is that each time it tries to inflict it it will do serious *injustice*?[13]

Convinced that practical difficulties in applying the *lex talionis* were unsurmountable, some philosophers who had set out as retributivists gave up the demand that punishment should fit the offense. Thus F.H. Bradley and B. Bosanquet opted for the view that it is the committing of an offense that gives the state the moral right to punish and imposes on it the duty to do so, but that the measure of punishment should be determined according to utilitarian criteria.[14] They believed that they were advancing a basically retributive standpoint, and saw no inconsistency in introducing utilitarian calculations at the level of measuring out punishments.

There would indeed be no inconsistency if the question of the right measure of punishment were logically independent of the question of its justification. That, however, is not the case. For the latter boils down to two more specific, but equally fundamental questions: What is the basis of the state's right to punish? and, What is the source of its duty to do so? Suppose we answer both these questions in terms of retribution: both the right and the duty are based on the offense committed. Suppose, further, that an offender is given a punishment which is going to be the most efficient, while still being economical, but is definitely harsher than what would fit the seriousness of the offense. Such punishment would clearly go beyond the right to punish, for this right is based on the offense committed, and accordingly is limited by the seriousness of the offense. Suppose, again, that in the case at hand the utilitarian aim of punishing would be secured in the most efficient way by a punishment that is clearly milder than the one that would match the gravity of the offense committed. To give such punishment would obviously mean to fall short of carrying out the duty to punish to the full, insofar as this duty, again, is imposed and determined by the offense. A judge cannot give a shoplifter five years in prison, and then go on to say that he is but executing the right to punish her, which is grounded solely in her own offense; nor can he give a murderer one month, and then claim that he has thereby carried out the duty to punish imposed on him by the murder committed. Both if the right to punish is not to be overstepped, and if the duty to punish is to be carried out, there has to be some sort of fit between the offense and the punishment given for it.[15]

This fit, admittedly, often cannot be achieved, if it is taken literally. If the offense committed is putting out an eye of the victim, and the offender has one eye only, "an eye for an eye" will not do; nor will it be relevant at all, if the offender is completely blind. Critics of the retributive theory have repeatedly referred to the verses from Exodus quoted at the beginning of this section, and then gone to pronounce the whole retributive tradition, and its biblical source in particular, cruel and barbaric. With regard to biblical retributivism, it should first be noted that such criticism testifies to poor understanding of the historical background. When the son of the ruler of Shechem defiled Dinah, her brothers retaliated by killing off all adult males of Shechem;[16] such outrageously disproportionate retribution was the rule in those times. Given such customs, the biblical demand for "life for life, eye for eye, tooth for tooth, hand for hand, foot for foot" did not encourage, but rather restrained the vengefulness of the wronged. Taken literally, it commands: for one life, take one, not ten lives; for one eye, take one, not both. Thus, even under a literal interpretation, the biblical law of retribution must have exerted a civilizing influence. But this is only a minor point. The main thing is that it was not meant to be taken literally. Rashi and other leading Bible commentators have repeatedly pointed out that the verses in Exodus and the parallel statement in Leviticus[17] express a demand for equivalence between the injury and material compensation determined as the punishment for it, not a demand that the offender should be punished by being made to suffer the same thing he did to the victim. Thus "tooth for tooth" means: if somebody knocks out somebody else's tooth, they should be punished by having to pay the compensation equivalent to the gravity of the injury and not a lesser one, say, one corresponding to a blow that leaves a bruise, nor a greater one, say, one corresponding to an eye knocked out.

In the Talmud it is also stressed that the *lex talionis* is not to be taken literally; interestingly enough, the reason for this is precisely the impossibility of applying it under a literal interpretation:

> R. Simon b. Yohai says: "*Eye for eye*" means pecuniary compensation. You say pecuniary compensation, but perhaps it is not so, but actual retaliation [by putting out an eye] is meant? What then will you say where a blind man put out the eye of another man, or where a cripple cut off the hand of another, or where a lame person broke the leg of another? How can I carry out in this case [the principle of retaliation of] "*eye for eye*," seeing that the Torah says, *Ye shall have one manner of law*, implying that the manner of law should be the same in all cases?[18]

The leading representatives of retributivism as a philosophical theory are no less alive to the difficulties and absurdities of a literal interpretation of the *lex talionis*. Thus Kant, in whose teachings on punishment one of the basic tenets is that "only the *law of retribution* (*ius talionis*) can determine exactly what quality and quantity of punishment is required," and that " all other criteria are inconstant; they cannot be reconciled with the findings of pure and strict justice, because they introduce other outside considerations,"[19] is careful to note the problems of its application. The upshot of his reflections on these problems is that the *lex talionis* should not be interpreted "according to the letter," but " in terms of effect": as a demand that the punishment should affect the offender as much as the offense affected the victim.[20] We have seen in the preceding chapter that Hegel takes the same view.[21] He writes that punishment "is retribution in so far as (a) retribution in *conception* is 'injury of the injury,' and (b) since as existent a crime is something determinate in its scope both qualitatively and quantitatively, its negation [i.e. punishment] as *existent* is similarly determinate," only to add that "this identity rests on the concept, but it is not an equality between the specific character of the crime and that of its negation; on the contrary, the two injuries are equal only in respect of their implicit character, i.e. in respect of their 'value'." And the value of both offenses and punishments is the degree in which they exhibit "their universal property of being injuries."[22]

The same point is sometimes made by saying that, properly understood, the *lex talionis* does not require that offense and punishment be equal, but that they be proportionate to one another. The notion of proportionality, however, is misleadingly ambiguous. Having rejected the *lex talionis* in its literal sense, one might be tempted to say, with J.G. Murphy, that " a retributivism grounded on fairness can at most demand a kind of *proportionality* between crime and punishment — i.e. demand that we rank acceptable punishments on a scale of seriousness, rank criminal offenses on a scale of seriousness, and then guarantee that the most serious punishments will be matched with the most serious crimes, the next most serious punishments with the next most serious crimes, and so on."[23] This kind of purely ordinal proportionality would rule out certain disproportionate and therefore unjust punishments. It would preclude punishing offenses of equal seriousness with penalties of differing severity, and the other way around; it would also make it impossible to punish less serious offenses with harsher punishments, and the other way around. The more serious an offense is, the more severe the punishment would be. But this kind of proportionality does not tell us anything about the severity of particular punishments for particular offenses. It allows for the possibility that we coordinate the scale of offenses, disorderly conduct being the least serious and murder the most serious, with the scale of punishments, beginning, say, with a year in prison as the lightest and ending with an aggravated death penalty as the harshest. It also allows for the possibility of coordinating the same scale of offenses with a scale of punishments in which a five-dollar fine is the least severe punishment and a year in prison the most severe. As long as the scales themselves were properly constructed, so that the more serious offense always got the more severe punishment, whatever the absolute degree of severity of the punishment, this kind of relative justice would be satisfied.

This kind of proportionality is necessary, to be sure; but it is not enough. If murder is punished by a year in prison, because that is the most severe punishment the law provides for, we should say that the punishment is proportionate to the offense in a way, but only in a way, and in a very formal and unsatisfactory way at that, and that it is at the same time disproportionate in another, more important, substantive sense: that it is too mild, given the absolute gravity of the crime. Having to spend a year in prison will affect the murderer incomparably less than his misdeed has affected the victim. Again, if disorderly conduct carries the penalty of a year in prison, because that is the mildest penalty the law knows of, we should have an analogous objection, only this time we should say that the punishment is too severe, even draconian, in view of the absolute seriousness of the offense. This means that drawing up the scale of punishments should not be seen as a procedure independent of the scale of offenses, but should rather be carried out with constant reference to the latter, as an attempt to prescribe punishments affecting the offender as much as the offense has affected the victim. (In many offenses there will be an individual victim; in some offenses, for example, treason, the only directly injured party is society as a whole. In cases of the latter sort the assessment of the severity of the injury will obviously be more complex and difficult, since it will be made in terms of society's interests and values; but the difficulty is of a practical, not logical nature.) Murder should be punished by the penalty of death;[24] disorderly conduct by a small fine. The proportionality to be aimed at should be substantive. Then, of course, it will be formal, ordinal, as well.

The demand for proportionality betweeen punishments and offenses thus construed — the demand that punishments be proportionate to offenses both in the relative, ordinal sense, and in the substantive sense of affecting the victim adversely in the same degree — is not all there is to it. When ranking offenses, we should first establish how much they injure the victim. Having taken this external side of an offense into account we should also attend to its inner , subjective side. This includes several things.

First, we should attend to the culpability of the offender. There is considerable difference in gravity between committing an offense deliberately and committing the same offense out of negligence. While in the first case justice would require that the punishment affect the offender adversely as much as the offense has affected the victim, the second case would deserve a penalty significantly less severe. (Of course, these two cases are merely extremes on a scale which a fully developed theory of culpability would offer, and which would include intermediate states calling for punishments of descending severity.)

In some cases the motive of the offender needs to be considered. Acts which are quite alike from the external point of view and affect those on receiving end in the same way, and which have been committed with the same degree of culpability, are sometimes judged morally very differently, depending on the motive of the actor. Assume three cases of deliberate battery which do not differ significantly from the external point of view in the methods applied, duration, and the kind and amount of physical pain and mental suffering caused to the victim. The first was committed out of a sense of serious and unredressed injury undeservedly suffered and the need to pay the malefactor back; the second, because that was the only way to rob the victim; the third, just for the fun of it. We should say that, their external equality notwithstanding, these three cases of battery are by no means equally grave, morally speaking: that the second is graver than the first, and the third graver still, precisely on account of the motives involved. For it is intrinsically worse to beat up someone in order to rob them than to do the same out of vengefulness caused by a real wrong undeservedly suffered; and to beat up someone just because one enjoys doing that is even more reprehensible, intrinsically, than to do the same out of reckless greed. Whether we would want to take the motives into account by way of describing such cases as belonging to different types of the same offense, or would rather keep to a single, externalistic classification of the offense, and treat the motives involved as aggravating or mitigating circumstances, is a technical matter. The main point is that in some cases there are differences of gravity due to differing motivation, which from the point of view of the retributive theory and the *lex talionis* amount to differences of deserts, on account of which justice demands punishments of differing severity.

Again, assume that we have two cases of the same offense which do not differ significantly from the external point of view, nor is there much difference with regard to culpability or motivation. Then we would be dealing with two cases of equal gravity and, other things being equal, the same punishment would be called for in both of them. But other things are not equal: one of them was committed in the face of very strong provocation by the victim, and thus with less than full responsibility on the part of the offender; the other was perpetrated with full responsibility. The provocation and the consequent diminished responsibility should be seen as *mitigating* circumstance, on account of which the offender deserves a punishment less severe than the one that would be appropriate for the same offense committed without provocation, that is, with full responsibility on the part of the offender. As H.L.A. Hart has put it,

the special features of Mitigation are that a good reason for adminis-
tering a less severe penalty is made out if the situation or mental state
of the convicted criminal is such that he was exposed to an unusual or
specially great temptation, or his ability to control his actions is
thought to have been impaired or weakened otherwise than by his
own action, so that conformity to the law which he has broken was a
matter of special difficulty for him as compared with normal persons
normally placed. . . . Justice requires that those who have special
difficulties to face in keeping the law which they have broken should
be punished less.[25]

Thus the *lex talionis* requires that the full measure of what is proportionate to the gravity of the offense committed — determined in terms of
the injury to the victim, the sort of culpability involved in the offense,
and in some cases the motive of the offender as well — should be given
as the punishment for it, if the offender was *fully responsible* for the act, if
no mitigating circumstance can be claimed. If her responsibility was
significantly diminished, her desert is thereby lessened too; accordingly,
the proportionate and just punishment should be less as well.

This, then, is how the *lex talionis* is to be construed and applied.[26] At
this point, further objections might be raised.

It has been said that a scale of offenses cannot be drawn up independently of a scale of punishments. How can we know that an offense is
more serious than another if not by the fact that the penalty provided for
it is more severe than that provided for the other? If capital punishment
is prescribed by law for a certain offense, it shows that that offense is
extremely grave; if another offense is to be punished only by a small
fine, it shows that it is almost trivial.[27]

It is not difficult to refute this argument. If we could not say of an
offense that it is more serious than another one not simply because the
punishment which is given for it is more severe than that prescribed for
the other, but independently of that, for some other reason, then we
could never say of a punishment that it is harsher or lighter than the offense
for which it is meted out; we could never evaluate the provisions of a
criminal law, or even a criminal code as a whole, as either too severe or
too mild. But, as a matter of fact, we do this.[28] Furthermore, it would not
be possible to draft a criminal code at all. Even if everyone who is not a
legislator could judge the relative gravity of offenses on the basis of the
severity of the punishments provided in law for them, what could the
legislator rely on when about to draft a criminal code? Criminal legislation is possible only if offenses can be judged as more or less grave *before*
the punishments for them are determined.

M.H. Mitias has claimed that the project of composing and coordinating the two scales cannot be carried out in a truly objective way; it will always be plagued by a certain arbitrariness. The scaling of offenses and punishments is to be made from the point of view of society. But this is not an objective standpoint, for societies and cultures differ in their assessment of the seriousness of crimes and gravity of punishments; there are significant differences even within a single culture, a single society. And whatever the punishment a society may choose for a particular offense, there is bound to be an element of imprecision and conventionality in the match; whatever system of such matchings it adopts, it will never be truly comprehensive and final.[29]

Admittedly, cultures and societies differ in their ranking of offenses and punishments, but is that really a problem for retributivism and the *lex talionis*? The demand that punishments should be measured out justly, that is proportionately to the gravity of offenses, does not imply that there is only one framework for carrying out this demand, valid throughout history, a framework identical for a postindustrial society of our day and a Greek *polis* of two and a half millennia ago. The sense of the seriousness of various injuries and of the morality or immorality of certain motives has changed historically. An adherent of the *lex talionis* will readily admit, together with Hegel, that "a criminal code cannot hold good for all time" and is "the child of its age and the state of civil society at the time."[30] She does not demand that society should go by some transhistorical and transcultural system of offenses and punishments. She demands rather that it should punish its offenders according to *its own* sense of what is deserved and just, *its own* sense of the seriousness of offenses and severity of punishments, articulated and codified after serious and thorough consideration, and not according to the criteria of social expediency in general, and the prevention of offenses in particular, which the utilitarian offers as the proper measure of punishment.

To be sure, there are societies whose assessment of the severity of certain offenses or punishments appears to us misguided, irrational, or even outrageous. When such a society metes out justice according to its own lights, we cannot help thinking of what it does as unjust and unacceptable. But if this is a problem, it is not specific to the retributive theory of punishment and its doctrine of *lex talionis*. It is rather a particular case of a much larger problem, the one of cultural and moral relativity. This latter, larger problem is liable to plague the discussion of any moral issue and set limits to the possibilities of coming to a rational, universally acceptable and compelling solution to it.

What of variations within a society? This may prove a source of real difficulties. Mitias cites a study by A.M. Rose and A.E. Prell which shows variations in the assessment of the seriousness of offenses and penalties by public opinion in the United States.[31] This particular society is an extremely heterogeneous and dynamic one, so variations of this kind should perhaps be expected; in less heterogeneous societies they may not be so pronounced. Even for the United States a more recent study by P.H. Rossi and others suggests a different picture, at least as far as the ranking of offenses is concerned: "There is considerable agreement from subgroup to subgroup on the relative ordering of the criminal acts rated and on the relative 'distance' between such acts on the scale used. . . . The norms defining how serious various criminal acts are considered to be, are quite widely distributed among blacks and whites, males and females, high and low socio-economic levels, and among levels of educational attainment."[32] Be that as it may, the point is well taken, and shows an important limitation of the *lex talionis* and the retributive theory of punishment as a whole: if they are to be applied, there has to be a measure of consensus on the gravity of offenses, the severity of punishments, and the proportion between the two. In a society where no such consensus can be attained for the legislator to articulate and codify and the judge to concretize and carry out in allotting punishments, the *lex talionis* becomes impracticable.

In all this there is nothing arbitrary, at least in the literal sense of the word. If, however, the objection is that the *lex talionis* is arbitrary, rather than objective, insofar as it is not a system of offenses and punishments transcending cultural relativity and historical change, the answer must be that this kind of objectivity cannot be achieved in the realm of morals and justice. For better or worse, in matters of legal punishment the only kind of justice attainable is human justice.

The same goes for the objection about the lack of precision, comprehensiveness, and finality. To ask for these is simply out of place in this matter, which resists attempts at an entirely precise formulation and complete and final systematization. As Hegel puts it, "no absolute determinacy is possible in this sphere . . . in the field of the finite, absolute determinacy remains only a demand, a demand which the Understanding has to meet by continually increasing determination — a fact of the greatest importance — but which continues *ad infinitum* and which allows only of perennially approximate satisfaction."[33] So, as retributivists will readily admit, we really cannot prove that a certain offense should carry a $99 rather than a $100 fine; but we should not be expected to exercise precision of this kind in the first place.[34]

3. Conservative

One of the arguments against the retributive theory is that it is basically conservative — committed to a defense of any existing social and political order, any positive law, however unreasonable, unjust, or otherwise objectionable. It is claimed that the theory, in the words of Marx, gives "a transcendental sanction to the rules of existing society."[35] According to this theory, punishment is justified solely, and fully, by the commission of an offense. Does this not entail that it is justified to punish transgressions of the laws regulating "separate development" in South Africa, various *delits d'opinion* enumerated in criminal codes of totalitarian states, or offenses against decency as defined by the most conservative interpretation of the religious tradition written into law in Saudi Arabia or Iran?

This objection testifies to a misunderstanding of the retributive theory of punishment. The theory would indeed imply that such punishments are justified if it were logically linked to a legal philosophy according to which *every* positive law ought to be obeyed, whatever its contents, simply because it is a positive law. This, however, is not the case. As I have already noted in the introductory chapter, when a retributivist puts forward the claim that the offense committed is the sole justification of punishment, by "offense" she does not mean any act that can be described as such in a neutral way, any act to which the word can be applied in its conventional, inverted-commas sense — that is, a violation of any criminal law whatsoever, including such laws as are unreasonable, unjust, illegitimate in any but the trivial, narrowly legalistic sense of legitimacy. On the contrary, she is using the word in a normative sense: she has in mind only violations of morally *legitimate* criminal laws. And there is a very good reason for this: otherwise she would have to embrace the unattractive, if not outrightly paradoxical position that it is sometimes morally *legitimate* to punish a person precisely — and exclusively — because he has offended against a morally *illegitimate* law.[36]

Which laws are to be accepted as legitimate, and which acts will consequently count as offenses in this normative sense — this is one of the fundamental questions of legal and political philosophy, which is raised beyond the comparatively narrow scope of the philosophy of punishment. The answer will set limits to the possibilities of justifying punishments in retributive terms. Given the content of her theory, a retributivist can be expected to accord paramount importance to principles of justice and liberty in her thinking of laws and their legitimacy or illegitimacy; she can also be expected to see criminal behavior as free and responsible human action, in some sense of the words. But over and above these very general points, she is not, *qua* retributivist, committed to any very specific answer to the question, which laws are legitimate, that is, what acts are to be considered offenses?

Thus, to go back to one of the examples mentioned above, if an adherent of the retributive theory of punishment is to justify punishments inflicted on those who offend against the *apartheid* laws in South Africa, not only will she have to be satisfied in each particular case that the person charged with the deed has really committed it, although he could have complied with the law, but will also have to hold that these laws are morally legitimate. If she does not accept them as legitimate, his judgment on the punishments meted out for offenses against them will be quite different. In that case she will say that what the accused have done is admittedly an offense from the point of view of the positive law of the Republic of South Africa and the agencies who enforce it, and of all those who accept the apartheid laws as legitimate. But she will hasten to add that, since she does not share that point of view and does not believe in the legitimacy of those laws, for her their violations are offenses only in a conventional, inverted-commas sense, but not in the normative sense of the word, which is relevant when a retributivist has to decide on the justification, or the lack of it, of particular punishments. In *that* sense, she will say, there have been no offenses; accordingly, there is no justification for punishing either.

4. Hypocritical

It is sometimes claimed that those who break the law are not really responsible for their offenses, are not really guilty. They are merely products of certain social conditions that breed criminal behavior, such as unemployment , poverty, bad housing, or alcoholism. Social environments in which such conditions prevail are actually "schools of crime"; every society that tolerates such conditions is responsible for their repercussions, and thus "has the criminals it deserves."[37] Not the offender, but the society in which he has grown up and lived in such conditions is the real culprit, or at least an accomplice in the offense. So it is hypocritical of society to put the blame on such an individual, and to claim that by punishing him it only treats him according to his deserts and carries out the demands of justice.

This objection can be interpreted in two different ways. It can be taken as claiming that offenders are not in the least responsible for their actions, that the whole responsibility is to be ascribed to the social conditions in which they have lived — that is, that society is quite literally the sole culprit. The extreme social determinism presupposed in this claim is very difficult to accept. The problem of responsibility is one of giving an analysis of the distinction between those actions that are and those are not responsible, and also an account of degrees of responsibility, that are both theoretically sound and workable in practice, both in our moral judgment and in courts of justice. To claim that there is no such thing as responsible action, and thus imply that both the distinction between action that is and action that is not responsible, and the related notions of mitigation and excuse, are untenable, and that we are completely misguided in applying them in our attempts at understanding human action in general, and in daily practice in courts in particular, is simply too farfetched to be plausible.[38]

Another difficulty encountered by the argument is the fact that not all offenders have lived in such social conditions as are said to breed crime, namely poverty, unemployment, and the like; some of them come from quite tolerable, even comfortable, social backgrounds. If these facts are not to be denied, and the argument is to be sustained in the face of them, the notion of crime-breeding social conditions will have to be extended so as to cover such cases as well. But if we do that, we shall end up with the thesis that the mere fact that someone has broken the law indicates that they come from a crime-breeding social background. To say this is not to say anything at all informative about social and psychological facts — it is merely to assert a useless tautology.

Interpreted another way, the argument would claim that social conditions are only partly responsible for offenses against the law — that society, to be sure, is not the sole culprit, but still is an accomplice in the deed. If so, however, we no longer have an argument against retributive punishment. For such punishment is by no means incompatible with the idea of degrees of responsibility; on the contrary, the retributivist will be the first to insist that we must take them into account when meting out punishments. Whenever it turns out that the social background of an offender is a highly important factor in determining action, she will demand that this be taken as a ground of mitigation. As we have seen, it is precisely the retributivist who insists on the requirement of justice that those who were faced with special difficulties in obeying the law they have broken deserve to be punished less severely than they otherwise should be.[39]

However, the extent to which the offender is really responsible for his deed is just one side of the matter. The other side is the moral standing of society. If society is to have the moral right to punish, its laws must be just. But that is not all; society must also be doing something about those social conditions that breed crime. Certainly, it can never eradicate them, but it must not be indifferent to them. If it does little or nothing about those social problems that generate law-breaking, and then goes on to punish the law-breakers, it will be rightly seen as both callous and hypocritical, and thus as lacking the moral standing requisite for punishing offenders in good faith.

If a society will be considered hypocritical when it punishes its offenders although it is itself guilty of sins of omission that make it an accomplice in their misdeeds, it will be seen as even more hypocritical if it is guilty of sins of commission such as systematically generating and nurturing the very motives that lead people to offend against the law. It has been argued that among the main sources of criminality in modern capitalist societies are selfishness, greed, excessive competitiveness, the ideal of success at any cost, and the lack of sympathy and care for others, and that these societies stimulate such motives and patterns of feeling and behavior in their members.[40] The accuracy of this diagnosis is not a philosophical, but a sociological and criminological question. But any society where it can convincingly be shown that those who break the law are acting out of the very motives which the society systematically generates and reinforces will be guilty of gross hypocrisy and will lose its moral license to punish.

None of this, however, tells against retributivism itself. The second part of the argument from hypocrisy, just as the argument about the allegedly conservative character of the retributive theory of punishment discussed in the preceding section, merely points out the conditions under which the theory can be properly applied.

5. Ascribing an Odd Right

Among other things, a fully developed retributive theory would claim that punishment is a right of the offender. As we have seen in the preceding chapter, this is one of the main tenets of Hegel's teaching on punishment.[41]

It has often been criticized. "It is an odd sort of right whose holders would strenuously resist its recognition," A.M. Quinton has remarked.[42] "One's response to this, of course, is that a right that cannot be escaped is an odd sort of right," writes T. Honderich. "Essays in the psychoanalysis of argument are not often profitable but it is hard to resist the feeling that the claiming of rights to punishment on behalf of others is most interesting as a projection of one's own feelings of guilt."[43]

One way of avoiding this objection would be to say that the thesis of punishment as a right of the offender does not claim that the right *belongs* to the offender, that he is the *holder* of this right, but something quite different: that the right to the offender's punishment belongs to somebody else, that somebody else (society, the state) is the holder of that right, and that the right is *his*, the offender's, in the sense that it is based on *his* act and *his* will. A few statements of Hegel's might be taken to support such an interpretation, in particular his words that the act of the ofender is " something universal and . . . by doing it [he] has laid down a law which he has explicitly recognized in his action and under which in consequence he should be brought as under his right."[44] But a defense of the thesis along these lines would not be helpful. Such an interpretation does not sound authentic, but rather like a reinterpretation imposed by the need to vindicate a thesis which cannot be defended in its most natural sense. It would be based on some of Hegel's wordings which do not point unequivocally in that direction, but would be inconsistent with many others, where Hegel explicitly and unambiguously speaks of punishment as an individual right of the offender.[45] Most importantly, such an interpretation would give us a thesis immune to the criticism mentioned, but at the cost of making it redundant; for, construed in this way, the thesis of the offender's right to punisment boils down to the claim that punishment is subjectively justified — that the state's right to punish is based on the act and will of the offender himself. This is a claim which Hegel need not make in this roundabout and unclear way, because he has already advanced it explicitly and clearly.[46]

P.G. Stillman's attempt to defend the thesis of the offender's right to punishment fails for similar reasons. For Stillman construes it as a thesis about something quite different: about the offender's *duty* to be punished. In his opinion, the criticism that the offender's right to punishment is something at least odd, since the offender himself, the alleged holder of that right, would be against having it ascribed to him, testifies to a misunderstanding of Hegel's notion of a right: "For the rights of 'Abstract Right' must be exercised; each person has the duty to exercise his rights. . . . What is a right is a duty. . . . Thus, the right to punishment is a duty to punishment. In order to be a person and free, one must be punished when one has done wrong; to preserve the rights of the person, all the rights — including the right to punishment — must be exercised as duties."[47] This interpretation certainly seems forced; its textual basis is very shaky.[48] It implies that all those rights which Hegel discusses in the section on "Abstract Right" of his *Philosophy of Right* (the rights to life, to property, to the making of contracts) are not rights in any usual sense of the word, but rather the exact opposite, duties. Thus Hegel's philosophy of law (of "abstract right") would know of no rights proper, but only of duties. Hegel, however, says explicitly that "in the sphere of abstract right, I have the right and another has the corresponding duty,"[49] which clearly shows that in this context he uses the word "right" in a sense in which it is different from, and opposed to, duty. Finally, Stillman's interpretation also makes the thesis of the offender's right to punishment redundant. It claims nothing more than that the offender has the duty of submitting to punishment, from which it follows that the state has the right to punish him, that is, that punishment is justified. And this is something Hegel says in so many words.

If Quinton's and Honderich's criticism of the thesis that punishment is the offender's right is to be rebutted in a convincing way, the thesis must be taken in its most natural interpretation — as referring to a right of which the offender himself is the holder, and not to somebody else's right, nor indeed to something which is not a right at all. The criticism has to be taken up head-on: it has to be shown that the assumption that must be made with regard to anything described as a right holds for punishment as well: that it can be meaningfully related to the choices of those on whose behalf it is claimed.

In his study of Hegel's theory of punishment J. McTaggart proposes an interpretation of the thesis of the offender's right to punishment which on the face of it satisfies these conditions. His point of departure is Hegel's insistence on the respect due the offender as a moral being. According to McTaggart, this means that the offender must be treated as "one who is potentially moral, however immoral he may be in fact, and one in whom this potential morality must be called into actual existence." The claim that punishment is the offender's right, says McTaggart, implies "that the punishment is in a sense for his sake." In his view, this is incompatible with retributivism and shows that Hegel's concept of punishment is not in fact retributive; for the retributive theory demands punishment not for the sake of the offender but just because he has committed an offense and deserves to be punished. Therefore, this theory does not respect the offender as a moral and rational being.[50]

According to McTaggart, the substance of Hegel's theory of punishment can be put in the following way:

> In sin, man rejects and defies the moral law. Punishment is pain inflicted on him because he has done this, and in order that he may, by the fact of his punishment, be forced into recognizing as valid the law which he rejected in sinning, and so repent of his sin — really repent, and not merely be frightened out of doing it again. Thus the object of punishment is that the criminal should repent of his crime and by so doing realise the moral character, which has been temporarily obscured by his wrong action, but which is, as Hegel asserts, really his truest and deepest nature.[51]

This sounds like the reformatory theory, but McTaggart claims that there is an essential difference between that theory and the doctrine he ascribes to Hegel:

> The reformatory theory says that we ought to reform our criminals *while* we are punishing them. Hegel says that punishment, as such, tends to reform them. The reformatory theory wishes to pain criminals as little as possible, and to improve them as much as possible. Hegel's theory says that it is the pain which will improve them, and therefore, although it looks on pain in itself as an evil, is by no means anxious to spare it.[52]

According to McTaggart Hegel's thesis about punishment as the offender's right ascribes to the offender a right to be persuaded by punishment to repent of his offense, and thus be helped toward moral rehabilitation — the victory of that which is higher and better in him over his lower nature, his subjective, egoistic, asocial, immoral urges, desires, and choices.[53] Some other commentators on Hegel's theory of punishment have advanced a similar interpretation of the thesis.[54] But they have not drawn from it the two conclusions which McTaggart himself does not hesitate to make. The first is that the criterion of desert has no significance whatever for punishment:

> There seems no reason why we should enquire about any punishment whether the criminal deserved it. For such a question really brings us back, if we press it far enough, to the old theory of vindictive punishment . . . On any other theory a man is to be punished, not to avenge the past evil, but to secure some future good. Of course, a punishment is only to be inflicted for a wrong action, for the effect of all punishment is to discourage the repetition of the action punished, and that would not be desirable unless the action were wrong. But to

enquire how far the criminal is to be blamed for his action seems irrelevant. If he has done wrong, and if the punishment will cure him, he has, as Hegel expresses it, a right to his punishment. If a dentist is asked to take out an aching tooth, he does not refuse to do so, on the ground that the patient did not deliberately cause the toothache, and that therefore it would be unjust to subject him to the pain of the extraction. And to refuse a man the chance of a moral advance, when the punishment appears to afford one, seems equally unreasonable.[55]

McTaggart's second conclusion is that Hegel's "chief mistake" is to believe that his theory applies to legal punishment. It does not, for two reasons. First, because the state must assign greater significance to the interests of the innocent than to those of the guilty, since there are far more of the former than the latter; accordingly, its primary aim when punishing must be to deter potential offenders. Second, given the state of penal establishments in contemporary society, it is unlikely that offenders can be persuaded through punishment to repent and thus be helped toward moral regeneration. Therefore, Hegel's teaching on punishment is not helpful with regard to criminal law, but there is much to be said for it in the field of education.[56]

However, McTaggart's interpretation is completely misguided. The distinction he makes between the conception he reads into Hegel and the reformatory theory is arbitrary and untenable. If he were right, Hegel's view would be but another variety of the reformatory theory, for any view which finds the essence of punishment and its justification in its reformatory effects must be characterized as such. When such a standpoint is taken, it makes no philosophically important difference whether it is claimed that punishment as such, that is, directly, has reformatory effects (Hegel as interpreted by McTaggart) or that punishment makes it possible to apply the means by which such effects are secured, that is, that punishment indirectly has such effects (McTaggart's definition of the reformatory theory). Hegel, however, does not approach the problem of punishment from such a standpoint; on the contrary, he expressly and repeatedly rejects it. His main objection to the reformatory view is that it does not respect the offender as a mature, responsible, free being; and one of his main claims for the retributive theory is that only this theory recognizes the offender as such a being.[57] Just how far off the mark McTaggart's interpretation is can be seen not only in all those passages in which Hegel expounds his standpoint as unambiguously retributive, but also from the fact that he believes so deeply in the justice and legitimacy of retribution, that he attempts to interpret and justify compulsion (including punishment) used in education as basically retributive.[58]

If the objection, that the offender's right to punishment does not make sense, as its alleged holder will be the first to deny that he has any such right, is to be answered in a convincing way, the answer will have to meet two conditions. It must not make the thesis refer to someone else's right and not the offender's, nor to something that is not a right at all; and it must not bring into question the retributive character of Hegel's theory of punishment, of which the thesis is an integral part.

Such an answer could be attempted along several lines.

First, by drawing on the theory of the general will. In the preceding chapter we have seen how, on Hegel's theory, punishment is justified "subjectively" by being anchored in the will of the offender himself. Laws are the embodiment of the general will, which is not some external, alien generality facing the individual, but rather his own "true" will expressing his higher and better nature, through which he participates in the realm of morality and right and thus attains to what Hegel calls "true" freedom. Accordingly, when a punishment prescribed by law follows an offense, it can be said to express not only the general will as the will of all and the law as its embodiment, but also the "true" will of the offender himself.[59] Both Kant[60] and Bosanquet[61] would have interpreted the thesis that punishment is a right of the offender in this way. The obvious limitation of this defense lies in its basic assumption: it will be found convincing only by those who subscribe to the general will theory.

Not many do. In the chapter on Hegel I gave a brief exposition of his doctrine of the general will; otherwise the account of his theory of punishment would have been seriously incomplete. There is much to be learned from Hegel on the morality of punishment, but that does not include this particular doctrine. Debates in political philosophy have shown how thoroughly unsatisfactory the doctrine of the general will is on the theoretical level, and how unattractive, even repugnant, some of its moral and political implications are.[62] As for punishment, I certainly would not want to rest the case for the offender's right to punishment on a view from which it follows that "when a thief runs down the street pursued by a policeman, the thief *really* wills that the policeman catch him, that the judge sentence him to prison so that he may expiate his crime against society — although his actual or apparent will is, of course, that he get away scot-free."[63]

Alternatively, the criticism could be countered by trying to base punishment in the offender's own will, but without recourse to the controversial conception of a general will: by interpreting it as an expression of his empirical, subjective will. Hegel's "subjective" justification of punishment is in part an attempt to show that the consent of the offender's subjective will to be punished is already pledged in his offense. If we want to see the offense as an act of a free, responsible, rational being, we must see it as the affirmation of a general rule. When we pay back the offender by punishing him, we are but applying to him his own rule of action, the rule implied in his own act.[64]

Hegel also has an answer to those who would not accept this view of the offender's action. It is true, as S.I. Benn points out, that the offender's "efforts to elude the police are evidence that he does not will his own punishment in any ordinary sense."[65] But it is also true that there are offenders who give themselves up to the police, who will not simulate mental incompetence in order to avoid punishment, who refuse to appeal for pardon. There are offenders who do not want to "get away with it," but would rather pay what they consider to be their debt to society by undergoing punishment. There are offenders who claim this as their right. They believe, as one such offender has written in a book on his prison experiences, that "to punish a man is to treat him as an equal. To be punished for an offence against rules is a sane man's right."[66] Retorting to claims like that of Benn, Hegel says: "With the same right we claim the opposite, because many have given themselves up, have not rested until their right has been granted them."[67] At this point, of course, the critic will protest that such cases are atypical, and that the standard attitude is that of trying to avoid punishment if that is at all possible. This brings up a wider question about rights. If a certain right is to be plausibly ascribed, does the choice to exercise it have to be typical of those to whom it is ascribed, or is it enough that at least some of them choose to do so?

However, I shall not take up this question here. For I think that there is still another, more promising way of defending the thesis that punishment is a right of the offender against the objection that this is an odd right. We should not try to assess the thesis in an abstract way, torn out from the context of the retributive theory as a whole, but should rather consider it in connection with other basic tenets of the theory. Then we shall no longer be dealing simply with a claim that those who offend against the law have a right to punishment, but with the more definite claim that they have a right to punishment because they have broken the law, and not for some other reason, and to a penalty measured out according to the seriousness of the offense, and not according to some other criterion for meting out punishments. In other words, the thesis claims that offenders have a right to *retributive* punishment.

The import of this claim will become clear when we consider retributive punishment along with alternative responses of society to violations of its laws, from the point of view of a person who might end up on the receiving end of the social response she has chosen. The position of such a person is similar to the Rawlsian "original position" in two important respects. First, she is not choosing between various courses of action open to society in a particular case, but between alternative institutions for dealing with offenses against the law. Second, a "veil of ignorance" prevents her from knowing whether she will ever have to face the response of the institution she has chosen; what she does know is that she *might*. What would such a person choose as the most acceptable option?

The complete list of options might be thought to include the following: (1) no reaction whatever on the part of the legal order to the commission of offenses; (2) verbal condemnation of them, made publicly and in an authoritative and solemn way; (3) restitution to the victim; (4) therapeutic treatment of offenders; (5) utilitarian punishment; (6) retributive punishment. Not all these possibilities are realistic, however. The first is ruled out *a priori*, by the very notions of "a right" and "law."[68] The second and the third would make sense neither in terms of the prevention of offenses nor from the point of view of justice.[69] So the choice would actually have to be made between the last three alternatives: therapy, utilitarian punishment, and retributive punishment.

Therapeutic response to law-breaking behavior is an alternative to punishment as we know it, proposed by a number of psychiatrists and psychologists such as K. Menninger or B.F. Skinner. The point of departure of these authors is the belief that the traditional way of coping with criminal behavior by punishing those who engage in it is completely discredited. Those who support the institution of punishment on retributive grounds are prisoners of religion or traditional morality, who operate with outdated, prescientific concepts of "responsibility," "guilt," "desert," and "justice," unable to see the causal background of criminal behavior that makes such concepts irrelevant. Those who support punishment for utilitarian reasons are unwilling to admit the obvious fact that it is not useful, that it does not prevent offenses. To understand criminal behavior scientifically means to see it as symptomatic of social maladjustment and personality disorder; accordingly, the only rational response to it is therapeutic. Offenders do not "deserve" to be punished, for they are not responsible for what they do; nor is punishment going to prevent them from breaking the law, for they are not open to persuasion, be it by way of deterrence, moral reformation, or education. They are disturbed, sick people, who need to be cured. Their place is not in prison, but in hospital.[70]

I believe that we would not opt for this approach to law-breaking behavior, for several reasons. Some of them are purely prudential. Any offense, however small, could prove to be an occasion for very long, even indefinite detention of its perpetrator. When an offender is punished, the measure of her punishment is basically determined at the trial, be it according to the seriousness of her offense or by utilitarian criteria of crime prevention (or by some combination of these, perhaps). But if she is not to be punished, but cured, then the time to release her will come when the psychiatrists in charge decide that she has been successfully cured. If it takes several years to rehabilitate a shoplifter, say, then several years of compulsory therapy will be the fate of a shoplifter caught; if she cannot be cured at all, she may have to be kept indefinitely. Again, prophylaxis is better than cure; so whenever it is possible to identify a sick, disturbed, socially unadapted person before she has demonstrated her condition by committing an offense, the rational thing to do will be to subject her to therapy at once, and not wait until she actually breaks the law. We would find it unacceptable to be exposed to such eventualities. More generally, we would find it unacceptable that our fate should depend so little on our own choices and actions, and that it should be so difficult to predict. Moreover, if we do not always share the views of the authorities and the psychiatric establishment as to what is normal and abnormal, healthy and sick, socially well adapted and disruptive of society, we would not want to authorize them in advance to shape and reshape our behavior and our personalities in accordance with their views. This is a complex reason, in part based on self-interest, in part expressive of the way we conceive of ourselves as mature, rational, free, self-determining beings. As C.S. Lewis has put it, "to be 'cured' against one's will and cured of states which we may not regard as disease is to be put on a level with those who have not yet reached the age of reason or those who never will; to be classed with infants, imbeciles, and domestic animals."[71] In the light of recent developments in some parts of the world, we would understandably be very apprehensive of the dangers of the "therapeutic state" which uses psychiatry as a means of political control and repression, labelling the dissident as mentally disturbed and forcing "rehabilitation" on her against her will.[72] On a more general level, we might be unable to accept the kind of paternalism presupposed by the whole therapeutic approach, according to which society and the state count so much, and the individual so little.

The second possibility would be the institution of punishment operated in accordance with the utilitarian rationale. People would be punished not because they deserve it, but for the sake of the common good, so as to prevent future offenses. Penalties would be measured out not in proportion to the severity of offenses, but in a way calculated to achieve this end in the most efficient way. In an earlier chapter we saw that a society with a system of utilitarian punishment would, under appropriate circumstances, mete out punishments disproportionately harsher than the seriousness of the offense committed would call for, especially hard punishments for offenses committed under provocation or in a passion, and collective punishments; that it would punish the mentally ill, and even those innocent of any offense; that the innocent "punished" for the sake of the common good would be required to collaborate in their condemnation and "punishment."[73] We would not choose the utilitarian system of punishment, for it would clearly be unacceptable to be exposed to such eventualities. More generally, we would not want to live in a society in which our fate depended so little on our own free decisions and actions, and so much on the requirements of the common good and the circumstances in which these requirements would have to be met by those in charge — circumstances which are beyond our control, and which we could hardly ever even predict. This unwillingness to live in a society which so dangerously limits the scope of our self-determination and the chances of predicting our future is sheer prudence; but it may also have to do with the way we understand ourselves as human beings. We may be unable to accept the collectivistic assumptions of utilitarian social philosophy, with its view of human beings as beings that may be used as means for promoting the ends of others, that make up the background of the utilitarian theory of punishment.[74]

The third option would be a system of retributive punishment, operating according to the criteria of justice and desert. Barring judicial errors, we would be punished if, and only if, we have deserved it, if we have brought punishment on ourselves by voluntarily breaking a morally legitimate law, and by a penalty proportionate in severity to what we deserve. Given that there must be some coercive social response to law-breaking, be it therapeutic or punitive, it is retributive punishment that provides for maximum liberty and predictability of our future. This, I believe, is the alternative we would choose.

This is not to say that the retributive punishment would be our choice in each and every case when, having broken the law, we must face society's response. In some cases it might be more advantageous to accept the punishment determined by utilitarian considerations; in others, perhaps, even the therapy suggested by a psychiatrist might seem more welcome than the full measure of deserved punishment. But if the choice had to be made on the level of alternative institutions and our individual futures were hidden behind a veil of ignorance, so that the only thing we knew was that we might commit an offense or in some other way get involved with the institution we choose for society to cope with law-breaking, I believe that we would not choose an institution which would treat us as irresponsible, sick creatures who must be cured even against their will, nor would we choose an institution which would see us as mere means for promoting the common good. We would rather choose the institution which would recognize us as mature, responsible beings, who to a considerable extent freely determine their fate and must be treated justly, according to their deserts — the institution which would relate to us as persons.

If this is true, then retributive punishment can be seen as based on the choice of the offender herself, and the right to such punishment is not odd after all.[75]

6. Incompatible with Mercy

One of the objections to the retributive theory is that it leaves no room for mercy and cannot accommodate the institution of pardon as the embodiment of this ideal. According to the theory, the offense committed is not only the ground of the right to punish, but the source of the duty to do so and the criterion of the severity of punishment due as well. If so, how can we ever be merciful to the offender, how can we pardon him, or even give him anything less than the full measure of deserved punishment, without failing to carry out a duty?[76]

An example of conflict between the duty of retributive punishment and the call for mercy would be a case where the offense committed calls for an extremely stiff fine as the proportionate punishment, but the imposition of such a fine would put an intolerable burden on the family of the offender. Retributive justice would entail that the fine ought to be exacted, while the fact that this would cause great suffering of innocent parties would call for mercy. Do such cases present an unsurmountable difficulty for retributivism?

They do for one of its classic formulations. Kant's theory of punishment would indeed prohibit us from showing mercy and reducing the penalty considerably, which we certainly would hold to be the right thing to do in some cases. It would imply that even in such cases, the full measure of just, deserved punishment must be meted out, and that the judge would fail to do her duty if she did anything less. This is made clear by Kant's account of the institution of pardon: the sovereign may pardon only when he himself has been the victim of the offense. To extend pardon to an offender who has wronged anyone else would be "the greatest injustice" to the citizens.[77] This might suggest that Kant subscribes to the principle *Fiat justitia, pereat mundus* (which, interestingly enough, he interprets in another connection as "let justice reign, even if all the rogues in the world must perish," adding that although it "may sound somewhat inflated . . . it is nonetheless true"[78]). It is perhaps too harsh to describe this view of retribution and of justice in general as an "inhumanly doctrinaire rigorism," and it is poor taste to compare it to sadism, as B. Blanshard does;[79] but it can safely be said that it is excessively severe, simplistic, and unacceptable.

However, the rigoristic view of justice in punishment is not the only one open to the retributivist. It is rather an idiosyncrasy of Kant's moral and legal philosophy, a result of his attempt to solve the problem of conflict of duties by claiming that "perfect" duties (those that refer to specific acts, such as promise-keeping) always override "imperfect" ones (which are not thus specified, such as the duty to help those in need). This solution, which in another context implies that we must not lie even to save an innocent person from the would-be murderer,[80] is notoriously implausible anyway. As I have emphasized in an earlier chapter, there is nothing in retributivism that entails that the duty to punish must be absolute; a retributivist is not necessarily a latter-day Michael Kohlhaas.[81] He can also conceive of this duty in a different manner, as a duty supervenient on the commission of an offense which, like all duties of justice, carries great moral weight and generally overrides other duties that conflict with it, but falls short of binding absolutely, and is thus sometimes itself overridden by another duty.[82]

The most typical case of conflict between the duty to punish and the call for mercy is when punishment inflicted on the offender indirectly causes suffering of the innocent. "It is obvious," says A.C. Ewing, "that in most cases the punishment of an offender brings suffering on his family and those closely connected with him, though they are innocent of the offence in question. A retributively just punishment for one person . . . would thus involve a retributively unjust punishment for several."[83] This is confused, for the suffering of the offender's family is not part of his punishment but an unintended and regrettable consequence of it. But it is a fact that punishment often has this consequence; whenever it does, this will be a consideration in favor of mercy. Now, the duties of justice are generally more binding than those of preventing suffering, so that most of the time the duty to punish will have to be carried out in full, notwithstanding the suffering of innocent third parties indirectly caused. But there will also be cases where the conflict of retributive justice and mercy will be resolved the other way round. Sometimes, when the offense committed is not very grave, and the suffering of the innocent parties involved that would be brought about by meting the full measure of deserved punishment would be very, very great, the call for mercy will override the duty to punish, and the penalty will be considerably reduced. There will also be cases in which the facts calling for mercy will be so weighty — say, the offender has sincerely and deeply repented of his misdeed and made great efforts to compensate the victim, and has been law-abiding generally ever since his offense — that the final decision will be a full pardon.

The latter view of the duty to punish is actually the dominant one in retributivism. This is the view of Hegel who, in opposition to Kant, stresses that *"fiat justitia* should not be followed by *pereat mundus,"*[84] and of contemporary retributivists such as H.J. McCloskey or Alwynne Smart. The duty is not seen as an absolute one, allowing for no exception and no mitigation, whatever the circumstances, but rather as a duty of paramount, but not absolute importance, which sometimes gives way to mercy and pardon.[85]

So the ideal of mercy, and pardon as its institutional expression, is not incompatible with the retributive view of punishment after all. Moreover — to repeat a point made in an earlier chapter — mercy and pardon only make sense in a retributive context, and exhibit a serious limitation of the alternative, utilitarian theory. For they logically presuppose a background of justice and desert as considerations different from, and irreducible to, those of the common good; and autonomy of this kind is ruled out by the very nature of utilitarianism.[86]

6. The Middle Way

1. The Idea of a Synthetic Theory

Through most of its history, the philosophy of punishment was marked by a deep division into two opposed and seemingly irreconcilable approaches. If one proposed to justify legal punishment, one had to choose between the claims of justice and desert, and those of the common good; one had to present punishment either as retribution, or as an indispensable means for attaining socially desirable objectives. No synthetic theory seemed possible, for each side in the debate totally repudiated the basic contentions of the other. Utilitarians tended to depict the retributive view as irrational, vindictive, and reactionary, and to deny it any intellectual or moral respectability, echoing the crushing verdict passed by Plato at the very beginning of the debate:

> In punishing wrongdoers, no one concentrates on the fact that a man has done wrong in the past, or punishes him on that account, unless taking blind vengeance like a beast. No, punishment is not inflicted by a rational man for the sake of the crime that has been committed — after all one cannot undo what is past — but for the sake of the future, to prevent either the same man or, by the spectacle of his punishment, someone else, from doing wrong again.[1]

Retributivists, on the other hand, pointed out the obliviousness of utilitarianism to the claims of justice as an autonomous principle, and the consequent tendency of its proponents to accept, and even call for, various types of obviously unjust punishment, whenever they turn out to be socially useful. Some of these unjust but expedient types of punishment are so appalling to anyone but the out-and-out utilitarian, that Westermarck wrote that "those who would venture to carry out all the consequences to which [the utilitarian theories of punishment] might lead would be regarded even as more criminal than those they punished, not only by the opponents, but probably by the very supporters of the theories in question."[2]

Still, there are philosophers who believe that both theories of punishment, over and above their undeniable difficulties, have an important

111

contribution to make. They hold that the way leading to a satisfactory theory is the middle way, that the theory of punishment must be a synthetic one which would avoid the one-sidedness, exaggerations, and outright mistakes of both utilitarianism and retributivism, while incorporating the important insights contained in both.

These attempts have one thing in common: the methodological point of departure. When philosophers set out to bridge a gap, to combine theories which seem to be mutually opposed and even irreconcilable, usually the first thing they do is introduce a distinction. This has been the case in all important attempts at a middle-of-the-road philosophy of punishment. All the attempts have proceeded from a distinction supposedly overlooked, or at least not fully appreciated, in the preceding debate: either the distinction between the question of the meaning of the word "punishment" and that of moral justification of what the word stands for; or between the ultimate end of punishment and the means indispensable for achieving it; or between the rationale of the institution of punishment and the principle, or principles, governing its application to particular cases. The synthesis is to be accomplished by working out a division of labor between the two theories, on the basis of the distinction seen as crucial.

In this chapter I shall discuss these attempts at a middle way in the philosophy of punishment, and try to show that none of them has been entirely satisfactory.

2. The Word and the Thing: A.M. Quinton

In an influential article, "On Punishment," Anthony M. Quinton attempts to solve what he calls "a prevailing antinomy" in the philosophy of punishment. The two traditional theories of punishment seem to be irreconcilably opposed to each other. If we believe that punishment is justified, we have to choose between the two. But the choice is difficult, for each has been shown by its opponents to be thoroughly unattractive. Retributivism is characterized by "vindictive barbarousness," which calls for the infliction of suffering for suffering's sake, while the utilitarian theory is plagued by "vicious opportunism," which culminates in the willingness to justify punishment of the innocent, whenever that would be expedient. No third option is available, for if punishment is justified, it is justified either intrinsically, as the retributivists submit, or extrinsically, as the utilitarians claim.

The antinomy can be solved if we attend to the distinction between two levels of discourse, the logical and the ethical; this will enable us to understand the real nature of the two theories, and to bridge the gap between them. The confrontation between them, which has been going on for centuries, is actually misleading and unnecessary, a result of a confusion of the two levels or, to be more precise, of "a confusion of modalities, of logical and moral necessity and possibility, of 'must' and 'can' with 'ought' and 'may'. In brief, the two theories answer different questions: retributivism the question 'when (logically) *can* we punish?', utilitarianism the question 'when (morally) *may* we or *ought* we to punish?'"[3]

As Quinton sees it, the retributive theory in its most complete form contains four tenets. There are the doctrine of punishment as "annulment" of the crime and the thesis that it is a right of the criminal himself. There is also the demand for proportion between crime and punishment. In Quinton's view, these three are clearly untenable. The main thesis of the theory, however, is a different matter. This thesis, which he formulates as the claim that "punishment is only justified by guilt" or, alternatively, that "it is necessary that a man be guilty if he is to be punished," strikes us as quite compelling.

> There is a very good reason for this difference in force. For the necessity of not punishing the innocent is not moral but logical. It is not, as some retributivists think, that we *may* not punish the innocent and *ought* only to punish the guilty, but that we *cannot* punish the innocent and *must* only punish the guilty. Of course, the suffering or harm in which punishment consists can be and is inflicted on innocent people but this is not punishment, it is judicial error or terrorism or . . . "social surgery." The infliction of suffering on a person is only properly described as punishment if that person is guilty. The retributivist thesis, therefore, is not a moral doctrine, but an account of the meaning of the word "punishment."[4]

This not only cuts retributivism down to size, but also takes care of the main objection to the utilitarian theory — the one on punishment of the innocent. Such a thing simply cannot happen; it is impossible in the strongest sense, that is, logically.

The general result is that

> the retributivist case against the utilitarians falls to the ground as soon as what is true and essential in retributivism is extracted from the rest. This may be unwelcome to the retributivists since it leaves the moral field in the possession of the utilitarians. But there is a compensation in the fact that what is essential in retributivism can at least be definitely established.[5]

It is established, and also contained in the utilitarian theory of punishment by virtue of the fact that the latter is a theory of *punishment*.

Quinton is right as to the meaning of the word "punishment," and therefore also as to the logical impossibility of punishing the innocent. Still, his interpretation of the main thesis of the retributive theory as an analytic statement, and the synthesis of the two theories based on it, is misconceived. He manages neither to trivialize the main retributivist tenet nor to save the utilitarian theory from the punishment-of-the-innocent objection.

Quinton phrases the main retributivist thesis in two alternative ways — "Punishment is only justified by guilt" and "It is necessary that a man be guilty if he is to be punished" — believing that these two formulations boil down to the same thing. They do not; only the first is an accurate expression of what the retributivists are saying. And it is certainly not an analytic statement. If this is not obvious, consider the following: (a) "Punishment is not justified only by guilt" and (b) "Is punishment justified only by guilt?" If the thesis were analytic, (a) would have to be a contradiction and (b) a self-answering question; clearly, neither is the case. When putting forward the thesis that "punishment is only justified by guilt," retributivists are not stating the logical truth that, in order that the word could be correctly applied, the person on the receiving end must be guilty; they are making a genuine ethical claim that the fact of his guilt is the sole justification of the evil inflicted on him, the sole ground of the state's right to punish him. They are not talking about a word, they are using it to say something about the morality of what it stands for.

On the other hand (and Quinton could see this as a compensation for the failure of his interpretation), if it were true that the main thesis of retributivism — that punishment is only justified by guilt — is an analytical truth, that would make the main thesis of the opposing, utilitarian theory, which he wishes to uphold — the thesis that punishment is justified by its good consequences — analytically false. The aim of trivializing the main thesis of the retributive theory in order to add it as an innocuous, logical appendix to the utilitarian theory of the moral basis of punishment would have been achieved at the price of doing away with the latter in the process.[6]

The second line of Quinton's argument — the attempt to rebut the crucial objection to the utilitarian view by reminding us of the meaning of the word "punishment" and the implication that punishment of the innocent is not really punishment — has been dealt with in an earlier chapter. As we saw, the "definitional stop" will not help. Punishment of the innocent is logically impossible, but something very similar to it is not: "punishment" of the innocent. That is precisely what the utilitarian would be committed to in the situation described in the argument: to say that we ought to inflict on the innocent person the evil which, if he were guilty, would be punishment; which, since he is not guilty, cannot be properly termed punishment; and which must be falsely presented to the public at large as punishment, that is, as an evil inflicted on the culprit , because only thus can the good results of the whole proceeding, which make for its moral justification, be achieved.[7]

3. The End and the Means: A.C. Ewing

A.C. Ewing's attempt at a reconciliation of the two theories[8] is also meant as a solution of an antinomy. Both theories have grasped an important truth, but these truths seem to be mutually opposed. Retributivism has the great merit of enabling us to make sense of the reference to the past in punishment, to talk of it in terms of guilt, desert, justice. But it absolutizes this perspective and denies any moral relevance to the good consequences of punishment. These are put forward as its justification by the utilitarian theory, but only at the cost of dissociating it completely from considerations of justice and desert and the retrospective reference implied in it. A satisfactory account of the moral basis of punishment will have to allow for the reference to the past implied in every punishment, its connection with the offense committed, and thus with desert and justice, while stopping short of the retributivist claim that just punishment is good in itself in any great measure. At the same time, it will have to justify punishment by the good it produces, but not at the price of ignoring justice and desert in pursuit of the good, which the traditional utilitarian doctrines of punishment were all too ready to pay.

These conditions, Ewing believes, can be met if we view punishment as a special kind of language. The evil involved in punishment is not evil pure and simple; it has a certain significance, a certain message to convey. Its distinctively moral function is to express the emphatic moral condemnation of the crime by society. This has a twofold purpose: to bring home to the offender the high degree of wrongness of her misdeed, and to teach the same lesson to all potential offenders in the public at large. This is not to be confused with the deterrent effects of punishment. The message is not about the dangers of breaking the law, but about the gross immorality of doing so. The aim is not to get both the actual offender and the public to accept the prudential rule that crime does not pay, but to strengthen in them those distinctively moral motives which will ensure that they do not commit crimes even when it pays to do so. Of course, it is not claimed that people need criminal law and punishment to teach them that such things as murder, rape, or theft are wrong; but the fact that some of them do commit such acts shows that they do not realize strongly and vividly enough just how very wrong they are. This is the lesson taught by punishment; it contributes to the reformation of the offender and the moral education of the public. In this way punishment helps prevent offenses. Given crime prevention as the ultimate goal of punishment, it is obviously much more important that the message be conveyed to, and the lesson impressed on, the public at large, than that the same effect be attained with regard to the actual offender. The function of punishment as a means of moral education of the public — which Ewing terms "educative," to distinguish it from the reformation of the offender — is its distinctively moral function and its true moral justification.

If it is to serve this purpose, punishment must satisfy certain conditions. As an expression of society's moral condemnation, punishment makes sense only if it is addressed to the offender and her offense. If it is inflicted upon an innocent person, it can have no desirable effects, either on her or on the public at large; it can only confuse and corrupt both the person "punished" and everyone else. This is where the reference to the past and the considerations of justice and desert come into the picture. They also come in when the severity of punishment has to be decided upon. There must be a certain proportion between the offense committed and the punishment meted out for it: more serious offenses ought to be punished by harsher punishments, and *vice versa*. For "in a given society a certain amount of pain is a suitable way of expressing a certain degree of disapproval, just as one tone of voice may be a more suitable way of expressing it than another."[9] If this proportion is not ensured, punishments will confound moral judgment about the comparative wrongness of offenses, and thus fail to achieve their purpose.

Thus a division of tasks is made, and a reconciliation of the utilitarian and retributive views of punishment effected, on the basis of the distinction between the end of punishment and the means indispensable for attaining that end. This is made possible by positing as its end the moral education of the public — something that had been almost entirely disregarded by the traditional utilitarian theories of punishment. This novel, "educative" theory solves what Ewing calls "the fundamental antinomy in the theory of punishment":

It seems an essential part of punishment that it should be inflicted for a past offence and not merely as a means to a better future like a surgical operation . . . Yet if it is inflicted for the past and not the future, what is the good of it? It cannot change the past and make the evil act undone. Hence the fundamental antinomy in the theory of punishment. One side says — punishment must be for a past act, otherwise it would be unjust; the other side says — punishment can only be justified by the good it does, but the good it does is not in the past, it can only be in the future. My solution would be that punishment is only justified by the good it does, but it can only do that good if it is for a past offence. If punishment serves as a kind of moral education for the community, it is far from purposeless, yet it can only serve this purpose if it is substantially just. . . . Because punishment is directed towards the past it does not follow that this is its ultimate end; on the contrary we have only justified the reference to the past by showing that without it the future effects desired by us cannot be obtained. It should be inflicted because of a past offence, but we must add also "as a means to a future good".[10]

However, this reconciliation is problematic; in certain circumstances it would prove to be merely apparent. That is so because of the status accorded to the considerations of justice and desert, which are first and foremost means to an end. Ewing concedes that justice in punishment may be valuable in itself, but emphasizes that its intrinsic value is very small compared to its value as a means. It is important as a means because only punishment which is seen as deserved and just will convey the message in which he finds the main moral purpose of punishment and its real justification. To be sure, a punishment will normally be seen as just if it *is* just — but then it ought to *be* just, essentially, so as to be *seen* as such. Thus, if it can be seen as just without being so, that will do well enough, for the intrinsic importance of justice in punishment is not great. This shows that Ewing would be committed to "punishing" the innocent no less than a traditional, Benthamite utilitarian. For the latter, the same as Ewing, could not accomplish his aim except by presenting the innocent person "punished" to the public at large as the culprit; this kind of merely apparent justice is presupposed in the argument. So long as the public is deceived into believing that the innocent person is guilty, her "punishment" will deter potential offenders; so long as it is so deceived, the "punishment" will carry the moral message to those in the public who need it. Ewing's "fresh purpose to justify [punishment]" can legitimize unjust punishment no less than the aim of deterrence which the traditional utilitarian theory saw as its main justification.

4. The Institution and the Particular Case (a):
Rule-Utilitarianism

Still another attempt at a synthetic theory of punishment, far more influential than those I have considered so far, has been made in the context of developing rule-utilitarianism.

Rule-utilitarianism is meant to attain two objectives: to provide an account of moral rules within a broadly utilitarian ethics and social philosophy and to enable the utilitarian to elude various damaging implications of the classical version of the theory (the most worrisome being the implication that it is justified to "punish" an innocent person whenever that is the option with the best consequences). The main principle of utilitarianism is that the good and bad consequences of our actions are the sole standard of their morality. The word "actions" can be taken in two different senses; depending on the sense given to it, a utilitarian theory belongs to the "act" or "rule" variety. If particular actions are meant, we have act-utilitarianism: the theory that we should decide on what is right and wrong, what we should do and what we must not do, by weighing the good and bad consequences of each and every action possible in a particular case, and opting for the one whose consequences are the best. This variety of utilitarianism applies the basic utilitarian principle directly to particular actions; the good and bad consequences to which the principle refers are taken to be the consequences of particular actions. But we can also understand the word "actions" in the sense of types or classes of actions. The result will be a different theory, rule-utilitarianism. According to this theory, the basic utilitarian principle does not normally come into the picture when we judge particular actions; these are evaluated by being subsumed under moral rules — rules which determine certain types or classes of actions as right or wrong, obligatory or prohibited. These rules, on their part, are justified in utilitarian terms: having them has better consequences than having alternative rules or no rules at all. The good and bad consequences of our actions referred to in the basic principle of utilitarianism are not the consequences of particular actions, but those of classes of actions. The principle itself is a second-order rule; it is normally applied to moral rules as rules of the first order, and only indirectly, through those rules, to particular actions.

Both main motives of rule-utilitarianism are clearly at work in various formulations of the rule-utilitarian rationale of punishment. In punishment, as elsewhere, we generally make use of rules, and if a utilitarian theory of punishment is to be plausible it must account for that. The traditional utilitarian theory of punishment, discussed in detail in chapters 2 and 3, is of the "act" variety. That theory's implication, that various unjust punishments, with "punishment" of the innocent understandably topping the list, are justified whenever they happen to be useful, is what the rule-utilitarian wishes to avoid. In addition, the rule-utilitarian theory of punishment is meant to transcend the confrontation of utilitarianism and retributivism by providing a synthesis that, while basically utilitarian, makes room for considerations of justice and desert as well.

The classic and still unsurpassed formulation of this theory is presented in "Two Concepts of Rules" by John Rawls.[11] Rawls' point of departure is the application of the distinction on which the rule-utilitarian theory is based — the one between justifying a moral rule and justifying a particular action falling under the rule — to the problem of punishment. Instead of simply asking what it is that justifies punishment, we should differentiate between two levels of justification and ask two separate questions: What is it that justifies the rules that make up the institution of punishment? and, What is it that justifies a particular act of punishing? Rawls' main thesis is that utilitarianism is the answer to the first question, and retributivism to the second. Thus the two theories are shown to be complementary, rather than opposed to each other.

> A particular man is punished, rather than some other man, because he is guilty, and he is guilty because he broke the law (past tense). In his case the law looks back, the judge looks back, the jury looks back, and a penalty is visited upon him for something he did. That a man is to be punished, and what his punishment is to be, is settled by its being shown that he broke the law and that the law assigns that penalty for the violation of it. On the other hand we have the institution of punishment itself, and recommend and accept various changes in it, because it is thought by the (ideal) legislator and by those to whom the law applies that, as a part of a system of law impartially applied from case to case arising under it, it will have the consequence, in the long run, of furthering the interests of society. One can say, then, that the judge and the legislator stand in different positions and look in different directions: one to the past, the other to the future. The justification of what the judge does, *qua* judge, sounds like the retributive view; the justification of what the (ideal) legislator does, *qua* legislator, sounds like the utilitarian view. Thus both views have a

point . . . and one's initial confusion [which is a result of their con-
frontation] disappears once one sees that these views apply to persons
holding different offices with different duties, and situated differently
with respect to the system of rules that make up the criminal law. . . .
One reconciles the two views by the time-honored device of making
them apply to different situations.[12]

The law is prior to particular cases falling under it; the role of the
legislator is prior to that of the judge. Accordingly, the rule-utilitarian
theory of punishment is basically utilitarian, while retributive considerations are assigned a secondary, subordinate role.

Is this a successful synthesis of utilitarianism and retributivism and a
plausible view of punishment? The answer depends on the capacity of
the theory to consistently rule out "punishment" of the innocent and
other kinds of unjust punishment which the traditional utilitarian theory
readily justifies whenever they are useful. It is certainly meant to do
that. An act-utilitarian goes by the consequences of options in particular
cases of choice; therefore, he is committed to "punishing" the innocent
in every particular case where that is the option with the best
consequences. A rule-utilitarian, in contrast, does not come to a decision
by weighing the consequences of particular actions, but by applying
moral rules to these actions. Even in such a case he will not consider it
justified to "punish" an innocent person, for he will go by the relevant
rule, and the rule, of course, says that the guilty, and only the guilty, are
to be punished. The rule provides for punishing the guilty and acquitting the innocent for good utilitarian reasons: accepting this rule and
acting on it will obviously have better consequences than having an
alternative rule of punishment, or having no rule at all.

At this point, however, a question must be raised: What is the reason
for keeping to the rule in cases where it is precisely the making of an
exception that will have the best consequences?

In order to answer this question, we must first examine the nature of
moral rules, for they can be understood in two very different ways.

One can view a moral rule as an empirical generalization which
condenses previous experience regarding the good and bad consequences of actions of a certain kind, previous decisions regarding such
actions taken by applying the basic principle of utilitarianism directly to
each particular case.[13] Understood in this way, moral rules have several
important characteristics. We need such rules because we often face
situations of the same kind, and it is much easier to make a decision if
we can refer to a relevant rule. But since decisions made in particular
cases are logically prior to such a rule, the rule can be formulated only

after a number of decisions have been taken in cases of the same kind. These cases can be identified as being of the same kind independently of the rule. In principle everyone is free to decide in a particular case whether to follow the rule or to make an exception, because the rule, like all generalizations, allows for exceptions. As for the fundamental principle of utilitarianism, its direct application to particular cases is not excluded in principle; the existence of moral rules merely makes it uneconomical and unnecessary most of the time. But whenever there is reason to doubt that the rule fits the case at hand, we are again referred to that principle. By applying the principle directly to the particular case, we can then decide that we ought to make an exception to the rule.[14]

If the rule-utilitarian conceived of moral rules in this way, he would still be exposed to the argument on "punishment" of the innocent. The rule that only the guilty ought to be punished would be seen as the condensation of the experience that punishment of the guilty and acquittal of the innocent has had better consequences than any other alternative action: a summary of previous decisions that the guilty should be punished and the innocent acquitted, made on the basis of these consequences through the direct application of the fundamental principle of utilitarianism in each particular case. Relying on the experience condensed in the rule, whenever the judge satisfies herself as to someone's guilt she will be able to assume that the best consequences are highly likely to come from punishing; when the accused is proven innocent, she will be able to assume that the best consequences will come from acquitting him. The rule relieves her of the need to weigh the good and bad consequences of alternatives in each case. However, when she knows that the rule does not fit the case at hand, she can put it aside and come to a decision by applying the fundamental utilitarian principle directly to the different courses of action open to her. The argument on "punishment" of the innocent hypothesizes just such a case: the judge already knows that the rule that the guilty should be punished and the innocent acquitted is unsuitable to the case at hand, that it is precisely by making an exception to the rule and "punishing" the innocent person that the best possible results will be produced. In such a case the existence of a moral rule according to which only the guilty ought to be punished makes no difference. If one knows that in *this* case "punishment" of the innocent will have the best results, then referring to the rule which says that such results are *most often* produced by an alternative action is no argument against it. The conclusion is still that the right thing to do is to "punish" the innocent.

This is only an instance of a more general point: rule-utilitarianism that sees moral rules as empirical generalizations is practically no different from act-utilitarianism. Such rules are nothing but a shortcut in the majority of cases to the same conclusion that would be reached by weighing all the good and bad consequences of every alternative available in the particular case. The adherent of this kind of rule-utilitarianism and the advocate of act-utilitarianism would come to the same judgment in all cases in which the relevant moral rule fitted the circumstances. They would also reach the same conclusion — that the rule should be broken — in all other cases, when the rule would not fit the circumstances. The only difference would be that the act-utilitarian would reach this conclusion by directly applying the fundamental principle of utilitarianism to the particular case, while the rule-utilitarian would first have to realize that in the case at hand the rule does not help, and then he too would have to apply the principle. It is understandable that advocates of act-utilitarianism have nothing against the use of moral rules viewed in *this* way.[15]

Moral rules can also be understood in a rather different way, as institutional rules. Such rules and the institutions they make up help coordinate and predict human conduct; without them society could not exist. In order to ensure the predictability and coordination of human behavior and thus attain various social objectives, rules are adopted and systems of rules are set up to define and prescribe activities and roles within institutions. Institutional rules are not summaries of previous experience in similar cases nor of previous decisions taken in such cases; they are rather logically prior to particular cases falling under them, and the latter can be identified as being of the same kind only on the basis of these rules. With the establishing of these rules, new activities and new roles emerge which would not exist but for the rules. Those who participate in these activities and assume these roles are not authorized to decide in particular cases to which the rules apply whether to comply with them or not. As opposed to the rules formulated by empirical generalization, which hold only generally and allow for exceptions, institutional rules apply universally, without exceptions.[16]

Punishment is one such institution, and the rule that only the guilty ought to be punished is one of its constitutive, defining rules. Still, one can again raise the question: Why not break this rule in a case where it is by doing so that the best possible results will be achieved? What can a rule-utilitarian who sees the rules of morality as institutional rules give as a reason for following the rule in such a case?

He can refer to the logical nature of institutional rules and argue that they do not authorize the person participating in an institution constituted by the rules to decide in particular cases whether to abide by them, but make it mandatory to do so in all cases to which they apply without exception. He can also point out that the action specified by the institution is logically possible only if the relevant institutional rules are respected, and that an action violating a constitutive, defining rule of the institution is no longer an action of the type specified, but something essentially different. In the case of punishment, this means that the institution of punishment does not authorize the judge, the person performing a specific role within the institution, to decide in particular cases whether to go by the rules of the institution, such as the rule that only the guilty are to be punished. The institution makes it incumbent on her to follow the rule in all cases of punishment without exception; it also implies that, were the judge to break this rule, what she did would not be punishment but something importantly different.[17]

This defense is not convincing. The critic of rule-utilitarianism need not deny that the rule in question aspires to universal validity and that the judge is not authorized by this rule (or any other rule of the institution of punishment) to decide for herself whether to comply with the rule in a case where its violation would have better results. The import of the argument against a rule-utilitarian view of punishment is that in such a case the judge has no good utilitarian reason not to *ignore* the claim to universal validity of the rule "only the guilty shall be punished," not to do something her role does *not* authorize her to do — namely, to break the rule and "punish" the innocent defendant. As for the second part of the argument — the claim that if the judge did that, it would not be punishment — we have already seen that this kind of "definitional stop" does not work. What the judge ought to do in such a case, if she is a rule-utilitarian, will not be punishment, to be sure, it will be "punishment" only. But for the purpose of critique of rule-utilitarianism, nothing more is needed.[18]

Another way in which the adherent of rule-utilitarianism can defend the theory is by referring to certain indirect, long-term effects of "punishment" of the innocent. These are alleged to be so bad as to outweigh by far any good results of such "punishment," and therefore are said to tip the final balance against it. These are the undesirable, even disastrous consequences of breaking one of the constitutive rules of the institution of punishment — the rule that only the guilty ought to be punished — which are damaging to the institution and, hence, to society as a whole. Punishment is one of the most important institutions in every society. The good results of its effective functioning are far-reaching and can hardly be overestimated: the legal security of each citizen, as well as many of society's interests and values, depends on it. Therefore, in the case described in the argument, the conclusion that the innocent person ought to be "punished" could be reached only by a superficial utilitarian, who would see no further than the immediate consequences of such an action — that it would for the moment restore public confidence in the legal order and prevent a number of offenses which would otherwise be committed in the near future. He would completely overlook the fact that the deliberate "punishment" of an innocent would, after a time, most likely come to the ears of the public, and that the bad effects which would *then* come about, compromising the whole institution of punishment, would outweigh any possible benefit this could have produced. Because of these indirect, long-term consequences, the final conclusion of the rule-utilitarian will be that the innocent person should not be "punished" after all.[19]

This defence of rule-utilitarianism is not convincing either. First of all, it can be claimed that the utilitarian is overestimating the bad consequences a single breach of a rule would have for the whole institution. Would public awareness of the fact that, on an earlier occasion, an innocent person had been deliberately "punished" for the sake of the common good really shake the foundations of the entire institution of punishment? The utilitarian can warn that "a series of exceptions in single cases can add up to the effective abandonment of a general rule,"[20] but one can reply that "this . . . is irrelevant, and is the old confusion between single act and systematical evasion [of a rule]."[21]

It would be difficult to bring this discussion to a close as long as it is conducted on an empirical level. Only research in the sociology of law could resolve the issue in a satisfactory manner. Far more important, and in my view conclusive, is another point to be made here against rule-utilitarianism. The indirect consequences of "punishing" an innocent person, which are so bad as to outweigh the immediate good effects of such an action and therefore give the utilitarian good reason to decide against "punishing", are not the consequences of the act itself, but rather of the fact becoming a matter of public knowledge. The public could lose confidence in the institution of punishment, with the result that the institution would no longer be able to function effectively, only if it learned that the person "punished" had in fact been innocent, and that the judge had been aware of that. This means that the argument on "punishing" the innocent can easily be made proof against the attempt to rebut it by bringing in the indirect consequences of such "punishment." It is enough to introduce the assumption that the judge has a way of ensuring that the truth will never get out. Such a case precludes the indirect consequences which a breach of the rule that only the guilty should be punished could have for the institution of punishment, so that only the direct consequences count. And these are *ex hypothesi* such that, from the utilitarian point of view, the thing to do is to break the rule and "punish" the innocent.[22]

The upshot of the discussion so far is that the rule-utilitarian, just like the adherent of act-utilitarianism, is committed to "punishing" the innocent whenever that is the option having the best consequences: the utility of having the rule that only the guilty are to be punished cannot help escape this conclusion. If he persists with the claim that we must stick to the rule, although he cannot come up with a good utilitarian reason for doing so, I think we should agree with the judgment shared by both H.J. McCloskey, a sharp critic of utilitarianism of any kind, and J.J.C. Smart, who rejects rule-utilitarianism in favor of the "act" variety of the theory: such a claim would be irrational and untenable. It would be but "the absurd insistence on conformity with the rule, with no good reason for this being offered,"[23] "a form of superstitious rule-worship (easily explicable psychologically) and not the rational thought of a philosopher."[24]

Up to this point the discussion has been in terms of a choice between keeping to the rule that only the guilty shall be punished and making an exception to it. In "Two Concepts of Rules" Rawls defends rule-utilitarianism by pointing out that the theory does not focus on particular actions but rather on moral rules. Therefore, the discussion should not be conducted in terms of the rule/exception dilemma; the relevant dilemma is that between a rule and an alternative rule. Faced with the argument on "punishment" of the innocent, the rule-utilitarian "must describe more carefully what the *institution* is which [the argument] suggests, and then ask . . . whether or not it is likely that having this institution would be for the benefit of society in the long run."[25]

Rawls describes this institution in the following way:

Try to imagine, then, an institution (which we may call "telishment") which is such that the officials set up by it have authority to arrange a trial for the condemnation of an innocent man whenever they are of the opinion that doing so would be in the best interests of society. The discretion of officials is limited, however, by the rule that they may not condemn an innocent man to undergo such an ordeal unless there is, at the time, a wave of offenses similar to that with which they charge him and telish him for. We may imagine that the officials having the discretionary authority are the judges of the higher courts in consultation with the chief of police, the minister of justice, and a committee of the legislature.[26]

In order to show that the argument on "punishing" the innocent really strikes at rule-utilitarianism, Rawls holds that the critic would have to show that such an institution could be justified in utilitarian terms. But when we consider all the risks of abuse which would plague this institution, and then add the uncertainty which would replace the legal security provided by the institution of punishment as we know it, and weigh heavily on every citizen, it becomes clear that "a utilitarian justification for this institution is most unlikely."[27]

This defense of rule-utilitarianism is equally weak. It seems to be either a result of misunderstanding the argument on "punishment" of the innocent, or yet another instance of that "rule-worship" which is so utterly unutilitarian, but to which rule-utilitarians tend to resort when trying to evade objections of this sort. For the argument is not that the rule-utilitarian would have to favor replacing the institution of punishment by the institution Rawls calls "telishment." The argument is rather that whenever the best consequences would be attained by breaking one of the constitutive rules of the institution of punishment, the rule that only the guilty should be punished, he could bring up no good reason against doing so — on the contrary, he would have to decide that the rule should be broken. And as I have already said, it is not at all clear that one breach of the rule would threaten the rule itself or the whole institution. It is obvious that making one exception to a rule does not amount to setting up an alternative rule or an alternative institution. Even if a series of violations were to undermine a rule or a whole institution and eventually lead to its breakdown, this in itself would still not establish an alternative rule or institution. Therefore, the critic of utilitarianism does not have to show that, from the utilitarian point of view, the institution of "telishment" is preferable to that of punishment as we know it. Quite the contrary to what Rawls claims, the relevant dilemma is not the institution of punishment vs. the institution of "telishment," but rather the institution of punishment with its constitutive rule that only the guilty shall be punished vs. a breach of this rule in a particular case.[28]

This sufficiently shows the failure of Rawls' defense of rule-utilitarianism, but it is only a part of the reply to his argument. Even if we grant him the (unsound) point that the discussion should be exclusively in terms of rules and institutions, the outcome will not favor utilitarianism. Rawls' thesis that it is "most unlikely" that the institution of "telishment" could have a utilitarian justification simply will not stand. Rawls bases this thesis on the dangers of the abuse of such an institution, and on the claim that the rules of the institution could not be public. His first reason does not carry great weight, for we can assume, for the sake of argument, that enough reliable, honest, and intelligent people can be found to assume office within the institution to reduce the likelihood of abuse to an acceptable minimum. Alternatively, we can assume for the sake of argument that the good consequences of having the institution of "telishment" far outweigh the harm of its occasional abuse.

Rawls' second reason is *prima facie* very strong: "people will come to have a very different attitude towards their penal system when telishment is adjoined to it. They will be uncertain as to whether a convicted man has been punished or telished. They will wonder whether or not they should feel sorry for him. They will wonder whether the same fate won't at any time fall on them."[29] But this is not a consequence of "telishment" as such, but of public knowledge of it: it will come to pass only if the rules of the institution are known to one and all, or at least to the majority. That, however, need not be the case. Rawls insists that it is a logical characteristic of institutional rules that they have to be "publicly known."[30] He is right in that an institutional rule cannot be private. It is possible to have private rules of conduct (maxims, as Kant would say), but not private institutions or private institutional rules, since institutions are by definition social phenomena. But while it follows from the concept of an institutional rule that it cannot be private, this does not mean that it must be public in the widest sense of the word, that is, known to the whole public at large; for these are not the only possibilities. *Internal* institutional rules are also possible, that is, rules which are known to those who hold offices within an institution and to them only. Some institutions, the secret police, for instance, have just such internal rules; the effective functioning of such institutions depends to a considerable degree on whether the secrecy of these rules is preserved. The rules of "telishment" could be internal institutional rules, known only to officials of the institution, while remaining a secret to the public. The officials would inform those whom it befell to be "telished" about the rules at appropriate moments in order to assure them that what is being done to them is morally right and that, moreover, they themselves are morally bound to cooperate.

From this it becomes clear that, just as one can imagine a particular case in which "punishment" of the innocent would have a utilitarian justification, so one can imagine circumstances in which the institution for "punishing" the innocent, which Rawls terms "telishment," would be morally justified from the utilitarian point of view. There could be circumstances such as those described in an earlier chapter,[31] except that they would not be transient, but would have a degree of permanence. A permanent social need would arise, which could be met effectively only by setting up the appropriate institution.[32]

Of course, just as particular cases of punishment of the guilty and acquittal of the innocent with utilitarian justification are typical, and cases of "punishment" of the innocent with good utilitarian reason, while possible, are atypical, so, generally speaking, social conditions in which the institution of punishment as we know it has a utilitarian justification are typical, while social conditions in which the common interest would best be served by setting up an institution for "punishing" the innocent are possible, but atypical. Unfortunately, as in the case of particular instances, this is not only a logical, but an empirical possibility as well. This is strikingly illustrated by the apparatus which populated the Gulag Archipelago with people deliberately "punished" although innocent. This apparatus had been operating for decades, according to internal institutional rules, and its victims were millions. That is why it can properly be described as an institution for "punishing" the innocent. Given certain empirical assumptions, the institution can be morally justified from the standpoint of the same "revolutionary Machiavellianism" which could give moral sanction to individual judicial murders at the Moscow trials in the thirties.[33]

Thus rule-utilitarianism does not really effect a synthesis of the utilitarian and retributive views of punishment; it does not really integrate retributive considerations in such a way as to avoid the commitment to socially expedient injustice in punishment, which vitiates the old, "act" variety of the theory. Rules or no rules, a utilitarian will have to put aside considerations of justice and desert when that is the option with the best consequences.

5. The Institution and the Particular Case (b): R.M. Hare's Two-Level Theory

Hare's two-level theory of moral thinking, developed in a series of articles over the seventies and systematically elaborated in his book *Moral Thinking: Its Levels, Method and Point*,[34] is based on the same distinction on which the rule-utilitarian builds his case. But it would be a mistake to take it for but another formulation of rule-utilitarianism, for it is much more complex and sophisticated. A recent review of contemporary utilitarianism praises it, without exaggeration, I think, as "the most rigorous and lucid account of utilitarianism in our century — and the most important since Sidgwick's classic work, *The Methods of Ethics*."[35] Hare applies his theory to a number of problems in moral and social philosophy, including that of the justification of punishment.

His point of departure is the claim that the philosopher must not ignore the human limitations of the moral agent. Our knowledge is limited, and so are our capacities for clear, logical thinking. Our sympathy for others and the ability to be impartial are rather limited too. In addition, we often have to arrive at a moral decision within a short time span. For Hare, as for any utilitarian, morality has a purpose, and that is doing good and reducing evil in the world, but he emphasizes that, in view of the limitations inherent to our everyday moral life, this purpose will not be promoted if we go for it directly, the way act-utilitarians advise us to do: by coming to a decision in each particular case on the basis of weighing and balancing good and bad consequences of options. The utilitarian aim of morality is much more likely to be served if we keep to the basic, simple, fairly general moral rules, such as those that enjoin us to keep our promises or tell the truth. We need not (and cannot) take them as absolute and observe each one of them on every occasion, but we should go by them most of the time. In order to be able to do that, we ought also to develop in ourselves, and help inculcate and strengthen in others, firm dispositions for acting in accordance with the rules and for feeling guilty whenever we offend against one of them.

There is a certain compellingness to such basic, everyday moral rules, which may justify calling the kind of moral thinking that remains on the level of such rules and consists in comprehending them, marking their relevance to particular cases and applying them in those cases, *intuitive* thinking. But this cannot be the only kind of moral thinking. Such rules are not self-justifying, there are bound to be cases which they do not fit, and they occasionally come into conflict with one another. Therefore, a higher level of moral thinking is needed, at which we select and revise the first-order, intuitive rules and resolve conflicts between them. This is *critical* thinking, which is something of a moral luxury: we can afford to engage in it only when we are free from the constraints of our everyday moral life. Critical moral thinking is purely utilitarian: it selects and modifies first-order rules according to their acceptance-utility and settles conflicts between them by calculating good and bad consequences of alternatives in concrete situations of moral choice. Of course, if we had superhuman powers of clear, logical thinking and were omniscient and completely impartial, we could safely think through each particular case of moral choice in this way and be sure always to find out what *is* right for us to do. But since we are only human, we should keep to the intuitive level of moral thinking most of the time and go by the rules. By doing so, we shall be sure to do what is *most likely* to be right.

Hare makes vivid the distinction between the types of moral thinking by introducing two figures to personify them. One is a person whose power of clear thinking is very weak, whose knowledge of the world is poor, and who is given to special pleading; he is called the *prole* (after Orwell's *Nineteen Eighty-Four*). A being completely free of all these human limitations — one endowed with superhuman intelligence, absolute knowledge, and complete impartiality — is called the *archangel*. The prole, quite incapable of critical moral thinking, must always keep to the intuitive level and go by the rules, having been taught to do so by someone else. The archangel will be able to provide the rules for him, but will not need them himself; he will never have occasion to descend to the intuitive level, for he is able to settle every moral question (and in no time at that) by critical thinking. Of course, these two figures are idealizations: "although the archangel and the prole are exaggerated versions of the top and bottom classes in Plato's Republic," says Hare, "it is far from my intention to divide up the human race into archangels and proles; we all share the characteristics of both to limited and varying degrees and at different times."[36]

One of the most important tasks of critical thinking is resolving moral conflicts, but we shall not leave the intuitive level and launch into such thinking in every case of such conflict. In some such cases "we may 'feel sure' that some principle or some feature of a situation is *in that situation* more important than others . . . We shall then be able to sort the matter out intuitively, letting one principle override the other in this case, without recourse to critical thinking."[37] In other cases we shall set aside the rules and consider only the concrete situation, bringing critical

thinking to bear on it and choosing the option that has better consequences. (The question when to deal with moral conflict intuitively, and
when to think it through critically — when to behave like a prole, and
when to imitate the archangel — admits of no general answer: "it
depends on how much each one of us, on some particular occasion or in
general, resembles one or the other of these two characters . . . on what
powers of thought and character each one of us, for the time being,
thinks he possesses."[38]) But no matter which way we settle the conflict,
we shall feel guilty for having broken a moral rule. That is as it should
be: the feelings of guilt will show that we have really adopted the rule
and are liable to go against it only rarely and with strong inner opposition. That is to say, there are good utilitarian reasons for developing and
nurturing these feelings.

These are the main contentions of Hare's two-level theory. The theory
is basically utilitarian, but it is much more complex than both act-
utilitarianism and the standard rule-utilitarian views. It includes ele-
ments of deontologism and rule-utilitarianism integrated at the first,
intuitive level of moral thinking, and those of act-utilitarianism, which
appear at the second, critical level. It is meant to incorporate the valid
insights of all these approaches, while steering clear of their mistakes
and exaggerations. Along with the deontologist and the rule-utilitarian,
Hare wants to do justice to the important role of rules in our moral life,
which is ignored and misunderstood by the act-utilitarian. Along with
the rule-utilitarian, and in opposition to the deontologist, he holds that
those rules cannot be accepted at their face value but need to be
justified, and provides this justification in terms of the good consequences of their acceptance. But he also emphasizes that there is more to
morality than moral rules — a fact beyond the scope of deontologism,
the consequence being that this approach is quite unhelpful when two
such rules come into conflict. It is in cases of moral conflict that the
act-utilitarian model of thinking comes into its own. The main mistake of
the act-utilitarian is to believe that his model applies to each and every
case of moral decision. Once this mistake is corrected and the model is
confined to its proper place, its role in moral thinking is fully safe-
guarded. The unacceptable permissiveness with regard to basic moral
rules that vitiates both act-utilitarianism and some rule-utilitarian views
seems to have been avoided: after taking account of the limitations and
difficulties inherent to everyday moral life, it becomes clear that we
ought to go by such rules most of the time. But we are by no means
invited to engage in the rule-worship typical of the deontologist and

sometimes embraced by the rule-utilitarian as well: there will be occasions when the right thing to do will be to break a moral rule.

What of punishment? As expected, Hare provides a two-level account that emphasizes the distinction between the laws that make up the institution of punishment and the role of the legislator, on the one hand, and the application of the law to particular cases, which is the task of the judge, on the other. The legislator is seen rather like an archangel and is expected to think critically, while the judge is rather like the prole and thus simply applies the rules provided by the legislator. But these rules will be much like the rules a retributivist would want to have, and for good utilitarian reasons:

> Prima facie moral principles are needed for the conduct of those who administer the law, and critical thinking has to select these principles. . . . Thus the grounds of selection will be utilitarian; but the principles selected may not themselves look utilitarian at all. They are likely to be, rather, of the sort dear to deontologists . . . they will insist on things like not punishing the innocent, not condemning people unheard, observing procedures in court which are calculated to elicit the truth from witnesses and cause the jury to attend to it, and so on.

Thus a division of labor between the two theories is established, and the problem of punishment is thereby "easily solved":

> The retributivists are right at the intuitive level, and the utilitarians at the critical level. It is proper and necessary for the judges to sentence in accordance with the law, and sentence only those who have been duly convicted. But the reason why this is proper and necessary is that a legal system in which judges have not been brought up to treat this principle as in practice unbreakable is likely to be a bad system for nearly everybody subject to it. And if a justification is demanded for the laws themselves, or for a particular law, with the penalties attached, it too will be utilitarian: these are the laws which it is best, in the general interest, to have.[39]

Does this most recent and sophisticated version of utilitarianism clearly and strongly enough rule out "punishment" of the innocent and other types of unjust punishment and provide a plausible reconciliation of the retributive and utilitarian theories of punishment?

Hare's response to the "punishment"-of-the-innocent argument (and others of the same kind) is two-pronged. On the one hand, he rejects the very method of criticizing an ethical theory by bringing up examples such as these, for they, in his view, are "unusual," "contrived," "jejune." On the other hand, he claims that a judge who accepted his theory would do nothing of the sort. As for the first move, to the extent that it is purely methodological, independent of the substance of Hare's two-level theory, I have already dealt with it in an earlier chapter. I have argued, first, that there is nothing wrong with using examples which have not been taken from, and may even be unlikely to happen in, real life; second, that cases when "punishing" an innocent person is the option with the best consequences attainable under the circumstances, regrettably enough, are by no means as unrealistic as utilitarians make out.[40]

The second line of Hare's retort to the "punishment"-of-the-innocent objection is that his theory would not allow that. For the judge is not supposed to question the rules, but to go by them; that is what he has been brought up to do, and what makes him a good judge: "The good judge will not consider the possibility of the case before him being of such a sort. If he could consider it, he would certainly be a worse judge — one who would not act for the best in *other* cases."[41] That is, the judge is supposed to be rather like the prole.

This argument is not convincing, for two reasons. The first can be stated quite briefly: normally, a judge is not at all like the prole. The model of the prole may well be applicable to most people most of the time as they live their private lives, and to a great many roles that have to be played and jobs that have to be done in society. But there are also social roles that by their nature presuppose a different way of thinking and decision-making, one much closer to the archangel's. The role of the judge is certainly among those on all four counts in terms of which Hare distinguishes between the two. A judge is supposed to be capable of clear thinking and to exercise it to the utmost when in court; muddled thinking would be certain to lose him the job. It is incumbent on him to establish all the facts relevant to the case at hand with great care. Impartiality is *the* virtue of a judge; he must exemplify it as much as a human being can. Finally, a judge is allowed, and expected, to take his time when coming to a judgment. (This does not apply to a judge sitting in a drumhead court-martial or a special court set up to mete out summary "justice" in times of revolution or civil war. But such courts are the exceptions that prove the rule.) So if anyone is ever in an archangelic position, a judge sitting in court is. Therefore, he will deal with his cases by thinking them through critically, that is, according to the act-utilitarian model. This means that Hare's judge will decide to "punish" the innocent on each and every occasion on which a judge who adheres to the old, crude act-utilitarian theory will: whenever that happens to be the option with the best consequences. To argue that he will not because his limited capability of clear thinking, his insufficient knowledge of relevant facts, his tendency to be partial, and the pressure of time make it unadvisable for him to try to think critically, and leave him no alternative but to stick to the simple, intuitive rule prohibiting such "punishment," seems to me quite implausible.

Even if what I have just said were not true — if the notion of the judge as someone who can and should deal with every issue he has to settle on its merits, by thinking it through in a highly lucid manner, not in a hurry, and come to a decision that is based on a wide range of facts and is not tainted by his personal or group sympathies and prejudices, were unduly optimistic, and if judges were in reality as prole-like as most of us — the "punishment"-of-the-innocent argument still would not have been rebutted. This is so because of a difficulty of a general nature that vitiates the two-level structure as a whole.

Let us assume a rather prole-like judge who resists the temptation to think about his cases critically, and sticks to the rules, including, of course, the rule that prohibits "punishing" the innocent. If the rules he is to go by have been well selected by critical thinking, this should come naturally and present no difficulty. In particular, in a well-selected set, the rules would only exceptionally come into conflict with one another. Is Hare's theory likely to ensure this? As examples of the sort of basic, fairly general rules that make up the first, intuitive level, Hare mentions those that prohibit violence, murder, stealing, lying, the breaking of promises, "punishing" the innocent — and also the rule of bene- ficence.[42] If beneficence is one of such rules, on an equal footing with the rule that prohibits "punishing" the innocent, every case in which to acquit the innocent defendant is not at the same time the option with the best consequences attainable under the circumstances will involve a *conflict* of the two rules.[43] The judge could easily go by the rule pro- hibiting "punishment" of the innocent most of the time, as Hare expects him to do, if all other basic rules were similarly specific; for most of the time this rule does not come into conflict with any other, and when it does, it is clear that there is such conflict. Then the usual situation of a judge facing a defendant who is innocent would be such that only one moral rule is relevant — the rule that enjoins acquittal. But when the rule of beneficence is brought in at the same level, in every case when it is not quite clear that to acquit the innocent defendant is the course of action that will have the best consequences — and that is often *not* quite clear, for otherwise the two-level theory would not demand that there should be such a rule — the judge will have to consider the possibility that the two rules conflict with each other. Thus the rule of not "punishing" the innocent is likely to be called in question much more frequently than Hare expects.

Sometimes the judge will resolve this conflict intuitively, without taking to critical thinking. Nothing can be said in general about the proportion of cases in which either of the two conflicting rules will prevail as the judge "feels sure" that it should. In other cases he will take up the case on its merits and think about it critically, that is, weigh the good and bad consequences of "punishing" the innocent person and of acquitting her, the way an act-utilitarian would. On such occasions, whenever it turns out that to acquit the innocent defendant is actually the alternative with the best consequences — which is to say, whenever it turns out that there is no conflict after all between the rule which enjoins this and the rule of beneficence — the judge will acquit her. On the other hand, whenever it turns out that "punishing" her would have the best consequences, that is, that there *is* a conflict between the two rules, the judge will decide to "punish." Beneficence figures on both levels, first as one of the two conflicting first-order rules and again as the principle of critical thinking for settling conflicts of first-level rules; it is both a litigant and the arbiter. Therefore, it is bound to prevail in every case of this sort. Accordingly, in all such cases, Hare's judge will be just as committed to "punishing" the innocent as an act-utilitarian judge would be.

Nor should Hare expect his judge to feel guilty about it. Having accepted the two-level theory, the judge will hold that it would be good for him to have the feelings of guilt for the utilitarian reasons the theory brings forward. But at the same time he will know that, from the point of view of the theory, he is *not* guilty. The fact that Hare nevertheless wants to induce such feelings in the judge only goes to show that in this respect his version of utilitarianism is even more compromised than other utilitarian views. While those are liable to justify the undeserved, unjust suffering of one person — the innocent person who gets "punished" for the sake of the common good — Hare calls for that *and* for the undeserved, unjust suffering of another: the judge who has done what his theory pronounces to be right under the circumstances and who is therefore equally innocent.[44]

This point about guilt is secondary, however. The main point is the unexpectedly far-reaching scope of the rule of beneficence which, against Hare's intentions, gives his two-level theory a strong push in the direction of act-utilitarian permissiveness with regard to moral rules. In the context of punishment this means a pull away from the principles of justice and desert, in the direction of "punishing" the innocent and committing other sorts of injustice in the field of punishment. To be sure, Hare does not draw anything like a list of simple, everyday moral rules for the intuitive level of moral thinking; he only cites a few examples of such rules. Could it be, then, that the rule of beneficence is no more than an unfortunate example, and that all will be well if we simply forget about beneficence as a first-order rule? It will not, since the difficulty here is not one of providing good illustrations of how a basically sound structure is to be filled out; it is rather a structural flaw of the whole two-level edifice. It was only to be expected that some such rule would come up at the first level. Once one takes the view that the point of morality is to promote the good and minimize the bad in the world — a view definitive of utilitarianism of all hues — one has to introduce some rule to that effect, alongside rules on truth-telling, promise-keeping, abstaining from violence, acquitting the innocent, and the like. For these latter, more specific rules can never effectively cover the whole range of possible beneficence.

Nor will it help to try to assign a special, residual status to the rule of beneficence, making it relevant only in those cases where no other, more specific moral rule applies, in order to eliminate the threat it poses to every other rule on every turn. Doing so would mean introducing a hierarchy of first-order moral rules. Hare rightly rejects the idea of such a hierarchy, not only for practical reasons, which are not relevant in this case (for the proposed hierarchy would be quite simple and easy to master and apply), but also because "we are unlikely to be able always to put [these rules] in the same order of priority."[45] Even retributivists — with the exception of Kant and one or two others — would not want to go so far as to maintain that the prohibition of "punishing" the innocent must *always* override considerations of beneficence, come what may.[46]

Thus Hare has not managed to overcome the far-reaching permissiveness with regard to "punishment" of the innocent and other sorts of unjust punishment that vitiates other utilitarian views. If my first objection to his account of punishment is valid, that is, if a judge is much more like the archangel than like the prole, there will be no difference whatsoever in practical implications between those views and Hare's two-level theory. If that is not granted, there will be a difference, but only in those cases when Hare's prole-like judge deals with the conflict between the rule that prohibits "punishing" the innocent and the one that enjoins beneficence at the intuitive level *and* resolves it in favor of the first rule. This is certainly not a big difference. In either case, Hare does not seem to have succeeded in bridging the gap between the retributive and utilitarian theories of punishment and providing a stable, plausible synthesis of the two.

6. The Institution and the Particular Case (c): H.L.A. Hart

In some respects, H.L.A. Hart's widely influential views on punishment are rather similar to the rule-utilitarian account. Hart sets out by claiming that a "morally tolerable" theory must display the complexity of punishment and "exhibit it as a compromise between distinct and partly conflicting principles."[47] The way to do that is by distinguishing the question of justification of the institution of punishment or, as he puts it, or its "general justifying aim," and those questions that arise in particular cases of punishing, that is, questions of its distribution: Who gets punished and how much? As an answer to the first question, retributivism will not do; the institution of punishment has to be legitimized by its justifying aim, which is the prevention of offenses by way of general deterrence. At the level of distribution, however, both utilitarian and retributive considerations are relevant. The question of liability to punishment has to be answered in purely retributivist terms: only those who have broken the law, and have done so voluntarily, may legitimately be punished. The amount of punishment is to be decided on partly by considerations of deterrence, which are entailed by the purpose and justification of the institution of punishment, and partly by criteria on which the retributivist would insist. Punishments ought to be measured out so as to serve the end of deterrence in an efficient but also economical way. At the same time, there ought to be some proportion between offenses and punishments. In cases of diminished responsibility, the severity of punishment ought to be mitigated.

On the face of it, this looks rather like the rule-utilitarian view I have already discussed.[48] Whether it is but another formulation of that view, open to the same objections, depends on the status of those principles of justice which, according to the theory, have an important role to play at the level of distribution of punishment. If the basis of these principles were their utility, they would have no autonomous status *vis-à-vis* the general justifying aim of punishment and could not come into conflict with that aim in any serious way. It is a distinctive and crucial contention of Hart's theory of punishment, however, that the principles of justice or fairness which, in combination with utilitarian considerations, determine the distribution of punishment, are to be understood as *different* from, *independent* of, and partly *conflicting* with its general justifying aim. And it is no accident that they conflict with it, for they are meant to limit the pursuit of the utilitarian aim, to make sure that it is not sought in unjust ways, that the individual is not denied his rights and unjustly used by society, or even sacrificed to it, in ways which the unqualified pursuit of deterrence would call for. In this respect, punishment is like other major social institutions: "Just because the pursuit of any single social aim has its restrictive qualifier, our main social institutions always possess a plurality of features which can only be understood as a compromise between partly discrepant principles."[49]

Thus, with regard to liability to punishment, the principle that only those who have broken the law, and have done so voluntarily, may legitimately be punished, cannot be established on utilitarian grounds. To try to show that "punishment" of the innocent could not possibly be socially expedient in the long run is to miss the point: "though such answers *can* be made they do not seem to account for the character of the normal unwillingness to 'punish' those who have not broken the law at all . . . " This unwillingness "would still remain even if we were certain that in the case of the 'punishment' of one who had not broken the law the fact of his innocence would not get out or would not cause great alarm if it did."[50] Nor can the requirement of culpability be plausibly defended by the argument from "inefficaciousness" of punishment of the insane or those who have violated the law unintentionally; Bentham's rationale of excuses is a "spectacular *non sequitur*." Such punishment would not make sense in terms of particular deterrence, but it could contribute significantly to general deterrence, which is the main purpose of punishing.[51] Our rejection of such punishment implies our willingness to do without that contribution. Generally, the option of "punishing" the innocent for the sake of the common good, and programs of abolishing the culpability requirement and meting out punishment in accordance with "objective liability,"[52] or of doing away with the institution of punishment altogether and replacing it by some therapeutic system of social control, cannot be plausibly rejected from a utilitarian point of view; they have to be repudiated in the name of justice or fairness as an irreducible, independent principle of considerable weight. This principle can be supported by arguments from liberty as a paramount moral and social value. Only a system of crime control incorporating the principle that those who have broken the law, while having a fair opportunity not to do so, may alone be punished, safe-

guards the greatest freedom of the individual possible within the coercive framework of law. It lets the individual's own decisions determine
his future, and also enables him to predict it, in a way and to a degree
which would not be possible were this principle to be discarded.

With regard to the severity of punishment, over and above the
utilitarian concern for economical deterrence entailed by the general
justifying aim of the institution, there are some requirements of justice
to be met. First, there ought to be a certain proportion between the
punishment and the offense; disproportionately harsh punishments are
unacceptable, not because they would be uneconomical (they might not
be), but just because they would be disproportionate. The demand for
proportion is supported both by considerations of utility and those of
justice:

> There are many reasons why we might wish the legal gradation of the
> seriousness of crimes, expressed in the scale of punishments, not to
> conflict with common estimates of their comparative wickedness. One
> reason is that such a conflict is undesirable on simple utilitarian
> grounds: it might either confuse moral judgments or bring the law
> into disrepute, or both. Another reason is that principles of justice or
> fairness between different offenders require morally distinguishable
> offences to be treated differently and morally similar offences to be
> treated alike.[53]

Second, there are considerations of mitigation. It is justice, not utility,
that requires that those who faced special difficulties in obeying the law
they have broken should be punished less severely. If utility were all, it
would have to be the other way round.[54]

These, then, are the main points of Hart's theory of punishment. It
has been criticized on several counts.

The notion of a "general justifying aim" has been objected to. It is
ambiguous between an aim or purpose of punishment and its justification, and these are not the same, "except in the eyes of those who have
travelled so far down the utilitarian road that they never question the
means if the end is desirable."[55] Hart certainly does not fit this description. The criticism misses the mark, for the notion is not used in order to
advance a utilitarian rationale of the institution of punishment, under
the guise of a normatively innocuous formulation of the problem; the
claim that the institution has to be justified in terms of deterrence is put

forward as an expressly normative one, and the alternative, retributivist solution of the same problem is explicitly rejected on the same, normative level.

It has also been pointed out that the mere fact that we can ask those particular questions distinguished by Hart

> is consistent with *all* the answers being solely in terms of prevention, or solely in terms of desert. There is no reason for thinking that some separate-questions procedure inevitably or logically leads one to a compromise theory. The existence of separate questions does not constitute an *argument* for the conclusion that punishment must be justified by several principles.[56]

This is not a valid objection either. The compromise view which Hart advances as the right solution to the problem of justification of punishment is not presented as following from the division of the relevant questions, nor are those out-and-out utilitarian and retributive theories dismissed as somehow logically flawed, because they allegedly do not recognize that there are several distinct questions involved. On the contrary, Hart repudiates both purely retributive and purely utilitarian theories of punishment for expressly moral reasons. The separation of questions does not logically lead to a compromise, but opens up a possibility of it; it is not a sufficient, but merely a necessary condition of a synthetic, middle-of-the-road theory.

Finally, this synthesis itself has been questioned; it has been asserted that it is based on a distinction which Hart, as a utilitarian, is not entitled to make. If one opts for utilitarianism as the answer to the question of the general justifying aim of punishment, one is thereby committed to going by utilitarian considerations, and such considerations only, at the level of distribution. A "thoroughgoing utilitarian" may not introduce restrictions on the pursuit of the aim which justifies the institution, except those which may themselves be based on utilitarian grounds.[57] This criticism is beside the point, which is precisely that Hart is not a thoroughgoing but a qualified utilitarian. He is not trying to "append" a principle of justice onto the principle of utility, but offers a theory which allows for both, conceived as distinct and independent principles.

Other attempts at a middle way in the philosophy of punishment, discussed in preceding sections, have in common a willingness to find room for considerations of justice and desert, but justice is never seen as a truly independent moral principle. It is either a mere logical appendix to a utilitarian ethical theory (Quinton), or a means to a utilitarian end

(Ewing), or a rule of an institution justified by its utility, and accordingly a rule predicated on its own utility (rule-utilitarianism, Hare's two-level theory). Having been given such a low status, justice proves incapable of ensuring that unjust but expedient punishment is ruled out. With Hart things are significantly different. Justice is introduced expressly as an independent principle, irreducible to utility and based on grounds other than utility; therefore Hart's theory rules out injustice in punishment such as disproportionately harsh penalties, punishment of the irresponsible, or "punishment" of the innocent. This has been accomplished by giving up the simplicity of a thoroughgoing utilitarianism, which is the source of most of its problems but also one of the main reasons for its wide appeal, and developing a qualified utilitarian theory of punishment, which is complex but also much more plausible. This theory has "delineated a middle ground, whose existence had not before been so clearly perceived, between the retributivists and the utilitarians."[58] It has been widely influential; it has been said that it "clearly shows how in philosophy — and all the more in the philosophy of punishment, which deals with an institution affecting so closely the dignity, liberty and security of men — balance and moderation are worth more than absolute and exclusive fidelity to a single principle."[59]

Still, Hart's theory of punishment is exposed to some objections.

According to the theory, the severity of punishment is to be determined partly by considerations of deterrence and partly by those of justice. The utilitarian view of punishment has been charged, *inter alia*, with committing us to disproportionately harsh punishment.[60] In Hart's theory, the upper limit of the severity of punishment is determined by considerations of utilitarian economy, on the one hand, and by the demand for some sort of proportion between punishments and offenses, on the other. Even when efficient in an economical way, disproportionately harsh punishments may not be meted out, for they would be unjust. But this principle of proportion is merely negative, a constraint upon the pursuit of the aim of punishment. So it does not at the same time determine the *lower* limit of the severity of punishment — that is decided upon on the grounds of deterrence only. Interestingly enough, this purely negative interpretation of the principle of proportion can also be met in the writings of some self-styled retributivists.[61] Its consequence is that, for instance, if a few months in prison turned out to be deterrent enough with regard to rape, or if a year turned out to be enough to deter potential murderers, these would be punishments appropriate for such crimes. We would not be justified in going beyond them. Thus Hart's theory would not justify disproportionately severe punishment, but it would justify disproportionately lenient penalties.[62]

With regard to liability to punishment, the theory advances only considerations of justice and desert, on which the retributivist insists. Only the voluntary commission of an offense gives the state the *right* to punish or — as Hart puts it — the moral license to use an individual for promoting the aim of deterrence. This effectively rules out "punishment" of the innocent. But this negative significance of the fact that someone has committed an offense is all the moral significance which the fact by itself has. It by no means entails the *duty* of the state to punish, which is based on the deterrent effects of punishment, and on these effects only. Hart repeatedly and emphatically repudiates retribution as a principle calling for punishment to be meted out independently of whether it will help deter offenders in the future. Thus the theory entails that in cases where considerations of deterrence do not apply, the guilty may not be justifiably punished. No matter how grave and morally reprehensible a crime is, if by punishing for it no deterrent results are to be attained, it ought to remain unpunished.

This argument on non-punishment of the guilty seems to carry the greatest weight in cases of the gravest crimes of all — those committed against humanity.[63] Was it, for example, justified to punish Adolf Eichmann? The answer suggested by Hart's theory is that it was, provided that punishing him served the purpose of deterring potential Eichmanns from committing genocidal acts in the future. This does not seem to be a very satisfactory answer. We can assume, for the sake of argument, that there are no potential Eichmanns left in the world or, alternatively, that those remaining and those still to come are beyond deterrence. Not that the history of the last forty years or so has convincingly testified to the deterrent efficiency of such punishments. The death sentences meted out at Nuremberg or the one given to Eichmann did not deter mass murderers who came later, such as Amin, Pot, or Macias, and their henchmen. If, from the point of view of deterrence, these punishments have failed, are we to conclude that the defendants at Nuremberg or Adolf Eichmann ought not to have been punished? Or that we should not bother to search out and bring to justice those who have committed mass murder, nor punish those who might do the same in the future?

In connection with Hart's claim that the institution of punishment is to be justified solely in terms of deterrence, R.A. Wasserstrom says the following:

There is a real sense in which Hart's position is less a justification of punishment than a justification of the threat of punishment. It is clear that if we could convince the rest of society that we were in fact punishing offenders we would accomplish all that Hart sees us as achieving through punishment. This is so because it is the *belief* that punishment will follow the commission of an offense that deters potential offenders. The actual punishment of persons is necessary only to keep the threat of punishment credible. Punishment is, therefore, in Hart's view, to be conceived as a necessary evil rather than a positive good. It follows, and this, too, is surely one of the merits of Hart's view, that punishment is something that society ought always seek to minimize if not eradicate.[64]

Rather than being a merit of the theory, I should say that this brings its dangerously close to the old Benthamite view of punishment, with its distinction between real and apparent punishment and the thesis that with regard to general deterrence, which is the main aim of punishing, the latter actually does the job, while the former is needed only for the sake of the latter and, being in itself an evil, ought to be minimized or avoided altogether whenever possible. Therefore, for instance, if the desirable deterrent effects of capital punishment could be secured by hanging someone in effigy, to hang them in person would be both stupid and cruel.[65] This example, taken from Bentham, may not be entirely felicitous here, for Hart does not believe in the deterrent effectiveness of the death penalty; but it does illustrate the kind of deception and manipulation of the public that could be justified by a theory which sees the positive value of punishment exclusively in its utility as a means of preventing offenses.[66]

7. Retribution as a Positive Principle

1. Retributive Convictions

The upshot of the discussion so far is that the purely utilitarian view of punishment is very difficult to accept. It ignores the connection of punishment with the notions of justice and desert, and commits us to various unjust punishments (or "punishments"). The same goes for most attempts to strike a "middle way" between utilitarianism and retributivism: they are unacceptable as well, for when one takes a closer look at them, they either completely collapse, or turn out to be very close to collapsing, back into the old, out-and-out utilitarian theory of punishment. There is one middle-of-the-road theory, though, to which this does not apply: that of H.L.A. Hart. So by the end of the preceding chapter the search for a convincing rationale of punishment brought us to the point at which a choice is to be made between a full-fledged retributive view and Hart's combination of utilitarianism and retributivism. It should be noted that the Rawlsian choice between alternative societal responses to crime, discussed in connection with the retributivist thesis that punishment is a right of the offender, rules out the therapeutic response and utilitarian punishment (and, by implication, all views which collapse back into utilitarianism), but seems to be undecided between pure retributivism and Hart's theory.[1]

In contrast to other attempts at a synthesis of utilitarianism and retributivism, which do not take retributive considerations seriously enough and therefore do not effectively rule out those unjust punishments which compromise utilitarianism pure and simple, Hart's theory does provide for an autonomous and significant role for considerations of justice and desert, and is therefore immune to most arguments against the utilitarian view of punishment. But it has one thing in common with other middle-of-the-road theories: it seeks to accommodate the retributive principle as a *negative* principle only. The principle of just deserts figures merely as a constraint upon the pursuit of the aim of punishment, by grounding and at the same time delimiting the state's right to punish. So it precludes "punishment" of the innocent, but does not call for punishing the guilty; it sets an upper limit to the severity of punishment, thus prohibiting disproportionately harsh punishments, but does not relate to the lower limit of punishment, does not call for the full measure of proportion to be secured when punishing. The duty of the state to punish and the lower limit of punishment are determined by entirely different considerations — those of deterrence.

To say that retribution not only gives the right to punish, but also imposes the duty to do so, and not only sets the upper, but also the lower limit to the severity of punishment would for all practical purposes mean to embrace the idea as the justification of the institution of punishment.[2] About this kind of retributivism as a distinctive theory of punishment (and not merely part of the case for legal moralism) Hart does not have much to say. He calls it "stern," "severe," even "fierce,"[3] and sometimes seems to imply that it is enough to display it for what it is, namely, a theory which would call for punishing and giving the full measure of deserved punishment even in cases when no utilitarian aim would be served by doing so — in order to dispose of it.[4] Apart from that, his main objection seems to be that it avoids the question of justification of punishment rather than providing an answer to it.[5] This is an old argument but not a very strong one, for it is based on a narrow notion of justification as a procedure showing that the *justificandum* has instrumental value. There is no reason why we should conceive of justification in such a narrow utilitarian manner. Still, the argument does point at something that might be seen as a disadvantage of retributivism: while the utilitarian view of punishment follows from a more general ethical theory, the retributive view seems somehow to stand on its own, to lack more general theoretical support.

A way of providing such support which has had a number of adherents is to interpret retributive punishment as a particular case of a wider conception of justice as an equilibrium of benefits and burdens. Criminal law determines a balance of certain benefits and burdens; provided most of us assume burdens involved in abiding by the law, we shall also be able to enjoy the benefits the legal order secures. In such a framework, to commit an offense means to throw off the burden the law-abiding carry and thus to be unfair to them; it means to gain an illegitimate benefit. When that happens, justice or fairness requires that things be put right again, that the disturbed equilibrium be reestablished. This is done by punishment.

It is just to punish those who have violated the rules and caused the unfair distribution of benefits and burdens. A person who violates the rules has something others have — the benefits of the system — but by renouncing what others have assumed, the burdens of self-restraint, he has acquired an unfair advantage. Matters are not even until this advantage is in some way erased. Another way of putting it is that he owes something to others, for he has something that does not rightfully belong to him. Justice — that is, punishing such individuals — restores the equilibrium of benefits and burdens by taking from the individual what he owes, that is, exacting the debt.[6]

But this variety of retributivism is not without its problems. As its critics have pointed out, it is by no means clear what exactly is the unfair benefit gained by the offender. Is it the ill-gotten gain, or the satisfaction involved in committing the offense, or renouncing the burden of self-restraint, or the protection the offender enjoyed from the very law he breaks? Critics have brought up serious obstacles that stand in the way of applying the model of an equilibrium of benefits and burdens to criminal law and explaining punishment as the restoration of that equilibrium after it has been disturbed — obstacles that arise under any of these interpretations of the notion of an unfair benefit. Offenses such as theft or robbery can perhaps be plausibly construed as cases of gain secured in an unjust way; but what is the gain in assault or rape? How can a rapist or murderer be said to enjoy an unfair advantage over others when, for various reasons quite independent of the criminal law, most of those others are not seriously tempted to commit such crimes and thus are not restraining themselves from committing them, nor would they reap any satisfaction if they somehow brought themselves to commit them? If the benefit unfairly gained is taken to refer to the protection by the law broken, how can we justify punishing for slander a person who has never enjoyed any good reputation to speak of?[7]

I am not sure that these problems can be solved in a satisfactory way.[8] But I shall not recount the debate about them, nor try to pursue it further, for I do not see why offering a general theory of justice into which the retributive view of punishment is to be fitted should be a precondition for advancing this view. I see nothing methodologically unsound in putting forward the crucial tenet of retributivism, that punishment is morally justified insofar as it is just, that justice is *the* moral consideration with regard to punishment, as a fundamental moral principle — fundamental in the sense of not being deduced from a more general ethical theory. A retributivist can put forward his basic thesis in this way, and then go on to explain it and to support it in a non-deductive way. By way of elucidating it he will say that punishment is just when it is deserved, and it is deserved by the commission of an offense. The offense committed is the sole ground of the state's right and duty to punish, and accordingly the measure of the severity of punishment as well. "Justice" and "just deserts" are not meant merely negatively, as constraints, but also positively, as demands for punishment of the guilty and the full measure of proportion between the punishment and the offense. It is unjust to "punish" the innocent, or to punish the guilty by disproportionately harsh punishments; but justice is also not being done when the guilty go unpunished, or when they are punished in a disproportionately lenient way. Justice in these matters is to treat offenders according to their deserts, to give them what they deserve, not more, and not less. By way of arguing in favor of his theory, the retributivist can set out from the assumption that the institution of punishment is not unjustifiable in principle, that at least some punishments are legitimate and called for, and then display the particular implications of the competing justifications of punishment. With regard to the utilitarian theory, he will point out those unjust punishments which could be expedient and thus also justifiable in utilitarian terms. As to Hart's "middle way" in the philosophy of punishment, he will note that it would justify disproportionately lenient punishment, non-punishment of the guilty, including those guilty of extremely heinous crimes, and making a show of punishment instead of actually inflicting it. Then he will submit that his theory, and his theory only, ensures that none of this is justified.

Admittedly, this will work only with those who hold that such unjust punishments as a thoroughgoing utilitarian is committed to, as well as disproportionately lenient punishment, non-punishment of the guilty, and shows of punishment, are morally unacceptable. Those who do not will easily outsmart the retributivist at this point, by saying that such courses of action *are* justified if and when they are options with the best consequences. Hart himself is alive to the weight of the argument on non-punishment of the guilty, at least:

> Even the most faithful adherents of utilitarian doctrine must have felt tempted at times to acknowledge the simple claim that it is right or just that one who has intentionally inflicted suffering on others should himself be made to suffer. I doubt if anyone, reading the records of Auschwitz or Buchenwald, has failed to feel the powerful appeal of this principle; perhaps even the most reflective of those who

supported the punishment of the criminals concerned were moved by this principle rather than by the thought that punishment would have beneficial future consequences.[9]

If we accept this claim with regard to the crimes committed in Auschwitz and Buchenwald, why not accept it with regard to crimes against humanity of lesser magnitude? And if we accept the claim with regard to the latter as well, why not with regard to murder of a single human being? And with regard to other crimes, less serious than murder? Or, if we are not willing to go all the way with this demand that justice be done and the criminal paid back in full, where, precisely, shall we draw the line? Why at that particular point, and not a degree or two higher, or lower, on the scale of crimes?

Admittedly, retribution as a positive principle seems to have greater force in cases of more serious crimes than in those of petty offenses. In cases of the latter sort we may be more inclined to let the offender "get away with it" if no effects of deterrence are to be achieved by punishment. If so, we should be able to account for the difference in our moral judgment in terms of a general theory of the gravity of offenses which would justify the different treatment: a theory which would allow, and even call for, the application of the principle of just retribution regarding the most heinous crimes, and others somewhat less abominable, and then others less abominable still — and then suspend the principle at a certain point on the scale of crimes and replace it by considerations of an entirely different nature: those of deterrence. Lacking such a theory,[10] we seem to have two options. Faced with the records of Auschwitz and Buchenwald, we can appeal to the idea of justice as a positive principle, which not only allows us to punish criminals but demands that we do so, independently of the effects in terms of deterrence to be reaped from the punishment, and then proceed to apply the principle to other crimes, serious and not so serious. Or we can stick to the position that retribution ought not to be exacted if no deterrent effects are to be expected from punishment, which may seem to come naturally in cases of petty offenses, and then go on to dismiss, along the same lines, the idea of punishing Eichmann.

2. Denunciation

In a review of the main varieties of retributivism, Hart points out that "in its most interesting form modern retributive theory has shifted the emphasis, from the alleged justice or intrinsic goodness of the return of suffering for the moral evil done, to the value of the authoritative expression, in the form of punishment, of moral condemnation for the moral wickedness involved in the offence."[11] The fact that punishment has something to do with expressing condemnation or denunciation of the offense by society has been recognized by several authors. Accounts that point out this dimension of punishment are sometimes termed "expressive" or "denunciatory" theories, but these labels are too indefinite and potentially misleading. One can analyze punishment as a practice that has this dimension, and even present it as the essence of punishment, without taking sides in the controversy about the moral justification of punishment thus analyzed. In such a case we have a view or an account or an analysis of punishment, but not a theory of punishment in the sense usually assumed in the debates on punishment in moral and legal philosophy.[12]

But even if this expressive aspect of punishment is brought up in the discussion of its moral basis, there are two different ways in which this can be done. It may be claimed that punishment is justified as the expression of condemnation or denunciation because that is how it serves its social purpose. This mechanism can then be described in more than one way. One could say, with J.F. Stephen, that society feels hatred and vengefulness toward the offender, that this is "a healthy natural sentiment,"[13] and that it ought to be given a socially recognized and regulated form in punishment rather than be left unchannelled and likely to break out in various disruptive ways. In this sense it could be said — to quote a famous formulation of Stephen — that "the criminal law stands to the passion of revenge in much the same relation as marriage to the sexual appetite."[14] Or one could see this expression of condemnation of the offense in the light of its contribution to the moral education of society, as in A.C. Ewing's "educative" theory of punishment. It could be claimed, with Durkheim, that the expression of moral condemnation through punishment serves to reinforce the "collective consciousness" of society. An offense is, first and foremost, a violation of this consciousness; the latter "would necessarily lose its energy if an emotional reaction of the community [i.e. punishment] did not come to compensate its loss, and [this] would result in a breakdown of social solidarity."[15] Another possibility would be to suggest some combination of these various uses of the expressive possibilities of punishment, as in *The Ethics of Punishment* by W. Moberly,[16] or in the view suggested by N. MacCormick, in his monograph on Hart, as one that would tie in nicely with Hart's analysis of "rules of obligation" and bring out the contribution of punishment to general prevention in a more sophisticated way than does the deterrent account pure and simple.[17]

However, one could also leave aside all such forward-looking, utilitarian considerations, and maintain that the expression of condemnation in the form of punishment is *intrinsically* right and called for. When discussing this view in his critique of legal moralism, Hart objects that it "represents as a value to be pursued at the cost of human suffering the *bare* expression of moral condemnation, and treats the infliction of suffering as a uniquely appropriate or 'emphatic' mode of expression. But . . . is the *mere* expression of moral condemnation a thing of value in itself to be pursued at this cost?"[18] To this it can be replied that to dissociate punishment as the expression of condemnation from the prospective considerations utilitarians would see as crucial is not to make it into a *bare* or *mere* expression. By expressing condemnation of the misdeed committed, punishment *vindicates* the law broken, *reaffirms* the right infringed, and *demonstrates* that the deed *was* an offense.

Rules which express standards of behavior and command categorically entail that their breaches are wrong, and that such breaches are to be condemned, denounced, repudiated. Expressions of such condemnation and repudiation are the index of the validity of these rules and of the acceptance of the notion that their violations are wrong. If actions of a certain kind can be carried out without meeting such a response, this shows that no rule prohibiting such actions is accepted as a valid standard of behavior. Moral standards, expressed by moral rules, evolve in a diffuse, noninstitutional way, rely on the moral authority of society and the conscience of its members, and are used as criteria of moral judgment by its members without special authorization or qualification. Whether a certain kind of action is seen as morally wrong in a society, whether a society adheres to a standard prohibiting that kind of action, can be established by finding out whether ordinary members of that society condemn actions of that sort. Their condemnation vindicates the standard, and demonstrates that its violations are held to be morally wrong. Criminal laws are similar to moral rules in that they also express standards of behavior and command categorically. But they express the standards of society organized into a state with its legal order; these standards rely on the authority of the state and its legal order, and are authoritatively formulated and applied solely through formalized procedures in appropriate institutions. Legislative institutions of the state pass criminal laws which determine some of our most important legal rights and make their violations into offenses. It is then up to criminal courts and institutions which carry out sentences passed to condemn actions that violate such laws and infringe the rights defined by them. This condemnation is expressed through punishment. By giving express-sion to it, punishment vindicates the law broken, reaffirms the right violated, and demonstrates that its violation was indeed an offense. If there are to be rights sanctioned by the criminal law, if some acts are to be offenses, if there is to be criminal law at all — there has to be punishment. If there is no punishment, there are no offenses, no criminal law, no rights determined and sanctioned by such law.

This, of course, does not mean to say that if, for instance, a thief who has stolen from me manages to escape the police and the court, this shows that his theft was not an offense, and that I actually had no right sanctioned by the criminal law to the piece of property stolen. But if the state and the legal order did not even try to punish him and other thieves, if thefts *as a rule* were not prosecuted and punished, the conclusion would have to be drawn that theft is not really an offense, and that property rights do not really obtain, at least in the sense of rights established and guaranteed by the criminal law.

There is a standard objection that arises at this point. Hart puts it in the following way:

> What is meant by the claim that the punishment of offenders is an appropriate way of expressing emphatic moral condemnation? The normal way in which moral condemnation is expressed is by *words*, and it is not clear, if denunciation is really what is required, why a solemn public statement of disapproval would not be the most "ap-propriate" or "emphatic" means of expressing this. Why should a denunciation take the form of punishment?[19]

But this is not quite accurate even of moral condemnation pure and simple. We express moral condemnation verbally most of the time, but this is not the only way of expressing it. We also give it expression by cooling and otherwise reducing our relations with the person who has commit-ted a serious moral misdeed, sometimes by breaking off all contact and communication. Ostracism is the ultimate moral sanction available to a community when it has to deal with an individual who has put himself beyond the moral pale. But this is a minor point.[20] The main point concerns the denunciation of violations of criminal laws and of rights, such as those relating to life, bodily integrity, or property, guaranteed by these laws. What would we think if the state and its legal order reacted to such actions only by issuing "solemn public statements of disapproval"? The state, which proclaimed the law giving validity and binding character to these rights, would desist from making use of its apparatus of coercion and force, which is one of its essential, defining features, in the face of their violations. There would be a pronounced dissimilarity and disproportion between those violations which affect their victims very palpably and the merely verbal reaction to them to which the state and the legal order would limit itself, which might not affect the person to whom it is addressed in the least. I think that both those whose rights were being violated and those who were violating them — and everyone else, for that matter — would be sure to conclude that these rights were not valid after all, were not really recognized, at least as rights defined and guaranteed by the criminal law, or in any serious manner. The notion of "taking X seriously" seems to preclude radical dissimilarity and disproportion between X and whatever one does by way of responding to it. A misdeed cannot be shown to be an offense, the right infringed and the law violated by it cannot be reasserted and vindicated if the act supposed to do this is so dissimilar to the deed, and so disproportionate to it in its weight, as a mere verbal condemnation, however solemn, would be. The necessary seriousness and weight can be secured only by punishment.

In order to avoid a possible misunderstanding at this point, let me emphasize that the connection between the expression of condemnation of the offense through punishment and the notions of an offense, a right defined by the criminal law, and the criminal law itself, is not predicated on the function of this condemnation as a means of prevention of future offenses.The thesis is entirely backward-looking. If by punishing we manage to prevent the commission of offenses, so much the better, but neither such effects nor the intention to attain them are inherent to the enterprise. We shall have demonstrated that an action was an offense, and reaffirmed the right violated and the law broken by it, even if the condemnation expressed by punishment proves inefficient in preventing future offenses of the same kind. We ought to punish in order to do this, for our failure to punish would be incompatible with our adherence to the law, respect for the right in question, and our belief that their violation is an offense.[21]

Still, it might be objected, to interpret and defend punishment as the condemnation of the offense in these purely retrospective terms is to put the cart before the horse. "We do nott live in society in order to condemn," says Hart, "though we may condemn in order to live."[22] But what kind of life in society would it be, if we could find it in ourselves to condemn, appropriately and seriously, only those wrongdoings — including the most reprehensible ones — whose condemnation could be justified in terms of *its* expediency?

8. Capital Punishment

1. The Ultimate Deterrent

The issue of capital punishment has been discussed for centuries by philosophers, theologians, legal scholars, social scientists, and reformers of all kinds. These discussions have involved a variety of types of reasoning: some are purely theoretical, some are highly technical statistical or, at a further remove, methodological analyses. But the crucial question, For or against? is a moral one. Since it has to do with moral considerations of a rather general nature for abolishing or retaining a legal institution, it also presents a problem for moral and legal philosophy. The best way to avoid the confusion which sometimes results from the great variety of arguments used both in favor of and against capital punishment is to keep the discussion within its proper philosophical context — the debate on the moral justification of punishment in general. For the nature of the arguments we see as relevant for deciding the issue of capital punishment depends on whether we subscribe to the utilitarian or the retributive rationale of punishment.

If we accept the utilitarian theory of punishment — that is, if we hold that the sole justification of punishment is in its good consequences — the issue of capital punishment boils down to the following question: Does this punishment really have those far-reaching desirable consequences its advocates have claimed for it? Is it true that through the threat of this punishment, and this punishment only, the most serious of crimes can be prevented? It somehow seems obvious that premature and violent death at the hands of the executioner is the worst thing that can happen to a human being, and that, consequently, the threat of execution is the most formidable one, the most efficient of all that could be used as a means of deterrence. This is nicely captured in the words of J.F. Stephen, written more than a century ago:

> No other punishment deters men so effectually from committing crimes as the punishment of death. This is one of those propositions which it is difficult to prove, simply because they are in themselves more obvious than any proof can make them. It is possible to display

ingenuity in arguing against it, but that is all. The whole experience of mankind is in the other direction.[1]

However, the experience of mankind has been much less clear, and much more disappointing, than Stephen was willing to allow, as one example will suffice to show. By the beginning of the last century, the criminal law of England was known as "the bloody code," and with good reason. It prescribed the punishment of death for more than 220 offenses, including, for instance, cutting down a tree in a public park, damaging a fishpond, or associating with Gypsies. And, of course, for picking pockets, if the money stolen was more than one shilling. But the threat did not work:

> If the argument in favour of the gallows as the supreme deterrent were true, then public executions would have the maximum discouraging effect on the criminal. Yet these public exhibitions, intended to prove that "crime does not pay", were known to be the occasion when pickpockets gathered their richest harvest among the crowd. A contemporary author explains why: "The thieves selected the moment when the strangled man was swinging above them as the happiest opportunity, because they knew that everybody's eyes were on that person and all were looking up."[2]

Some explanations of the baffling ineffectiveness of this threat which plain common sense tells us should be the most frightening of all were offered long ago. Beccaria proposed a psychological one: when it comes to deterring people from breaking the law by means of punishment, it is not so much the intensity of punishment that does the job, as its duration. So even a public execution — and in Beccaria's time executions were held in public — will not make a sufficiently strong and lasting impression, while the spectacle of convicts serving life sentences most probably will.

> For our sensibility is more easily and more permanently affected by slight but repeated impressions than by a powerful but momentary action. . . . It is not the terrible yet momentary spectacle of the death of a wretch, but the long and painful example of a man deprived of liberty, who, having become a beast of burden, recompenses with his labors the society he has offended, which is the strongest curb against crimes.[3]

Bentham differed from Beccaria on psychology, holding that the intensity of punishment is yet more important than its duration. He offered a piece of armchair sociology instead: capital punishment does deter, but in the wrong direction. It deters the majority of people, who have reason enough to fear death, because they have reason enough to appreciate life. But they are not likely to commit capital crimes anyway, so there is no need to deter *them*. On the other hand, we have the "criminal class" — those whose social position and way of life are such that they set no great store by life, and are not so terribly afraid of losing it. To "the wretched class of beings that furnish the most atrocious criminals" execution is by far less horrible than to the majority of ordinary, law-abiding citizens; it is but "a speedy termination to an uneasy, unhappy, dishonoured existence, stript of all true worth . . ."[4]

In our own time the social sciences have replaced speculations of armchair psychologists and sociologists. Empirical research, conducted by application of scientific methods, has shown that there is no significant correlation between the presence or absence of capital punishment and the rates of those crimes for which it is prescribed and meted out. Already in the sixties, T. Sellin could summarize research results in the following way:

> Regarding deterrence, it is well established by statistical studies that (1) when comparisons are made between contiguous states with similar populations and similar social, economic and political conditions — some of these states lacking and others retaining capital punishment — homicide rates are the same and follow the same trend over a long period of time, regardless of the use or nonuse of capital punishment; (2) the abolition, introduction or reintroduction of this penalty is not accompanied by the effect on the homicide rates that is postulated by the advocates of capital punishment; (3) even in communities where the deterrent effect should be greatest because the offender and his victim lived there and trial and execution were well publicized, homicide rates are not affected by the execution; (4) the rate of policemen killed by criminals is no higher in abolition states than in comparable death-penalty states. Capital punishment, then, does not appear to have a specific influence on the amount or trend of the kind of crime it is supposed to deter people from committing.[5]

These conclusions are no less valid today. Advocates of capital punishment have tried in various ways to deny the reliability or conclusive character of these findings, but their efforts have not been successful.[6] Thus, whoever subscribes either to a purely utilitarian view of punishment in general or to the Hartian variety of utilitarianism within certain retributive constraints cannot in all consistency defend the death pen-

alty any longer. This kind of punishment simply does not have consequences good enough to justify its infliction, and therefore ought to be
abolished.[7]

2. A Life for a Life

The conclusion of the preceding section is not in the least binding on
those retentionists who approach the problem of the moral basis of
punishment in general from the retributive standpoint. According to the
retributive theory, consequences of punishment, however important
from the practical point of view, are irrelevant when it comes to its
justification; *the* moral consideration is its justice. Punishment is morally
justified insofar as it is meted out as retribution for the offense committed. When someone has committed an offense, he deserves to be
punished: it is just, and consequently justified, that he be punished. The
offense is the sole ground of the state's right and duty to punish. It is
also the measure of legitimate punishment: the two ought to be proportionate. So the issue of capital punishment within the retributive
approach comes down to the question, Is this punishment ever proportionate retribution for the offense committed, and thus deserved, just,
and justified?

The classic representatives of retributivism believed that it was, and
that it was the only proportionate and hence appropriate punishment, if
the offense was *murder* — that is, criminal homicide perpetrated voluntarily and intentionally or in wanton disregard of human life. In other
cases, the demand for proportionality between offense and punishment
can be satisfied by fines or prison terms;[8] the crime of murder, however,
is an exception in this respect, and calls for the literal interpretation of
the *lex talionis*. The uniqueness of this crime has to do with the uniqueness of the value which has been deliberately or recklessly destroyed.
We come across this idea as early as the original formulation of the
retributive view — the biblical teaching on punishment: "You shall
accept no ransom for the life of a murderer who is guilty of death; but he
shall be put to death."[9] The rationale of this command — one that
clearly distinguishes the biblical conception of the criminal law from
contemporaneous criminal law systems in the Middle East — is that man
was not only created *by* God, like every other creature, but also, alone
among all the creatures, *in the image of God*:

That man was made in the image of God . . . is expressive of the
peculiar and supreme worth of man. Of all creatures, Genesis 1

relates, he alone possesses this attribute, bringing him into closer relation to God than all the rest and conferring upon him the highest value. . . . This view of the uniqueness and supremacy of human life . . . places life beyond the reach of other values. The idea that life may be measured in terms of money or other property . . . is excluded. Compensation of any kind is ruled out. The guilt of the murderer is infinite because the murdered life is invaluable; the kinsmen of the slain man are not competent to say when he has been paid for. An absolute wrong has been committed, a sin against God which is not subject to human discussion. . . . Because human life is invaluable, to take it entails the death penalty.[10]

This view that the value of human life is not commensurable with other values, and that consequently there is only one truly equivalent punishment for murder, namely death, does not necessarily presuppose a theistic outlook. It can be claimed that, simply because we have to be alive if we are to experience and realize any other value at all, there is nothing equivalent to the murderous destruction of a human life except the destruction of the life of the murderer. Any other retribution, no matter how severe, would still be less than what is proportionate, deserved, and just. As long as the murderer is alive, no matter how bad the conditions of his life may be, there are always at least *some* values he can experience and realize. This provides a plausible interpretation of what the classical representatives of retributivism as a philosophical theory of punishment, such as Kant and Hegel, had to say on the subject.[11]

It seems to me that this is essentially correct. With respect to the larger question of the justification of punishment in general, it is the retributive theory that gives the right answer. Accordingly, capital punishment ought to be retained where it obtains, and reintroduced in those jurisdictions that have abolished it, although we have no reason to believe that, as a means of deterrence, it is any better than a very long prison term. It ought to be retained, or reintroduced, for one simple reason: that justice be done in cases of murder, that murderers be punished according to their deserts.

There are a number of arguments that have been advanced against this rationale of capital punishment.

Two of these arguments have to do, in different ways, with the idea of the right to life. The first is the famous argument of Beccaria that the state cannot have the right to take away the life of its citizen, because its rights in relation to him are based on the social contract, and it cannot be assumed that he has transferred his right to life to the state and consented to be executed.

> What manner of right can men attribute to themselves to slaughter their fellow beings? Certainly not that from which sovereignty and the laws derive. These are nothing but the sum of the least portions of the private liberty of each person; they represent the general will, which is the aggregate of particular wills. Was there ever a man who can have wished to leave to other men the choice of killing him? Is it conceivable that the least sacrifice of each person's liberty should include sacrifice of the greatest of all goods, life? And if that were the case, how could such a principle be reconciled with the other, that man is not entitled to take his own life? He must be, if he can surrender that right to others or to society as a whole.[12]

The most obvious way of attacking Beccaria's argument would be to call into question its philosophical basis, the social contract theory of political obligation. This is what Hegel does, for instance; he conceives of the nature and grounds of political obligation in a completely different manner, so he can do away with Beccaria with a single sentence: "The state is not a contract at all."[13] I shall not argue along these lines, however. This is not the place to take up the problem of political obligation and to assess the social contract theory as a solution to it. What Beccaria is saying here can in any case be refuted even within the framework of that theory.

Both steps in his argument are wrong, and for the same reason. The act of consenting to be executed if one commits murder is presented as a kind of suicide. Against the background of this conflation, it seems convincing to claim that it would be utterly unreasonable to do that, and the case appears to be strengthened even further by the appeal to the moral prohibition of suicide. This latter prohibition is, of course, rather controversial, to say the least; it was controversial in Beccaria's time as well. But his argument fails even if we grant him this point. For by consenting to be executed if I murder someone, I do not commit a kind of suicide — I do not "sacrifice the greatest of all goods" I have, my own life. My consent could be described in these terms if it were unconditional, if it implied that others were entitled to do with my life whatever they chose, quite independently of my own choices and actions. In order to show that capital punishment is legitimate from the standpoint of the contract theory of political obligation, however, we need not assume that citizens have agreed to *that*. All that is needed is the assumption of a conditional consent — consent to be executed *if* one commits murder; and it is, of course, up to everyone to choose whether to commit such a crime or not. To agree to this, obviously, is not the same as to sacrifice one's life, to commit a suicide of sorts. And it is not so unreasonable to assume that citizens have agreed to this if, against the background of the social contract theory, we grant, first, that the laws, including criminal laws, ought to be just, and second, that the only proportionate and hence just punishment for murder is capital punishment.[14]

The second abolitionist argument makes use of the idea of a right to life in a more straightforward manner: it simply says that capital punishment is illegitimate because it violates the right to life, which is a fundamental, absolute, sacred right belonging to each and every human being, and therefore ought to be respected even in a murderer.[15]

If any rights are fundamental, the right to life is certainly one of them; but to claim that it is absolute, inviolable under any circumstances and for any reason, is a different matter. If an abolitionist wants to argue his case by asserting an absolute right to life, she will also have to deny moral legitimacy to taking human life in war, revolution, and self-defense. This kind of pacifism is a consistent but farfetched and hence implausible position.

I do not believe that the right to life (nor, for that matter, any other right) is absolute. I have no general theory of rights to fall back upon here; instead, let me pose a question. Would we take seriously the claim to an absolute, sacred, inviolable right to life — coming from the mouth of a *confessed murderer*? I submit that we would not, for the obvious reason that it is being put forward by the person who confessedly denied another human being this very right. But if the murderer cannot plausibly claim such a right for himself, neither can *anyone else* do that in his behalf. This suggests that there is an element of reciprocity in our general rights, such as the right to life or property. I can convincingly claim these rights only so long as I acknowledge and respect the same rights of others. If I violate the rights of others, I thereby lose the same rights. If I am a murderer, I have no *right* to live.

Some opponents of capital punishment claim that a criminal law system which includes this punishment is contradictory, in that it prohibits murder and at the same time provides for its perpetration: "It is one and the same legal regulation which prohibits the individual from murdering, while allowing the state to murder. . . . This is obviously a terrible irony, an abnormal and immoral logic, against which everything in us revolts."[16]

This seems to be one of the more popular arguments against the death penalty, but it is not a good one. If it were valid, it would prove too much. Exactly the same might be claimed of other kinds of punishment: of prison terms, that they are "contradictory" to the legal protection of liberty; of fines, that they are "contradictory" to the legal protection of property. Fortunately enough, it is not valid, for it begs the question at issue. In order to be able to talk of the state as "murdering" the person it executes, and to claim that there is "an abnormal and immoral logic" at work here, which thrives on a "contradiction," one has to use the word "murder" in the very same sense — that is, in the usual sense, which implies the idea of the *wrongful* taking the life of another — both when speaking of what the murderer has done to the victim and of what the state is doing to him by way of punishment. But this is precisely the question at issue: whether capital punishment *is* "murder," whether it is wrongful or morally justified and right.

The next two arguments attack the retributive rationale of capital punishment by questioning the claim that it is only this punishment that satisfies the demand for proportion between offense and punishment in the case of murder. The first points out that any two human lives are different in many important respects, such as age, health, physical and mental capability, so that it does not make much sense to consider them equally valuable. What if the murdered person was very old, practically at the very end of her natural life, while the murderer is young, with most of his life still ahead of him, for instance? Or if the victim was gravely and incurably ill, and thus doomed to live her life in suffering and hopelessness, without being able to experience almost anything that makes a human life worth living, while the murderer is in every respect capable of experiencing and enjoying things life has to offer? Or the other way round? Would not the death penalty in such cases amount either to taking a more valuable life as a punishment for destroying a less valuable one, or *vice versa*? Would it not be either too much, or too little, and in both cases disproportionate, and thus unjust and wrong, from the standpoint of the retributive theory itself?[17]

Any plausibility this argument might appear to have is the result of a conflation of differences between, and value of, human lives. No doubt, any two human lives are *different* in innumerable ways, but this does not entail that they are not *equally valuable*. I have no worked-out general theory of equality to refer to here, but I do not think that one is necessary in order to do away with this argument. The modern humanistic and democratic tradition in ethical, social, and political thought is based on the idea that all human beings are equal. This finds its legal expression in the principle of equality of people under the law. If we are not willing to give up this principle, we have to stick to the assumption that, all differences notwithstanding, any two human lives, *qua* human lives, are equally valuable. If, on the other hand, we allow that, on the basis of such criteria as age, health, or mental or physical ability, it can be claimed that the life of one person is more or less valuable than the life of another, and we admit such claims in the sphere of law, including criminal law, we shall thereby give up the principle of equality of people under the law. In all consistency, we shall not be able to demand that property, physical and personal integrity, and all other rights and interests of individuals be given equal consideration in courts of law either — that is, we shall have to accept systematic discrimination between individuals on the basis of the same criteria across the whole field. I do not think anyone would seriously contemplate an overhaul of the whole legal system along these lines.

The second argument having to do with the issue of proportionality between murder and capital punishment draws our attention to the fact that the law normally provides for a certain period of time to elapse between the passing of a death sentence and its execution. It is a period of several weeks or months; in some cases it extends to years. This period is bound to be one of constant mental anguish for the condemned. And thus, all things considered, what is inflicted on him is disproportionately hard and hence unjust. It would be proportionate and just only in the case of "a criminal who had warned his victim of the date at which he would inflict a horrible death on him and who, from that moment onward, had confined him at his mercy for months."[18]

The first thing to note about this argument is that it does not support a full-fledged abolitionist stand; if it were valid, it would not show that capital punishment is *never* proportionate and just, but only that it is *very rarely* so. Consequently, the conclusion would not be that it ought to be abolished outright, but only that it ought to be restricted to those cases that would satisfy the condition cited above. Such cases do happen, although, to be sure, not very often; the murder of Aldo Moro, for instance, was of this kind. But this is not the main point. The main point is that the argument actually does not hit at capital punishment itself, although it is presented with that aim in view. It hits at something else: a particular way of carrying out this punishment, which is widely adopted in our time. Some hundred years ago and more, in the Wild West, they frequently hanged the man convicted to die almost immediately after pronouncing the sentence. I am not arguing here that we should follow this example today; I mention this piece of historical fact only in order to show that the interval between sentencing someone to death and carrying out the sentence is not a *part* of capital punishment itself. However unpalatable we might find those Wild West hangings, whatever objections we might want to voice against the speed with which they followed the sentencing, surely we shall not deny them the *description* of "executions." So the implication of the argument is not that we ought to do away with capital punishment altogether, nor that we ought to restrict it to those cases of murder where the murderer had warned the victim weeks or months in advance of what he was going to do to her, but that we ought to reexamine the procedure of carrying out this kind of punishment. We ought to weigh the reasons for having this interval between the sentencing and executing, against the moral and human significance of the repercussions such an interval inevitably carries with it.

These reasons, in part, have to do with the possibility of miscarriages of justice and the need to rectify them. Thus we come to the argument against capital punishment which, historically, has been the most effective of all: many advances of the abolitionist movement have been connected with discoveries of cases of judicial errors. Judges and jurors are only human, and consequently some of their beliefs and decisions are bound to be mistaken. Some of their mistakes can be corrected upon discovery; but precisely those with most disastrous repercussions — those which result in innocent people being executed — can never be rectified. In all other cases of mistaken sentencing we can revoke the punishment, either completely or in part, or at least extend compensation. In addition, by exonerating the accused we give moral satisfaction. None of this is possible after an innocent person has been executed; capital punishment is essentially different from all other penalties by being completely irrevocable and irreparable.[19] Therefore, it ought to be abolished.

A part of my reply to this argument goes along the same lines as what I had to say on the previous one. It is not so far-reaching as abolitionists assume; for it would be quite implausible, even fanciful, to claim that there have *never* been cases of murder which left no room whatever for reasonable doubt as to the guilt and full responsibility of the accused. Such cases may not be more frequent than those others, but they do happen. Why not retain the death penalty at least for them?

Actually, this argument, just as the preceding one, does not speak out against capital punishment itself, but against the existing procedures for trying capital cases. Miscarriages of justice result in innocent people being sentenced to death and executed, even in the criminal-law systems in which greatest care is taken to ensure that it never comes to that. But this does not stem from the intrinsic nature of the institution of capital punishment; it results from deficiencies, limitations, and imperfections of the criminal law procedures in which this punishment is meted out. Errors of justice do not demonstrate the need to do away with capital punishment; they simply make it incumbent on us to do everything possible to improve even further procedures of meting it out.

To be sure, this conclusion will not find favor with a diehard abolitionist. "I shall ask for the abolition of Capital Punishment until I have the infallibility of human judgement demonstrated to me," that is, as long as there is even the slightest possibility that innocent people may be executed because of judicial errors, Lafayette said in his day.[20] Many an opponent of this kind of punishment will say the same today. The demand to do away with capital punishment altogether, so as to eliminate even the smallest chance of that ever happening — the chance which, admittedly, would remain even after everything humanly possible has been done to perfect the procedure, although then it would be very slight indeed — is actually a demand to give a privileged position to murderers as against all other offenders, big and small. For if we acted on this demand, we would bring about a situation in which proportionate penalties would be meted out for all offenses, *except* for murder. Murderers would not be receiving the only punishment truly proportionate to their crimes, the punishment of death, but some other, lighter, and thus disproportionate penalty. All other offenders would be punished according to their deserts; only murderers would be receiving less than *they* deserve. In all other cases justice would be done in full; only in cases of the gravest of offenses, the crime of murder, justice would not be carried out in full measure. It is a great and tragic miscarriage of justice when an innocent person is mistakenly sentenced to death and executed, but systematically giving murderers advantage over all other offenders would also be a grave injustice. Is the fact that, as long as capital punishment is retained, there is a possibility that over a number of years, or even decades, an injustice of the first kind may be committed, unintentionally and unconsciously, reason enough to abolish it altogether, and thus end up with a system of punishments in which injustices of the second kind are perpetrated daily, consciously, and inevitably?[21]

There is still another abolitionist argument that actually does not hit out against capital punishment itself, but against something else. Figures are sometimes quoted which show that this punishment is much more often meted out to the uneducated and poor than to the educated, rich, and influential people; in the United States, much more often to blacks than to whites. These figures are adduced as a proof of the inherent injustice of this kind of punishment. On account of them, it is claimed that capital punishment is not a way of doing justice by meting out deserved punishment to murderers, but rather a means of social discrimination and perpetuation of social injustice.

I shall not question these findings, which are quite convincing, and anyway, there is no need to do that in order to defend the institution of capital punishment. For there seems to be a certain amount of discrimination and injustice not only in sentencing people to death and executing them, but also in meting out other penalties. The social structure of the death rows in American prisons, for instance, does not seem to be basically different from the general social structure of American penitentiaries. If this argument were valid, it would call not only for abolition of the penalty of death, but for doing away with other penalties as well.

> But it is not valid; as Burton Leiser has pointed out, ... this is not an argument, either against the death penalty or against any other form of punishment. It is an argument against the unjust and inequitable distribution of penalties. If the trials of wealthy men are less likely to result in convictions than those of poor men, then something must be done to reform the procedure in criminal courts. If those who have money and standing in the community are less likely to be charged with serious offenses than their less affluent fellow citizens, then there should be a major overhaul of the entire system of criminal justice . . . But the maldistribution of penalties is no argument against any particular form of penalty.[22]

There is, finally, the argument that the moral illegitimacy of capital punishment is obvious from the widespread contempt for those who carry it out: "Logically, if the Death Penalty *were* morally justified, the executioner's calling would be considered an honourable one. The fact that even its keenest supporters shrink from such a man with loathing and exclude him from their circle, is in itself an indication that Capital Punishment stands morally condemned."[23]

This is also a poor argument, for several reasons. The contempt for the executioner and the accompanying social ostracism is by no means a universal phenomenon in history; on the contrary, it is a comparatively modern one. In earlier ages, the person who carried out capital punishment — whether the professional executioner or, before this became an occupation in its own right, the judge, or some other high-ranking official, sometimes even the ruler himself, or a relative of the murdered person — was always regarded with respect.[24] Quite apart from this, the so-called common moral consciousness, to which the argument appeals is not to be seen as some kind of supreme tribunal in moral matters. Among reasons of general nature for this is that it would be an unreliable, inconsistent, confused, and confusing tribunal. On the one hand, when viewed historically, it hardly seems a very good guide to the moral status of various occupations, for in earlier ages it used to condemn very resolutely and strongly the merchant, the banker, the actor, which no one would think of disparaging today, abolitionists included. On the other hand, it has proved itself quite inconsistent on the issue of the moral basis of punishment in general, voicing incompatible views, now retributive, now utilitarian.[25] It is not at all surprising that both advocates and opponents of capital punishment have claimed its support for their views.[26] But if it supports both sides in this more restricted dispute as well, then it actually supports neither.

There is still another facet of this illogical, irrational streak inherent to the common moral consciousness that comes to the fore in connection with this dispute. If the contempt for the executioner is really rooted in the belief that what he carries out is morally reprehensible, then it is surely heaped upon the wrong person. For he merely carries out decisions on which he has no say whatsoever. Those who are responsible are, in the first instance, the judge and members of the jury. They, on their part, act as they do against the background of criminal laws for which responsibility lies at a further remove still — with the legislators. These, again, legislate in the name of the people, if the political system is a representative one. But for some reason the common moral consciousness has never evinced contempt of any of these.

3. Retributivism without Capital Punishment?

Everything I have said in the preceding section has had a pronounced defensive ring to it. I have attempted to show that none of the standard arguments against the death penalty, which would be relevant within the retributive approach to punishment in general, are really convincing. But I shall end on a conciliatory note. I can envisage a way for a retributivist to take an abolitionist stand, without thereby being inconsistent. Let me explain this in just a few words.

The Eighth Amendment to the Constitution of the United States says that "excessive bail shall not be required, nor excessive fines imposed, nor cruel and unusual punishments inflicted."[27] I do not find the idea of a "usual" or "unusual" punishment very helpful. But I do think that punishments ought not to be *cruel*. They ought not to be cruel in the relative sense, by being considerably more severe than what is proportionate to the offense committed, what is deserved and just; but they also ought not to be cruel in an absolute sense — that is, severe beyond a certain threshold.

Admittedly, it would be very difficult to determine that threshold precisely, but it is not necessary for my purpose here. It will be enough to provide a paradigmatic case of something that is surely beyond that threshold: torture. I do not believe that a torturer has a *right* not to be tortured. If we could bring ourselves to torture him, as a punishment for what he has done to the victim, I do not think that it could be plausibly claimed that what we were doing to him was something undeserved and unjust. But I also do not think that we should try to bring ourselves to do that, in pursuit of proportion between offense and punishment and in striving to execute justice. Justice is one of the most important moral principles — perhaps the most important one — but it is not *absolute*. On the other hand, I feel that torture is something *absolutely wrong* from the moral point of view: something indecent and inhuman, something immensely and unredeemably degrading both to the man tortured and to the torturer himself, something that is morally "beyond the pale." So to sentence a torturer to be tortured would not mean to give him a punishment which is undeserved and unjust, and hence cruel in the relative sense of the word; but it *would* mean to punish him in a way that is cruel in this second, absolute sense. On account of this, I would say that, when punishing a torturer, we ought to desist from giving him the full measure of what he has deserved by his deed, that we ought to settle for less than what in his case would be the full measure of justice. One of the moral principles limiting the striving to do justice is this prohibition of cruelty in the absolute sense of the word. We ought not to execute justice to the full, if that means that we shall have to be cruel.

I do not feel about executing a person in a swift and relatively painless manner the same way I feel about torturing him. But a person, or a society, could come to feel the same way about both. A person or a society that adhered to the retributive view of punishment, but at the same time felt this way about executing a human being, could decide that capital punishment is cruel and therefore unacceptable without being in any way inconsistent.

Notes

Chapter 1. Introduction

1. For a discussion of this question see H.J. McCloskey, "The Complexity of the Concepts of Punishment," *Philosophy* 37 (1962). McCloskey's conclusion is that "there is not one paradigm concept of punishment, but a family of distinct but related concepts (distinct from the parasitic concepts), these concepts varying from non-institutional to fully institutional punishment, with the notion of an offence or alleged offence being relevant but relevant in different ways and interpreted in different senses" (pp. 315–316).

2. Or, rather, legal punishment proper. Practices which are similar to legal punishment proper in some respects and dissimilar in other respects, such as administrative and disciplinary sanctions which have a basis in law, remain outside the scope of the definition. But this does not tell against the definition; for, although such practices may raise certain ethical questions, they are not important in their own right in the context of philosophical discussion of the rationale of legal punishment.

3. A. Flew, "The Justification of Punishment," in H.B. Acton (ed.), *The Philosophy of Punishment* (London: Macmillan, 1969); S.I. Benn, "An Approach to the Problems of Punishment," *Philosophy* 33 (1958); H.L.A. Hart, "Prolegomenon to the Principles of Punishment," *Punishment and Responsibility* (Oxford: Oxford University Press, 1973).

4. T. Honderich, *Punishment: The Supposed Justifications*, rev.ed. (Harmondsworth: Penguin, 1976), pp. 18–19.

5. S. Gendin, "The Meaning of 'Punishment'," *Philosophy and Phenomenological Research* 28 (1967/8), pp. 237–238.

Chapter 2. The Utility of Punishment: Bentham

1. J.S. Mill, "Bentham," *Essays on Ethics, Religion and Society*, ed. J.M. Robson, *Collected Works*, ed. F.E.L. Priestley et al. (Toronto: University of Toronto Press, 1969), vol. 10, p. 111.

2. J.S. Mill, "Obituary of Bentham," *Essays on Ethics*, p. 497.

3. J. Bentham, *An Introduction to the Principles of Morals and Legislation*, ed. W. Harrison (Oxford: Basil Blackwell, 1960), p. 125.

4. Ibid., p. 126.

5. Ibid., p. 189.

6. Ibid., p. 205.

7. Ibid., p. 127.

8. Ibid., p. 136.

9. Ibid., pp. 138–139.

10. Ibid., p. 140.
11. J. Bentham, *Theory of Legislation*, trans. from the French of E. Dumont by R. Hildreth, 2d ed. (London: Trübner, 1871), p. 76.
12. J. Bentham, *An Introduction to the Principles of Morals and Legislation*, p. 281.
13. J. Bentham, *Principles of Penal Law*, *The Works of Jeremy Bentham*, ed. J. Bowring (New York: Russell & Russell, 1962), vol. 1, p. 396.
14. Ibid., p. 367.
15. Ibid., p. 396.
16. J. Bentham, *An Introduction to the Principles of Morals and Legislation*, p. 298. "There are few madmen," Bentham adds in a footnote, "but what are observed to be afraid of the strait waistcoat."
17. J. Bentham, *Principles of Penal Law*, p. 396.
18. Ibid., p. 371.
19. J. Bentham, *Theory of Legislation*, p. 309.
20. See Bentham's analysis of hate and its consequences, ibid., pp. 55–57.
21. For a qualification of this, see *infra*, pp. 59–61.
22. J. Bentham, *Principles of Penal Law*, p. 391.
23. However, see *supra*, p. 3; *infra*, pp. 51–53.
24. J. Bentham, *Principles of Penal Law*, p. 476.
25. Ibid.
26. Ibid.
27. J. Bentham, *An Introduction to the Principles of Morals and Legislation*, p. 290, n. 1.
28. Ibid., pp. 291–292.
29. J. Bentham, *Principles of Penal Law*, p. 400.
30. Ibid., pp. 398–399.
31. J. Bentham, *Theory of Legislation*, p. 337.
32. J. Bentham, *Principles of Penal Law*, p. 398.
33. J. Bentham, *An Introduction to the Principles of Morals and Legislation*, p. 308.
34. *Supra*, pp. 24–26.

Chapter 3. Arguments Against the Utilitarian Theory

1. J. Bentham, *Theory of Legislation*, trans. from the French of E. Dumont by R. Hildreth, 2d ed. (London: Trübner, 1871), p. 54.
2. G.W.F. Hegel, *Philosophy of Right*, trans. T.M. Knox (Oxford: Oxford University Press, 1965), p. 246.
3. J. Bentham, *An Introduction to the Principles of Morals and Legislation*, ed. W. Harrison (Oxford: Basil Blackwell, 1960), pp. 240–241, n. 2. For a discussion of the utilitarian approach to justice, see H.A. Bedau, "Justice and Classical Utilitarianism," in C.J. Friedrich and J.W. Chapman (eds.), *Justice*, "Nomos" 6 (New York: Atherton Press, 1963).
4. J. Plamenatz, *The English Utilitarians*, 2d ed. (Oxford: Basil Blackwell, 1966), p. 80.
5. For an analysis of the concept of mercy see A. Smart, "Mercy," in H.B. Acton (ed.), *The Philosophy of Punishment* (London: Macmillan, 1969).
6. Ibid., pp. 224–225.
7. J. Bentham, *Principles of Penal Law*, *The Works of Jeremy Bentham*, ed. J.

Bowring (New York: Russell & Russell, 1962), vol. 1, p. 529.

8. K.G. Armstrong, "The Retributivist Hits Back," in Acton, *Philosophy of Punishment*, p. 152.

9. *Supra*, pp. 27–28.

10. E. Westermarck, *The Origin and Development of the Moral Ideas*, 2d ed. (London: Macmillan, 1912), vol. 1, p. 83. See A.C. Ewing, *The Morality of Punishment* (London: Kegan Paul, Trench, Trubner & Co., 1929), p. 53. For an attempt at a (partial) defense of utilitarianism on this point, see F.W. Maitland, "The Relation of Punishment to Temptation," *Mind* 5 (1880).

11. Cf. *supra*, p. 23. This rationale of excusing the mentally ill is not consistent with Bentham's claim that would-be offenders always calculate the desirable and undesirable effects of what they consider doing, and that even the insane do so (*supra*, p. 21).

12. Cf. H.L.A. Hart, *Punishment and Responsibility* (Oxford: Oxford University Press, 1973), pp. 19–20, 40–44; O.S. Walker, "Why Should Irresponsible Offenders Be Excused?," *Journal of Philosophy* 66 (1969), p. 280; J.J.C. Smart, "Utilitarianism and Criminal Justice," *Bulletin of the Australian Society of Legal Philosophy* (Special Issue, 1981), 12–14.

13. Cf. D.F. Thomson, "Retribution and the Distribution of Punishment," *Philosophical Quarterly* 16 (1966), p. 59.

14. Cf. H.L.A. Hart, *Punishment and Responsibility*, pp. 20–21.

15. T.L.S. Sprigge, "A Utilitarian Reply to Dr. McCloskey," in M.D. Bayles (ed.), *Contemporary Utilitarianism* (Garden City, N.Y.: Doubleday, 1968), pp. 290–291.

16. H.J. McCloskey, "A Non-Utilitarian Approach to Punishment," in Bayles, *Contemporary Utilitarianism*, p. 252.

17. J. Bentham, *Theory of Legislation*, p. 345.

18. *Supra*, p. 23.

19. I. Kant, "The Metaphysics of Morals," *Kant's Political Writings*, ed. H. Reiss, trans. H.B. Nisbet (Cambridge: Cambridge University Press, 1970), p. 155.

20. See *supra*, pp. 28–29.

21. J. Bentham, *Principles of Penal Law*, p. 398.

22. See *supra*, pp. 24–26.

23. Cf. H.J. McCloskey, "Non-Utilitarian Approach," p. 250.

24. T.L.S. Sprigge, "Utilitarian Reply," p. 275; cf. pp. 272–276, 278–282.

25. H.J. McCloskey, "Non-Utilitarian Approach," p. 247.

26. A. Donagan, "Is There a Credible Form of Utilitarianism?," in Bayles, *Contemporary Utilitarianism*, pp. 188–189.

27. T.L.S. Sprigge, "Utilitarian Reply," pp. 274–275.

28. K. Nielsen, "Against Moral Conservativism," *Ethics* 82 (1971/2), pp. 226–227.

29. See R. Conquest, *The Great Terror: Stalin's Purge of the Thirties* (Harmondsworth: Penguin, 1971), pp. 179–191.

30. V.I. Lenin, "The Tasks of the Youth Leagues," in R.C. Tucker (ed.), *The Lenin Anthology* (New York: W.W. Norton, 1975), pp. 668–669.

31. L. Trotsky, "Moralists and Sycophants against Marxism," in L. Trotsky, J. Dewey and G. Novack, *Their Morals and Ours: Marxist versus Liberal Views on*

Morality, 5th ed. (New York: Pathfinder Press, 1973), p. 65.
32. L. Trotsky, *Terrorism and Communism: A Reply to Karl Kautsky* (Ann Arbor: University of Michigan Press, 1963), p. 63.
33. Cf. A. Solzhenitsyn, *The Gulag Archipelago*, trans. T.P. Whitney (London: Fontana/Collins, 1974), vol. 1, pp. 282–283, 308.
34. Ibid., pp. 100–101.
35. Ibid., p. 100.
36. Quoted ibid., pp. 307–308.
37. Striking examples of this line of argument can be found in A. Koestler's *Darkness at Noon*, a philosophical novel inspired by the Moscow trials. See A. Koestler, *Darkness at Noon*, trans. D. Hardy (London: Longmans, 1968), pp. 125–127, 156, 189–191.
38. H.L.A. Hart, *Punishment and Responsibility*, pp. 5–6.
39. S.I. Benn, "An Approach to the Problems of Punishment," *Philosophy* 33 (1958), p. 332.
40. T. Hobbes, *Leviathan*, ed. M. Oakeshott (Oxford: Basil Blackwell, n.d.), p. 207.
41. I. Kant, *The Doctrine of Virtue*, trans. M.J. Gregor (Philadelphia: University of Pennsylvania Press, 1964), p. 166; "The Metaphysics of Morals," p. 155.
42. Cf. H.J. McCloskey, "The Complexity of the Concepts of Punishment," *Philosophy* 37 (1962), pp. 316–325; "A Non-Utilitarian Approach to Punishment," pp. 244–245.
43. See A.M. Quinton, "On Punishment," in Acton, *Philosophy of Punishment*, pp. 59–61.
44. See *supra*, p. 3. *Cf.* K.E. Baier, "Is Punishment Retributive?," in Acton, *Philosophy of Punishment*; T.S. Champlin, "Punishment without Offence," *American Philosophical Quarterly* 13 (1976); A.C. Ewing, "Armstrong on the Retributive Theory," *Mind* 72 (1963), pp. 121–122; D. Locke, "The Many Faces of Punishment," ibid., pp. 568–569; S. Gendin, "The Meaning of 'Punishment'," *Philosophy and Phenomenological Research* 28 (1967/8), p. 235.
45. This possibility also poses certain moral questions; see A. Wertheimer, "Punishing the Innocent — Unintentionally," *Inquiry* 20 (1977).
46. Cf. J. Rawls, "Two Concepts of Rules," in J.J. Thomson and G. Dworkin (eds.), *Ethics* (New York: Harper & Row), 1968, pp. 110–111; K.G. Armstrong, "Retributivist Hits Back," pp. 153–154, 158; T. Honderich, *Punishment: The Supposed Justifications*, rev.ed. (Harmondsworth: Penguin, 1976), pp. 62–64.
47. D. Dennet (ed.), *The Philosophical Lexicon*, 8th ed. (Newark: American Philosophical Association, 1987), p. 14.
48. A. Donagan, "Credible Form," p. 198.
49. G.E.M. Anscombe, "Modern Moral Philosophy," in Thomson and Dworkin, *Ethics*, pp. 206–207.
50. G. Schedler, *Behavior Modification and "Punishment" of the Innocent: Towards a Justification of the Institution of Legal Punishment* (Amsterdam: B.R. Grüner, 1977), pp. 11–20, 73–99.
51. Ibid., p. 15.
52. F.H. Bradley, "The Vulgar Notion of Responsibility in Connexion with the Theories of Free-Will and Necessity," *Ethical Studies*, 2d ed. (London: Oxford University Press, 1962), pp. 28–31.

53. F.C. Sharp and M.C. Otto, "A Study of the Popular Attitude towards Retributive Punishment," *International Journal of Ethics* 20 (1909/10); "Retribution and Deterrence in the Moral Judgments of Common Sense," ibid.

54. F.C. Sharp and M.C. Otto, "Retribution and Deterrence in the Moral Judgments of Common Sense," p. 444.

55. J.J.C. Smart, *An Outline of a System of Utilitarian Ethics* (Parkville: Melbourne University Press, 1961), pp. 40–41. Cf. J.J.C. Smart, *Ethics and Science*, University of Tasmania Occasional Paper 30 (Hobart: University of Tasmania, 1981), pp. 13–17.

56. Cf. J.J.C. Smart, *An Outline of a System of Utilitarian Ethics*, p. 19. This was pointed out by Smart's critic R.T. Garner in "Some Remarks on Act Utilitarianism," *Mind* 78 (1969), pp. 125–126.

57. See J. Rawls, *A Theory of Justice* (Cambridge, Mass.: Belknap Press, 1981), pp. 19–21, 46–51; N. Daniels, "Wide Reflective Equilibrium and Theory Acceptance in Ethics," *Journal of Philosophy* 75 (1979); W. Sadurski, *Giving Desert Its Due* (Dordrecht: D. Reidel, 1985), pp. 64–76.

58. J.J.C. Smart, "The Methods of Ethics and the Methods of Science," *Journal of Philosophy* 62 (1965), pp. 347–348.

59. See John 11. 47–53.

60. Cf. T.L.S. Sprigge, "Utilitarian Reply," pp. 267, 269–270.

61. I. Kant, "The Metaphysics of Morals," p. 159.

62. W.D. Ross, *The Right and the Good* (Oxford: Oxford University Press, 1967), p. 61. Cf. H.J. McCloskey, "A Non-Utilitarian Approach to Punishment," pp. 243, 256–257; "Utilitarian and Retributive Punishment," *Journal of Philosophy* 64 (1967), pp. 91–93, 96–97.

63. N. Hartmann, *Ethics*, trans. S. Coit (London: George Allen & Unwin, 1932), vol. 2, pp. 284–285.

64. Cf. *infra*, pp.149–154.

65. J.J.C. Smart, *An Outline of a System of Utilitarian Ethics*, p. 35.

66. H. Sidgwick, *The Methods of Ethics*, 7th ed. (London: Macmillan, 1967), p. 489.

67. Ibid., p. 490.

68. S. Bok, *Secrets: On the Ethics of Concealment and Revelation* (New York: Vintage Books), 1984, p. 112.

69. A.M. Quinton, "On Punishment," p. 56.

70. For more on these subjects see I. Primoratz, "Lying and the 'Methods of Ethics'," *International Studies in Philosophy* 16 (1984); A.M.S. Piper, "Utilitarianism, Publicity, and Manipulation," *Ethics* 88 (1977/8); D. Locke, "Why the Utilitarians Shot President Kennedy," *Analysis* 36 (1975/6).

71. On this see, e.g., R.L. Lippke, "Why Persons Are the Ground of Rights (and Utility Isn't)," *Journal of Value Inquiry* 18 (1984).

72. J.J.C. Smart, *Outline*, p. 26.

73. See J. Rawls, *Theory of Justice*, pp. 22–33, 187–190.

Chapter 4. Punishment as Retribution: Hegel

1. G.W.F. Hegel, *Philosophy of Right*, trans. T.M. Knox (Oxford: Oxford University Press, 1965), p. 23.

2. Ibid., p. 20.
3. Ibid., p. 227.
4. G.W.F. Hegel, *Philosophische Propädeutik, Sämtliche Werke*, ed. H. Glockner (Stuttgart: Fr. Frommann Verlag, 1961), vol. 3, p. 55.
5. G.W.F. Hegel, *Philosophy of Right*, p. 38.
6. Ibid., pp. 15, 241.
7. Ibid., p. 134.
8. G.W.F. Hegel, *Philosophische Propädeutik*, p. 57.
9. Ibid., p. 56.
10. Plato, *Crito*, 49c (Jowett).
11. Plato, *The Republic*, 335e (D. Lee).
12. Matthew 5. 39–41 (R.S.V.).
13. G.W.F. Hegel, *Vorlesungen über die Rechtsphilosophie, 1818–1831*, ed. K.-H. Ilting (Stuttgart: Frommann-Holzboog, 1973–74), vol. 1, p. 274; 3, p. 319.
14. W. Moberly, *The Ethics of Punishment* (London: Faber & Faber, 1968), pp. 80–81.
15. G.W.F. Hegel, *Philosophy of Right*, p. 247.
16. G.W.F. Hegel, *Philosophische Propädeutik*, p. 218; *Philosophy of Right*, p. 73.
17. G.W.F. Hegel, *Vorlesungen über die Rechtsphilosophie, 1818–1831*, vol. 4, p. 556.
18. G.W.F. Hegel, *Philosophy of Right*, p. 246.
19. G.W.F. Hegel, *Science of Logic*, trans. W.H. Johnston and L.G. Struthers (London: George Allen & Unwin, 1929), vol. 2, p. 24.
20. G.W.F. Hegel, *Philosophy of Mind*, trans. W. Wallace and A.V. Miller (Oxford: Oxford University Press, 1971), p. 163.
21. G.W.F. Hegel, *Science of Logic*, vol. 1, p. 119. (Johnston and Struthers translate *aufheben* as "transcend.")
22. G.W.F. Hegel, *Philosophy of Right*, p. 244. In connection with the "annulment" thesis see also *infra*, pp. 149–154.
23. G.W.F. Hegel, *Philosophy of Right*, p. 274.
24. Ibid., p. 294.
25. Ibid., p. 87.
26. Ibid., p. 38–39.
27. G.W.F. Hegel, *Philosophische Propädeutik*, p. 47.
28. Ibid., p. 57.
29. W.H. Walsh, *Hegelian Ethics* (London: Macmillan, 1969), p. 68.
30. *Supra*, pp. 34–35.
31. J.-J. Rousseau, *The Social Contract*, pt. 1, ch. 7; C. Beccaria, *On Crimes and Punishments*, ch. 2.
32. G.W.F. Hegel, *Vorlesungen über die Rechtsphilosophie, 1818–1831*, vol. 3, pp. 316–317.
33. Ibid., vol. 3, pp. 318–319.
34. Ibid., vol. 4, p. 289.
35. O.K. Flechtheim, *Hegels Strafrechtstheorie*, 2d ed. (Berlin: Duncker & Humblot, 1975), p. 102.
36. G.W.F. Hegel, *Early Theological Writings*, trans. T.M. Knox and R. Kroner (Philadelphia: University of Pennsylvania Press, 1971), pp. 226, 229–230, 238.
37. G.W.F. Hegel, *Philosophy of Right*, p. 141.

38. See *infra*, pp. 86–87.
39. G.W.F. Hegel, *Philosophy of Right*, p. 72.
40. Ibid.
41. G.W.F. Hegel, *Vorlesungen über die Rechtsphilosophie, 1818–1831*, vol. 4, p. 293.
42. G.W.F. Hegel, *Philosophy of Right*, p. 137.

Chapter 5. Arguments Against the Retributive Theory

1. J. Popper-Lynkeus, *Philosophie des Strafrechts*, ed. M. Ornstein (Wien: R. Löwit, 1924), pp. 12, 18, 26.
2. Plato, *Crito*, 49c (Jowett).
3. I. Kant, *The Doctrine of Virtue*, trans. M.J. Gregor (Philadelphia: University of Pennsylvania Press, 1964), pp. 129–130; G.W.F. Hegel, *Philosophy of Right*, trans. T.M. Knox (Oxford: Oxford University Press, 1965), p. 247.
4. On this see, e.g., M. Elkins, *Forged in Fury* (New York: Ballantine Books, 1971).
5. K.G. Armstrong, "The Retributivist Hits Back," in H.B. Acton (ed.), *The Philosophy of Punishment* (London: Macmillan, 1969), p. 157.
6. Cf. *supra*, p. 4.
7. I. Kant, *Doctrine of Virtue*, p. 130.
8. G.W.F. Hegel, *Philosophy of Right*, p. 73.
9. Exodus 21. 23–25 (R.S.V.).
10. W. Blackstone, *Commentaries on the Laws of England*, 4th ed., ed. J. Dewitt Andrews (Chicago: Callaghan & Co., 1899), p. 1223.
11. Cf. *supra*, pp. 80–81.
12. T.H. Green, *Lectures on the Principles of Political Obligation* (London: Longmans, 1966), p. 191.
13. A.C. Ewing, *The Morality of Punishment* (London: Kegan Paul, Trench, Trubner & Co., 1929), pp. 39–40.
14. Cf. F.H. Bradley, "The Vulgar Notion of Responsibility in Connexion with the Theories of Free-Will and Necessity," *Ethical Studies*, 2d ed. (London: Oxford University Press, 1962), pp. 26–27; B. Bosanquet, *The Philosophical Theory of the State*, 4th ed. (London: Macmillan, 1965), p. 212.
15. Cf. A.C. Ewing, *Morality of Punishment*, p. 41.
16. Genesis 34.
17. Leviticus 24. 17, 19–21.
18. *Baba Kamma* 84a, trans. E.W. Kirzner, ed. I. Epstein, rev. M. Ginsberg, Hebrew-English edition of the Babylonian Talmud (London: Soncino Press), 1964.
19. I. Kant, "The Metaphysics of Morals." *Kant's Political Writings*, ed. H. Reiss, trans. H.B. Nisbet (Cambridge: Cambridge University Press, 1970), p. 155.
20. Ibid., pp. 155–156.
21. *Supra*, pp. 80–81.
22. G.W.F. Hegel, *Philosophy of Right*, pp. 71–72.
23. J.G. Murphy, *Retribution, Justice, and Therapy* (Dordrecht: D. Reidel, 1979), pp. 85–86; cf. C.W.K. Mundle, "Punishment and Desert," in Acton, *Philosophy of Punishment*, pp. 71–73.

24. I discuss capital punishment separately in some detail in chapter 8.

25. H.L.A. Hart, *Punishment and Responsibility* (Oxford: Oxford University Press, 1973), pp. 15, 24.

26. For a somewhat different, detailed and highly interesting account of the *lex talionis*, see M. Davis, "How to Make the Punishment Fit the Crime," *Ethics* 93 (1982/3).

27. S.I. Benn, "An Approach to the Problems of Punishment," *Philosophy* 33 (1958), p. 336.

28. H.J. McCloskey, "A Non-Utilitarian Approach to Punishment," in M.D. Bayles (ed.), *Contemporary Utilitarianism* (Garden City, N.Y.: Doubleday, 1968), pp. 257–258.

29. M.H. Mitias, "Is Retributivism Inconsistent without *Lex Talionis?*," *Rivista Internazionale di Filosofia del Diritto* 60 (1983).

30. G.W.F. Hegel, *Philosophy of Right*, pp. 274, 140.

31. A.M. Rose and A.E. Prell, "Does the Punishment Fit the Crime? A Study in Social Valuation," *American Journal of Sociology* 61 (1955).

32. P.H. Rossi, E. Waite, C.E. Bose and R.E. Berk, "The Seriousness of Crimes: Normative Structure and Individual Differences," *American Sociological Review* 39 (1974), p. 237.

33. G.W.F. Hegel, *Philosophy of Right*, p. 72.

34. Cf. *supra*, p. 81.

35. K. Marx, "Capital Punishment," in K. Marx and F. Engels, *Basic Writings*, ed. L.S. Feuer (London: Fontana/Collins, 1971), p. 525.

36. *Supra*, pp. 12–13.

37. A. Camus, "Reflections on the Guillotine," *Resistance, Rebellion and Death*, trans. J. O'Brien (London: Hamish Hamilton, 1961), p. 147.

38. See P.F. Strawson, "Freedom and Resentment," *Freedom and Resentment and Other Essays* (London: Methuen, 1976).

39. See *supra*, pp. 91–92.

40. See J.G. Murphy, *Retribution*, pp. 102–110.

41. *Supra*, p. 79.

42. A.M. Quinton, "On Punishment," in Acton, *Philosophy of Punishment*, p. 57.

43. T. Honderich, *Punishment: The Supposed Justifications*, rev. ed. (Harmondsworth: Penguin, 1976), p. 47.

44. G.W.F. Hegel, *Philosophy of Right*, p. 70.

45. Cf. ibid., p. 88; *Vorlesungen über die Rechtsphilosophie, 1818–1831*, ed. K.-H. Ilting (Stuttgart: Frommann-Holzboog, 1973–74), vol. 1, pp. 276–277; 3, p. 670.

46. *Supra*, pp. 75–79.

47. P.G. Stillman, "Hegel's Idea of Punishment," *Journal of the History of Philosophy* 14 (1976), p. 174, n. 11.

48. It seems to me that only one among the formulations Stillman cites (G.W.F. Hegel, *Philosophy of Mind*, trans. W. Wallace and A.V. Miller [Oxford: Oxford University Press, 1971], pp. 242–243) could give some support to his reading of Hegel.

49. G.W.F. Hegel, *Philosophy of Right*, pp. 109–110.

50. J. McTaggart Ellis McTaggart, "Punishment," *Studies in Hegelian Cosmology* (Cambridge: Cambridge University Press, 1901), pp. 132–133.

51. Ibid., p. 133.

52. Ibid., pp. 133–134.
53. Cf. ibid., pp. 134–144.
54. Cf. W.B. Wines, "On Hegel's Idea of the Nature and Sanction of Law," *Journal of Speculative Philosophy* 18 (1884), pp. 13–14, 19–20; B. Blanshard, "Retribution Revisited," in E.H. Madden, R.N. Handy and M. Farber (eds.), *Philosophical Perspectives on Punishment* (Springfield: Charles C. Thomas, 1968), pp. 72–74; G.R.G. Mure, *The Philosophy of Hegel* (Oxford: Oxford University Press, 1965), pp. 166–167.
55. McTaggart, *Hegelian Cosmology*, p. 140.
56. Cf. ibid., pp. 145–150.
57. *Supra*, p. 79.
58. G.W.F. Hegel, *Philosophy of Right*, p. 67; *Vorlesungen über die Rechtsphilosophie, 1818–1831*, vol. 3, p. 295; 4, pp. 273–274.
59. *Supra*, pp. 75–76.
60. I. Kant, "Metaphysics of Morals," p. 158.
61. B. Bosanquet, *Theory of the State*, pp. 210–211.
62. The classic critique is that by L.T. Hobhouse, *The Metaphysical Theory of the State* (London: George Allen & Unwin, 1960).
63. W.M. McGovern, *From Luther to Hitler: The History of Fascist-Nazi Political Philosophy* (Cambridge, Mass.: Houghton Mifflin, 1941), p. 303.
64. See *supra*, pp. 76–78.
65. S.I. Benn, "Problems of Punishment," p. 329.
66. W.F.R. Macartney, *Walls Have Mouths*, p. 165; quoted in J.D. Mabbott, "Punishment," in Acton, *Philosophy of Punishment*, pp. 45–46.
67. G.W.F. Hegel, *Vorlesungen über die Rechtsphilosophie, 1818–1831*, vol. 1, p. 276.
68. Cf. *infra*, pp. 151–152.
69. On verbal condemnation see *infra*, pp. 152–153.

The proposal that the institution of punishment as we know it be dismantled and replaced by a system of restitution the offender is made to pay to the victim has been motivated by reservations about retribution, the belief that punishment as a means of preventing offenses does not work, and concern for the victim, who is said to be completely neglected as things are. The most elaborate formulation of this proposal in recent philosophical literature is the paper by R.E. Barnett, "Restitution: A New Paradigm of Criminal Justice," *Ethics* 87 (1976/7).

The obvious objection that a system of restitution will not be very efficient in preventing offenses, for the well-off will see the compensation exacted from them as a price of indulging themselves they can afford to pay, is dismissed by Barnett as irrelevant, for "our goal is not the suppression of crime; it is doing justice to victims" (p. 296). If justice is the point, however, the program fails on its own terms. As one of Barnett's critics has pointed out, the whole proposal is predicated upon a misconception of a criminal offense:

> What, really, does the wealthy criminal care about having to compensate his victim? Or the wealthy victim about receiving compensation? If a rich man rapes a rich woman, are we really to suppose that monetary damages will restore the status quo, will satisfy the claims of justice? . . . The reduction of

criminal wrongs to civil wrongs . . . bespeaks an all too primitive view of what in fact is at issue in the matter of crime. . . . The civil remedy by itself is altogether inadequate in the case of criminal acts. For the element missing from the mere tort but present in the criminal act is the guilty mind. The criminal has not simply harmed you. *He has affronted your dignity.* He has *intentionally* used you, against your will, for his own ends. He cannot simply pay damages as though his action were accidental or unintentional. How would this right the wrong? . . . How would compensation make the victim whole again? For compensation does not reach the whole of what is involved — it does not reach the *mens rea* element. There is simply no amount of money that will rectify certain kinds of wrongs.

(R. Pilon, "Criminal Remedies: Restitution, Punishment, or Both?," *Ethics* 88 [1977/8], pp. 351–352.)

70. For the main varieties of the therapeutic alternative to punishment, see K. Menninger, *The Crime of Punishment* (New York: Viking Press, 1966); B.F. Skinner, *Science and Human Behavior* (New York: Macmillan, 1953).

71. C.S. Lewis, "The Humanitarian Theory of Punishment," in W. Sellars and J. Hospers (eds.), *Readings in Ethical Theory*, 2d ed. (New York: Appleton-Century-Crofts, 1970), p. 649. For critical discussions of therapy as an alternative to punishment, see C.S. Lewis, "Humanitarian Theory of Punishment"; A. Flew, *Crime or Disease?* (London: Macmillan, 1973); G. Schedler, *Behavior Modification and "Punishment" of the Innocent: Towards a Justification of the Institution of Legal Punishment* (Amsterdam: B.R. Grüner, 1977).

72. In this connection, see, e.g., M. Lader, *Psychiatry on Trial* (Harmondsworth: Penguin, 1977); S. Bloch and P. Reddaway, *Russia's Political Hospitals: The Abuse of Psychiatry in the Soviet Union* (London: Victor Gollancz, 1977).

73. *Supra*, pp. 37–41, 43–45.

74. Cf. *supra*, pp. 34–35.

75. Cf. *infra*, p. 145.

For somewhat different accounts of the right to punishment, see W.A. Miller, "Mr. Quinton on 'an Odd Sort of Right'," *Philosophy* 41 (1966); H. Morris, "Persons and Punishment," *The Monist*, 52 (1968); D.A. Hoekema, "The Right to Punish and the Right to Be Punished," in H.G. Blocker and E.H. Smith (eds.), *John Rawls' Theory of Social Justice* (Athens: Ohio University Press, 1980). See further M.R. Gardner, "The Right to Be Punished — A Suggested Constitutional Theory," *Rutgers Law Review* 33 (1980/1); J. Deigh, "On the Right to Be Punished: Some Doubts," *Ethics* 94 (1983/4).

76. B. Blanshard, "Retribution Revisited," pp. 77–78.

77. I. Kant, "Metaphysics of Morals," p. 160.

78. I. Kant, "Perpetual Peace," *Kant's Political Writings*, p. 123.

79. B. Blanshard, "Retribution Revisited," pp. 77–78.

80. I. Kant, "On a Supposed Right to Lie from Altruistic Motives," *Critique of Practical Reason and Other Writings in Moral Philosophy*, trans. and ed. L. W. Beck (Chicago: University of Chicago Press), 1950.

81. *Pace* B. Blanshard ("Retribution Revisited," p. 77), who says that a retributivist must consistently uphold the Kantian view of the duty to punish according

to justice and desert as an absolute one, allowing for no mitigation and no exception, but provides no argument in support of this claim.

82. Cf. *supra*, p. 60.
83. A.C. Ewing, *Morality of Punishment*, p. 43.
84. G.W.F. Hegel, *Philosophy of Right*, p. 87.
85. Cf. H.J. McCloskey, "Approach to Punishment," pp. 255–257; A. Smart, "Mercy," in Acton, *Philosophy of Punishment*, pp. 221–227.
86. Cf. *supra*, pp. 36–37.

Chapter 6. The Middle Way

1. Plato, *Protagoras*, 324ab (W.K.C. Guthrie).
2. E. Westermarck, *The Origin and Development of the Moral Ideas*, 2d ed. (London: Macmillan, 1912), vol. 1, pp. 81–82.
3. A.M. Quinton, "On Punishment," in H.B. Acton (ed.), *The Philosophy of Punishment* (London: Macmillan, 1969), pp. 55–56.
4. Ibid., pp. 58–59.
5. Ibid., p. 62.
6. For a more detailed discussion of Quinton's argument see I. Primoratz, "Is Retributivism Analytic?," *Philosophy* 56 (1981).
7. See *supra*, pp. 51–54.
8. A.C. Ewing, "Punishment as a Moral Agency: An Attempt to Reconcile the Retributive and the Utilitarian View," *Mind* 36 (1927); *The Morality of Punishment* (London: Kegan Paul, Trench, Trubner & Co.), 1929.
9. A.C. Ewing, *The Morality of Punishment*, p. 105.
10. A.C. Ewing, "Punishment as a Moral Agency," p. 300.
11. Another important early formulation is S.I. Benn, "An Approach to the Problems of Punishment," *Philosophy* 33 (1958).
12. J. Rawls, "Two Concepts of Rules," in J.J. Thomson and G. Dworkin (eds.), *Ethics* (New York: Harper & Row, 1968), pp. 107–108.
13. For a classic statement of this concept of moral rules, see J.S. Mill, "Utilitarianism," *Essays on Ethics, Religion and Society*, ed. J.M. Robson, *Collected Works*, ed. F.E.L. Priestley et al., (Toronto: University of Toronto Press, 1969), vol. 10, pp. 224–225.
14. Cf. J. Rawls, "Two Concepts," pp. 121–126.
15. Cf. J.J.C. Smart, "Extreme and Restricted Utilitarianism," in Thomson and Dworkin, *Ethics* pp. 140–142; *An Outline of a System of Utilitarian Ethics* (Parkville: Melbourne University Press, 1961), pp. 29–31.
16. Cf. J. Rawls, "Two Concepts," pp. 126–131.
17. Cf. ibid., pp. 118–119, 128–129, 131, 133.
18. Cf. *supra*, pp. 51–54.
19. Cf. W. Lyons, "Deterrent Theory and Punishment of the Innocent," *Ethics* 84 (1973/4).
20. A. Flew, "The Justification of Punishment," in Acton, *Philosophy of Punishment*, p. 97.
21. J.D. Mabbott, "Professor Flew on Punishment," in Acton, *Philosophy of Punishment*, p. 128.

22. J.D. Mabbott, "Punishment," in Acton, *Philosophy of Punishment*, pp. 42–44; A. Flew, "Justification of Punishment," pp. 97–98; J.D. Mabbott, "Professor Flew on Punishment," pp. 128–129; H.J. McCloskey, "An Examination of Restricted Utilitarianism," in M.D. Bayles (ed.), *Contemporary Utilitarianism* (Garden City, N.Y.: Doubleday, 1968), pp. 125, 132–133.

23. H.J. McCloskey, "Restricted Utilitarianism," p. 125.

24. J.J.C. Smart, "Extreme and Restricted Utilitarianism," p. 143; cf. *An Outline of a System of Utilitarian Ethics*, p. 5.

25. J. Rawls, "Two Concepts," p. 113; cf. ibid., pp. 112–113.

26. Ibid., p. 113. For an analysis of the concept of "telishment," see G. Schedler, "On Telishing the Guilty," *Ethics* 86 (1975/6).

27. J. Rawls, "Two Concepts," p. 114.

28. Cf. T. Honderich, *Punishment: The Supposed Justifications*, rev. ed. (Harmondsworth: Penguin, 1976), pp. 64–65; H.J. McCloskey, "Restricted Utilitarianism," p. 124; J.J.C. Smart, *An Outline of a System of Utilitarian Ethics*, p. 5.

29. J. Rawls, "Two Concepts," pp. 113–114.

30. Ibid., p. 127.

31. *Supra*, pp. 43–44.

32. Cf. H.J. McCloskey, "Restricted Utilitarianism," pp. 127–129; "A Non-Utilitarian Approach to Punishment," in Bayles, *Contemporary Utilitarianism*, pp. 253–254; A. Donagan, "Is There a Credible Form of Utilitarianism?," ibid., pp. 196–198.

33. Cf. *supra*, pp. 49–51. For a less familiar example of an established system for "punishing" the innocent, justified by reasons of social utility, see G.B. Wall, "Cultural Perspectives on the Punishment of the Innocent," *Philosophical Forum* 2 (1970/1), pp. 492–495.

34. R.M. Hare, *Moral Thinking: Its Levels, Method and Point* (Oxford: Oxford University Press, 1981). The most important among the articles preceding the book and leading to it are "Ethical Theory and Utilitarianism," in H.D. Lewis (ed.), *Contemporary British Philosophy*, 4th series (London: George Allen & Unwin, 1976), and "Moral Conflicts," in S. McMurrin (ed.), *The Tanner Lectures on Human Values*, vol. 1 (Salt Lake City: University of Utah Press, 1980).

35. J. Griffin, "Modern Utilitarianism," *Revue Internationale de Philosophie* 36 (1982), pp. 353.

36. R.M. Hare, *Moral Thinking: Its Levels, Method and Point*, p. 45.

37. Ibid., p. 50.

38. Ibid., p. 45.

39. Ibid., pp. 162–163. See also R.M. Hare, "Punishment and Retributive Justice," *Philosophical Topics* 14 (1986), pp. 218–222.

40. See *supra*, pp. 45–51.

41. R.M. Hare, *Moral Thinking: Its Levels, Method and Point*, p. 164.

42. Ibid., p. 121; also pp. 117–118, 193.

43. Cf. J.J.C. Smart, "Extreme and Restricted Utilitarianism," pp. 149–150.

44. Cf. M. Walzer, "Political Action: The Problem of Dirty Hands," *Philosophy and Public Affairs* 2 (1972/3), pp. 171–174.

45. R.M. Hare, *Moral Thinking*, p. 34.

46. *Supra*, pp. 59–61.

47. H.L.A. Hart, *Punishment and Responsibility* (Oxford: Oxford University Press, 1973), p. 1.

48. *Supra*, pp. 118–128.

49. H.L.A. Hart, *Punishment and Responsibility*, p. 10.

50. Ibid., pp. 76, 77–78.

51. Cf. *supra*, pp. 23, 38–39.

52. See H.L.A. Hart, *Punishment and Responsibility*, pp. 242–244.

53. H.L.A. Hart, *Law, Liberty, and Morality* (London: Oxford University Press, 1971), pp. 36–37.

54. Cf. *supra*, pp. 27–28, 38.

55. K.G. Armstrong, "The Retributivist Hits Back," in Acton, *Philosophy of Punishment*, p. 141.

56. T. Honderich, *Punishment*, p. 151.

57. S. Gendin, "A Plausible Theory of Retribution," *Journal of Value Inquiry* 6 (1972), pp. 10–11.

58. R.A. Wasserstrom, "H.L.A. Hart and the Doctrine of *Mens Rea* and Criminal Responsibility," *University of Chicago Law Review* 35 (1967/8), p. 125.

59. M.A. Cattaneo, "La Retribuzione Penale nell'Interpretazione e nella Critica di Herbert L.A. Hart," *Materiali per una Storia della Cultura Giuridica* 4 (1974), p. 699.

60. *Supra*, pp. 37–38.

61. Cf. K.G. Armstrong, "Retributivist Hits Back," pp. 154, 157–158.

62. Cf. *supra*, p. 38.

63. Cf. R.A. Wasserstrom, "Hart and the Doctrine of *Mens Rea*," pp. 109–110.

64. Ibid., p. 111.

65. Cf. *supra*, pp. 28–29, 42–43.

66. This objection carries less weight than the previous two, for it could be met by introducing an appropriate constraint. This could be done, at the level of the theory of punishment, by adding a prohibition of staging shows of punishment (instead of actually inflicting it) to the retributive principles already contained in the theory. Alternatively, a principle that deception and manipulation of the public are inadmissible in general could be posited at a more fundamental level — that of social or moral philosophy. As it stands, however, Hart's theory of punishment is exposed to this criticism.

   For still another attempt at a middle-of-the-road theory of punishment, which sets out in a rather Hartian way but ends up as a view that is for all practical purposes indistinguishable from retributivism pure and simple, see D.E. Scheid, "Kant's Retributivism," *Ethics* 93 (1982/3); I. Primoratz, "On 'Partial Retributivism'," *Archiv für Rechts- und Sozialphilosophie* 71 (1985); D.E. Scheid, "Kant's Retributivism Again," ibid., 72 (1986).

Chapter 7. Retribution as a Positive Principle

1. Cf. *supra*, pp. 104–108. For an argument that the result of this kind of choice would be something like the rationale of punishment advanced by Hart, see D.A. Hoekema, "The Right to Punish and the Right to Be Punished," in H.G. Blocker and E.H. Smith (eds.), *John Rawls' Theory of Social Justice* (Athens: Ohio University Press), 1980.

2. J.L. Mackie ("Morality and the Retributive Emotions," *Criminal Justice Ethics* 1 [1982], p. 4) has introduced the terms "negative" and "positive retributivism" to mark this distinction.

3. H.L.A. Hart, *Punishment and Responsibility* (Oxford: Oxford University Press, 1973), pp. 232, 236–237.

4. See ibid., p. 75.

5. Ibid., pp. 9, 235.

6. H. Morris, "Persons and Punishment," *The Monist* 52 (1968), p. 478. Other statements of this variety of retributivism are J.G. Murphy, *Retribution, Justice, and Therapy* (Dordrecht: D. Reidel, 1979), pp. 77–78, 83–84, 100–101; J. Finnis, "The Restoration of Retribution," *Analysis* 32 (1971/2).

7. See R.A. Wasserstrom, "Punishment," *Philosophy and Social Issues* (Notre Dame: University of Notre Dame Press, 1980), pp. 142–146; R.W. Burgh, "Do the Guilty Deserve Punishment?," *Journal of Philosophy* 79 (1982), pp. 202–210.

8. For further discussion and an impressive attempt to develop a general theory of justice as an equilibrium of benefits and burdens, which includes an account of punishment along the same lines, see W. Sadurski, *Giving Desert Its Due* (Dordrecht: D. Reidel, 1985), in particular chs. 4, 8.

9. H.L.A. Hart, *Law, Liberty, and Morality* (London: Oxford University Press, 1971), p. 59.

10. The distinction between legal offenses which are also morally wrong (*mala in se*) and those which are intrinsically morally indifferent (*mala prohibita*) (see P. Devlin, *The Enforcement of Morals* [London: Oxford University Press, 1973], ch. 2, and H.L.A. Hart, *Punishment and Responsibility*, pp. 235–236) will not help here, for many offenses regarding which we may be willing initially to desist from punishment if it would be useless in terms of crime control belong to the first category.

11. H.L.A. Hart, *Punishment and Responsibility*, p. 235.

12. Cf., e.g., J. Feinberg, "The Expressive Function of Punishment," *Doing and Deserving* (Princeton: Princeton University Press, 1970).

13. J.F. Stephen, *A History of the Criminal Law of England* (London: Macmillan, 1883), vol. 2, p. 82.

14. J.F. Stephen, *A General View of the Criminal Law of England*, 2d ed. (London: Macmillan, 1890), p. 99.

15. E. Durkheim, *The Division of Labor in Society*, trans. G. Simpson (New York: Free Press, 1964), p. 108.

16. W. Moberly, *The Ethics of Punishment* (London: Faber & Faber, 1968).

17. See N. MacCormick, *H.L.A. Hart* (London: Edward Arnold, 1981), pp. 66, 136–137, 141–143.

18. H.L.A. Hart, *Law, Liberty, and Morality*, p. 65 (emphasis added).

19. Ibid., p. 66.

20. It is noted by Hart himself in *The Concept of Law* (Oxford: Oxford University Press, 1961), pp. 175–176; see also *Law, Liberty, and Morality*, pp. 76–77.

21. This, I believe, is the true import of Hegel's thesis that punishment "annuls" the offense (cf. *supra*, pp. 73–74). It has been criticized and even ridiculed as a pathetic demand to undo the past (cf. W. Moberly, "Some Ambiguities in the Retributive Theory of Punishment," *Proceedings of the Aristotelian Society* 25 (1924/5), p. 303; *The Ethics of Punishment*, Ch. 7), and interpreted

as a utilitarian claim wrapped up in obscure, nonutilitarian phraseology (cf. A.M. Quinton, "On Punishment," in H.B. Acton (ed.), *The Philosophy of Punishment* [London: Macmillan, 1969], p. 56). The interpretation suggested above seems to me to capture what Hegel wants to say, and to make the thesis both intelligible and convincing.

22. H.L.A. Hart, *Punishment and Responsibility*, p. 172.

Chapter 8. Capital Punishment

1. J.F. Stephen, "Capital Punishments," in L. Blom-Cooper and G. Drewry (eds.), *Law and Morality* (London: Duckworth, 1976), p. 51.

2. A. Koestler, *Reflections on Hanging* (London: Victor Gollancz, 1956), p. 58.

3. C. Beccaria, *On Crimes and Punishments*, trans. H. Paolucci (Indianapolis: Bobbs-Merrill, 1977), p. 47.

4. J. Bentham, *Principles of Penal Law*, *The Works of Jeremy Bentham*, ed. J. Bowring (New York: Russell & Russell, 1962), vol. 1, p. 445.

5. T. Sellin, "Capital Punishment," *Encyclopaedia Britannica*, 1965 ed., vol. 4, pp. 848–849.

6. See, e.g., the debate between E. van den Haag and H.A. Bedau in *Ethics* 78 (1967/8); 80 (1969/70); 81 (1970/1).

The most recent important attempt at showing that the death penalty does have the deterrent effects requisite for its utilitarian justification, the paper "The Deterrent Effect of Capital Punishment: A Question of Life and Death" by I. Ehrlich (*American Economic Review* 65 [1975]), also does not seem convincing; see, e.g., the exchange between Ehrlich and his critics in *Yale Law Journal* 85 (1975/6).

7. For an interesting attempt to show that the proper method for dealing with the issue of capital punishment is not that of social science but "the method of common sense," and that the application of this method leads to the conclusion that the death penalty *is* the most effective deterrent, see M. Davis, "Death, Deterrence, and the Method of Common Sense," *Social Theory and Practice* 7 (1981).

8. Cf. *supra*, pp. 85–94.

9. Numbers 35.31 (R.S.V.).

10. M. Greenberg, "Some Postulates of Biblical Criminal Law," in J. Goldin (ed.), *The Jewish Expression* (New York: Bantam, 1970), pp. 25–26. (Post-biblical Jewish law evolved toward the virtual abolition of the death penalty, but that is of no concern here.)

11. "There is no *parallel* between death and even the most miserable life, so that there is no equality of crime and retribution [in the case of murder] unless the perpetrator is judicially put to death" (I. Kant, "The Metaphysics of Morals," *Kant's Political Writings*, ed. H. Reiss, trans. H.B. Nisbet [Cambridge: Cambridge University Press, 1970], p. 156). "Since life is the full compass of a man's existence, the punishment [for murder] cannot simply consist in a 'value', for none is great enough, but can consist only in taking away a second life" (G.W.F. Hegel, *Philosophy of Right*, trans. T.M. Knox [Oxford: Oxford University Press, 1965], p. 247).

12. C. Beccaria, *Crimes and Punishments*, p. 45.

13. G.W.F. Hegel, *Philosophy of Right*, p. 71; see also *supra*, pp. 76–79.

14. For critical comments on my analysis and refutation of Beccaria's argument, developed in the paper on "Kant und Beccaria," *Kant-Studien* 69 (1978) and summarized here in the briefest way possible, see M.A. Cattaneo, *Beccaria e Kant. Il valore dell'uomo nel diritto penale* (Sassari: Università di Sassari, 1981), pp. 20–30.

15. For an example of this view, see L.N. Tolstoy, *Smertnaya kazn i hristianstvo* (Berlin: I.P. Ladizhnikov, n.d.), pp. 40–41.

16. S.V. Vulović, *Problem smrtne kazne* (Belgrade: Geca Kon, 1925), pp. 23–24.

17. Cf. W. Blackstone, *Commentaries on the Laws of England*, 4th ed., ed. J. DeWitt Andrews (Chicago: Callaghan & Co., 1899), p. 1224.

18. A. Camus, "Reflections on the Guillotine," *Resistance, Rebellion and Death*, trans. J. O'Brien (London: Hamish Hamilton, 1961), p. 143.

19. For an interesting critical discussion of this point, see M. Davis, "Is the Death Penalty Irrevocable?," *Social Theory and Practice* 10 (1984).

20. Quoted in E.R. Calvert, *Capital Punishment in the Twentieth Century* (London: G.P. Putnam's Sons, 1927), p. 132.

21. For a criticism of this argument, see L. Sebba, "On Capital Punishment — A Comment," *Israel Law Review* 17 (1982), pp. 392–395.

22. B.M. Leiser, *Liberty, Justice and Morals: Contemporary Value Conflicts* (New York: Macmillan, 1973), p. 225.

23. E.R. Calvert, *Capital Punishment*, p. 172.

24. For a good review of the relevant historical data, see A.F. Kistyakovsky, *Izsledovanie o smertnoy kazni*, 2d ed. (St. Petersburg: L.F. Panteleev, 1896), pp. 260–267.

25. See *supra*, pp. 55–56.

26. Cf. I. Kant, "Metaphysics of Morals," p. 157, and C. Beccaria, *Crimes and Punishments*, p. 50.

27. On the question whether the death penalty is cruel and unusual within the meaning of the Eighth Amendment, see M.J. Radin, "The Jurisprudence of Death: Evolving Standards for the Cruel and Unusual Clause," *University of Pennsylvania Law Review* 126 (1978); H.A. Bedau, "Thinking of the Death Penalty as a Cruel and Unusual Punishment," *U.C. Davis Law Review* 18 (1985).

Bibliography*

Anscombe, G.E.M. "Modern Moral Philosophy," In J.J. Thomson and G. Dworkin (eds.), *Ethics*, 186–210. New York: Harper & Row, 1968.

Armstrong, K.G. "The Retributivist Hits Back." In H.B. Acton (ed.), *The Philosophy of Punishment*, 138–158. London: Macmillan, 1969.

Baier, K.E. "Is Punishment Retributive?" In H.B. Acton (ed.), *The Philosophy of Punishment*, 130–137. London: Macmillan, 1969.

Barnett, R.E. "Restitution: A New Paradigm of Criminal Justice." *Ethics* 87 (1976/7): 279–301.

Beccaria, C. *On Crimes and Punishments*, trans. H. Paolucci. Indianapolis: Bobbs-Merrill, 1977.

Bedau, H.A. "Justice and Classical Utilitarianism." In C.J. Friedrich and J.W. Chapman (eds.), *Justice*, "Nomos" 6, 284–305. New York: Atherton Press, 1963.

Benn, S.I. "An Approach to the Problems of Punishment." *Philosophy* 33 (1958): 325–341.

Bentham, J. *An Introduction to the Principles of Morals and Legislation*, ed. W. Harrison. Oxford: Basil Blackwell, 1960.

_____. *Theory of Legislation*, 2d ed., trans. from the French of E. Dumont by R. Hildreth. London: Trübner, 1871.

_____. *Principles of Penal Law, The Works of Jeremy Bentham*, ed. J. Bowring, vol. 1. New York: Russell & Russell, 1962.

Blackstone, W. *Commentaries on the Laws of England*, 4th ed., ed. J. DeWitt Andrews. Chicago: Callaghan & Co., 1899.

Blanshard, B. "Retribution Revisited." In E.H. Madden, R. Handy and M. Farber (eds.), *Philosophical Perspectives on Punishment*, 59–81. Springfield: Charles C. Thomas, 1968.

Bosanquet, B. *The Philosophical Theory of the State*, 4th ed. London: Macmillan, 1965.

Bradley, F.H. "The Vulgar Notion of Responsibility in Connexion with the Theories of Free-Will and Necessity." *Ethical Studies*, 2d ed. London: Oxford University Press, 1962.

Burgh, R.W. "Do the Guilty Deserve Punishment?" *Journal of Philosophy* 79 (1982): 193–210.

Calvert, E.R. *Capital Punishment in the Twentieth Century*. London: G.P. Putnam's Sons, 1927.

_____

*Two important recent books, R.A. Duff's *Trials and Punishments* (Cambridge: Cambridge University Press, 1986) and C.L. Ten's *Crime, Guilt, and Punishment* (Oxford: Oxford University Press, 1987), were published too late for me to be able to make use of them in working on my own.

Camus, A. "Reflections on the Guillotine." *Resistance, Rebellion and Death*, trans. J. O'Brien. London: Hamish Hamilton, 1961.

Cattaneo, M.A. "La Retribuzione Penale nell'Interpretazione e nella Critica di Herbert L.A. Hart." *Materiali per una Storia della Cultura Giuridica* 4 (1974): 639–699.

Champlin, T.S. "Punishment without Offence." *American Philosophical Quarterly* 13 (1976): 85–87.

Conquest, R. *The Great Terror: Stalin's Purge of the Thirties*. Harmondsworth: Penguin, 1971.

Davis, M. "How to Make Punishment Fit the Crime." *Ethics* 93 (1982/3): 726–752.

_____. "Death, Deterrence, and the Method of Common Sense." *Social Theory and Practice* 7 (1981): 145–177.

_____. "Is the Death Penalty Irrevocable?" *Social Theory and Practice* 10 (1984): 143–156.

Deigh, J. "On the Right to Be Punished: Some Doubts." *Ethics* 94 (1983/4): 191–211.

Donagan, A. "Is There a Credible Form of Utilitarianism?" In M.D. Bayles (ed.), *Contemporary Utilitarianism*, 187–202. Garden City, N.Y.: Doubleday, 1968.

Doyle, J.F. "Justice and Legal Punishment." In H.B. Acton (ed.), *The Philosophy of Punishment*, 159–171. London: Macmillan, 1969.

Durkheim, E. *The Division of Labor in Society*, trans. G. Simpson. New York: The Free Press, 1964.

Ewing, A.C. "Punishment as a Moral Agency: An Attempt to Reconcile the Retributive and the Utilitarian View." *Mind* 36 (1927): 292–305.

_____. *The Morality of Punishment*. London: Kegan Paul, Trench, Trubner & Co., 1929.

_____. "Armstrong on the Retributive Theory." *Mind* 72 (1963): 121–124.

Feinberg, J. "The Expressive Function of Punishment," *Doing and Deserving*. Princeton: Princeton University Press, 1970.

Finnis, J. "The Restoration of Retribution." *Analysis* 32 (1971/2): 131–135.

Flechtheim, O.K. *Hegels Strafrechtstheorie*, 2d ed. Berlin: Duncker & Humblot, 1975.

Flew, A. "The Justification of Punishment." In H.B. Acton (ed.), *The Philosophy of Punishment*, 83–104. London: Macmillan, 1969.

_____. *Crime or Disease?* London: Macmillan, 1973.

Gardner, M.R. "The Right to Be Punished — A Suggested Constitutional Theory." *Rutgers Law Review* 33 (1980/1): 838–864.

Garner, R.T. "Some Remarks on Act Utilitarianism." *Mind* 78 (1969): 124–128.

Gendin, S. "The Meaning of 'Punishment'." *Philosophy and Phenomenological Research* 28 (1967/8): 235–240.

_____. "A Plausible Theory of Retribution." *Journal of Value Inquiry* 6 (1972): 1–16.

Green, T.H. *Lectures on the Principles of Political Obligation*. London: Longmans, 1966.

Greenberg, M. "Some Postulates of Biblical Criminal Law." In J. Goldin (ed.), *The Jewish Expression*, 18–37. New York: Bantam, 1970.

Hare, R.M. *Moral Thinking: Its Levels, Method and Point*. Oxford: Oxford University Press, 1981.

_____. "Punishment and Retributive Justice." *Philosophical Topics* 14 (1986): 211–223.

Hart, H.L.A. *The Concept of Law*. Oxford: Oxford University Press, 1961.

_____. *Punishment and Responsibility*. Oxford: Oxford University Press, 1973.

_____. *The Morality of the Criminal Law*. Jerusalem: Magnes Press, 1964.

_____. *Law, Liberty, and Morality*. London: Oxford University Press, 1971.

Hegel, G.W.F. *Philosophy of Right*. Trans. T.M. Knox. Oxford: Oxford University Press, 1965.

_____. *Vorlesungen über die Rechtsphilosophie, 1818–1831*. ed. K.-H.Ilting, 4 Vols. Stuttgart: Frommann-Holzboog, 1973–74.

_____. *Philosophische Propädeutik, Sämtliche Werke*. ed. H. Glockner, Vol. 3. Stuttgart: Fr. Frommann Verlag, 1961.

_____. "The Spirit of Christianity and Its Fate." *Early Theological Writings*, trans. T.M. Knox and R. Kroner. Philadelphia: University of Pennsylvania Press, 1971.

Hobbes, T. *Leviathan*, ed. M. Oakeshott. Oxford: Basil Blackwell, n.d.

Hoekema, D.A. "The Right to Punish and the Right to Be Punished." In H.G. Blocker and E.H. Smith (eds.), *John Rawls' Theory of Social Justice*, 239–269. Athens: Ohio University Press, 1980.

Honderich, T. *Punishment: The Supposed Justifications*, rev. ed. Harmondsworth: Penguin, 1976.

Kant, I. "The Metaphysics of Morals," *Kant's Political Writings*, ed. H. Reiss, trans. H.B. Nisbet. Cambridge: Cambridge University Press, 1970.

_____. *The Doctrine of Virtue*, trans. M.J. Gregor. Philadelphia: University of Pennsylvania Press, 1964.

Kistyakovsky, A.F. *Izsledovanie o smertnoy kazni*, 2d ed., St. Petersburg: L.F. Panteleev, 1896.

Koestler, A. *Reflections on Hanging*. London: Victor Gollancz, 1956.

_____. *Darkness at Noon*, trans. D. Hardy. London: Longmans, 1968.

Leiser, B.M. *Liberty, Justice and Morals: Contemporary Value Conflicts*. New York: Macmillan, 1973.

Lenin, V.I. "The Tasks of the Youth Leagues." In R.C. Tucker (ed.), *The Lenin Anthology*. New York: W.W. Norton, 1975.

Lewis, C.S. "The Humanitarian Theory of Punishment." In W. Sellars and J. Hospers (eds.), *Readings in Ethical Theory*, 2d ed., 646–650. New York: Appleton-Century-Crofts, 1970.

Locke, D. "The Many Faces of Punishment." *Mind* 72 (1963): 568–572.

Lyons, W. "Deterrent Theory and Punishment of the Innocent." *Ethics* 84 (1973/4): 346–348.

Mabbott, J.D. "Punishment." In H.B. Acton (ed.), *The Philosophy of Punishment*, 39–54. London: Macmillan, 1969.

_____. "Professor Flew on Punishment." In H.B. Acton (ed.), *The Philosophy of Punishment*, 115–129. London: Macmillan, 1969.

Mackie, J.L. "Morality and the Retributive Emotions." *Criminal Justice Ethics* 1 (1982): 3–10.

MacCormick, N. *H.L.A.Hart*. London: Edward Arnold, 1981.

Maitland, F.W. "The Relation of Punishment to Temptation." *Mind* 5 (1880): 259–264.

Marx, K. "Capital Punishment." In K. Marx and F. Engels, *Basic Writings*, ed. L.S. Feuer, 485–489. London: Fontana/Collins, 1971.

McCloskey, H.J. "The Complexity of the Concepts of Punishment." *Philosophy* 37 (1962): 307–325.

_____. "An Examination of Restricted Utilitarianism." In M.D. Bayles (ed.), *Contemporary Utilitarianism*, 117–142. Garden City, N.Y.: Doubleday, 1968.

_____. "A Non-Utilitarian Approach to Punishment." In M.D. Bayles (ed.), *Contemporary Utilitarianism*, 239–259. Garden City, N.Y.: Doubleday, 1968.

_____. "A Note on Utilitarian Punishment." *Mind* 72 (1963): 599.

_____. "Utilitarian and Retributive Punishment." *Journal of Philosophy* 64 (1967): 91–110.

McTaggart Ellis McTaggart, J. "Punishment", *Studies in Hegelian Cosmology*. Cambridge: Cambridge University Press, 1901.

Menninger, K. *The Crime of Punishment*. New York: Viking Press, 1966.

Miller, W.A. "Mr. Quinton on 'an Odd Sort of Right'." *Philosophy* 41 (1966): 258–260.

Mitias, M.H. "Another Look at Hegel's Concept of Punishment." *Hegel-Studien* 13 (1978): 175–185.

_____. "Is Retributivism Inconsistent Without *Lex Talionis*?" *Rivista Internazionale di Filosofia del Diritto* 60 (1983): 211–230.

Moberly, W. "Some Ambiguities in the Retributive Theory of Punishment." *Proceedings of the Aristotelian Society* 25 (1924/5): 289–304.

_____. *The Ethics of Punishment*. London: Faber & Faber, 1968.

Morawetz, T. "Comment." In R. Gavison (ed.), *Issues in Contemporary Legal Philosophy: The Influence of H.L.A. Hart*, 221–237. Oxford: Oxford University Press, 1987.

Morris, H. "Persons and Punishment." *The Monist* 52 (1968): 475–501.

Mundle, C.W.K. "Punishment and Desert", in H.B. Acton (ed.), *The Philosophy of Punishment*, 65–82. London: Macmillan, 1969.

Murphy, J.G. *Retribution, Justice, and Therapy*. Dordrecht: D. Reidel, 1979.

Nielsen, K. "Against Moral Conservativism." *Ethics*, 82 (1971/2): 219–231.

Pilon, R. "Criminal Remedies: Restitution, Punishment, or Both?" *Ethics* 88 (1977/8): 348–357.

Popper-Lynkeus, J. *Philosophie des Strafrechts*, ed. M. Ornstein. Wien: R. Löwit, 1924.

Primoratz, I. "Utilitarianism and Self-Sacrifice of the Innocent." *Analysis* 38 (1978): 194–199.

_____. "Kant und Beccaria." *Kant-Studien* 69 (1978): 403–421.

_____. "On Some Arguments against the Retributive Theory of Punishment." *Rivista Internazionale di Filosofia del Diritto* 56 (1979): 43–60.

_____. "Utilitarianism and Punishment of the Innocent." *Rivista Internazionale di Filosofia del Diritto* 57 (1980): 582–625.

_____. "Punishment as the Criminal's Right." *Hegel-Studien* 15 (1980): 187–198.

_____. "Is Retributivism Analytic?" *Philosophy* 56 (1981): 203–211.

_____. "Utilitarianism and Punishment." *International Philosophical Quarterly* 22 (1982): 241–254.

_____. "Life for Life: Arguments against Capital Punishment." *Philosophical Studies* 29 (1982/3): 186–201.

_____. "On Capital Punishment." *Israel Law Review*, 17 (1982): 133–150.

_____. "On Retributivism and the *lex talionis*." *Rivista Internazionale di Filosofia del Diritto* 61 (1984): 83–94.

_____. "On 'Partial Retributivism'." *Archiv für Rechts- und Sozialphilosophie* 71 (1985): 373–377.

_____. "The Judge as a Prole: Hare's 'Two-Level Theory' and the Problem of Punishment." *Archiv für Rechts- und Sozialphilosophie* 74 (1988): 93–101.

_____. *Banquos Geist. Hegels Theorie der Strafe.* Hegel-Studien, Beiheft 29. Bonn: Bouvier Verlag Herbert Grundmann, 1986.

_____. "The Middle Way in the Philosophy of Punishment." In R. Gavison (ed.), *Issues in Contemporary Legal Philosophy: The Influence of H.L.A. Hart*, 193–220. Oxford: Oxford University Press, 1987.

Quinton, A.M. "On Punishment." In H.B. Acton (ed.), *The Philosophy of Punishment*, 55–64. London: Macmillan, 1969.

Rawls, J. "Two Concepts of Rules." In J.J. Thomson and G. Dworkin (eds.), *Ethics*, 104–135. New York: Harper & Row, 1968.

_____. *A Theory of Justice.* Cambridge, Mass.: Belknap Press, 1971.

Ross, W.D. *The Right and the Good.* Oxford: Oxford University Press, 1967.

Sadurski, W. *Giving Desert Its Due.* Dordrecht: D. Reidel, 1985.

Schedler, G. "On Telishing the Guilty." *Ethics* 86 (1975/6): 256–260.

_____. *Behavior Modification and "Punishment" of the Innocent: Towards a Justification of the Institution of Legal Punishment*, Amsterdam: B.R. Grüner, 1977.

Scheid, D.E. "Kant's Retributivism." *Ethics* 93 (1982/3): 262–282.

_____. "Kant's Retributivism Again." *Archiv für Rechts- und Sozialphilosophie* 72 (1986): 224–230.

Sebba, L. "On Capital Punishment — A Comment." *Israel Law Review* 17 (1982): 391–398.

Sharp F.C. and M.C. Otto. "A Study of the Popular Attitude towards Retributive Punishment." *International Journal of Ethics* 20 (1909/10): 341–357.

_____. "Retribution and Deterrence in the Moral Judgments of Common Sense." *International Journal of Ethics* 20 (1909/10): 438–453.

Sidgwick, H. *The Methods of Ethics*, 7th ed. London: Macmillan, 1967.

Skinner, B.F. *Science and Human Behavior.* New York: Macmillan, 1953.

Smart, A. "Mercy." In H.B. Acton (ed.), *The Philosophy of Punishment*, 212–227. London: Macmillan, 1969.

Smart, J.J.C. "Extreme and Restricted Utilitarianism." In J.J. Thomson and G. Dworkin (eds.), *Ethics*, 136–150. New York: Harper & Row.

_____. *An Outline of a System of Utilitarian Ethics.* Parkville: Melbourne University Press, 1961.

_____. "Utilitarianism and Criminal Justice." *Bulletin of the Australian Society of Legal Philosophy* (Special Issue 1981): 1–19.

_____. "The Methods of Ethics and the Methods of Science." *Journal of Philosophy* 62 (1965): 344–348.

_____. *Ethics and Science*. University of Tasmania Occasional Paper 30. Hobart: University of Tasmania, 1981.

Solzhenitsyn, A. *The Gulag Archipelago*, vol. 1, trans. T.P. Whitney. London: Fontana/Collins, 1974.

Sprigge, T.L.S. "A Utilitarian Reply to Dr. McCloskey." in M.D. Bayles (ed.), *Contemporary Utilitarianism*, 261–299. Garden City, N.Y.: Doubleday 1968.

Stephen, J.F. *A History of the Criminal Law of England*. London: Macmillan, 1883.

_____. *A General View of the Criminal Law of England*, 2d ed. London: Macmillan, 1890.

_____. "Capital Punishments." In L. Blom-Cooper and G. Drewry (eds.), *Law and Morality*, 51–53. London: Duckworth, 1976.

Stillman, P.G. "Hegel's Idea of Punishment." *Journal of the History of Philosophy* 14 (1976): 169–182.

Thompson, D.F. "Retribution and the Distribution of Punishment." *Philosophical Quarterly* 16 (1966): 59–63.

Tolstoy, L.N. *Smertnaya kazn i hristianstvo*. Berlin: I.P. Ladizhnikov, n.d.

Trotsky, L., J. Dewey and G. Novack, *Their Morals and Ours: Marxist versus Liberal Views on Morality*, 5th ed. New York: Pathfinder Press, 1973.

Vulović, S.V. *Problem smrtne kazne*. Belgrade: Geca Kon, 1925.

Walker, O.S. "Why Should Irresponsible Offenders Be Excused?" *Journal of Philosophy* 66 (1969): 279–290.

Wall, G.B. "Cultural Perspectives on the Punishment of the Innocent." *Philosophical Forum* 2 (1970/1): 489–499.

Wasserstrom, R.A. "Punishment," *Philosophy and Social Issues*. Notre Dame: University of Notre Dame Press, 1980.

_____. "H.L.A. Hart and the Doctrines of *Mens Rea* and Criminal Responsibility." *University of Chicago Law Review* 35 (1967/8): 92–126.

Wertheimer, A. "Punishing the Innocent — Unintentionally." *Inquiry* 20 (1977): 45–65.

Westermarck, E. *The Origin and Development of the Moral Ideas*, 2d ed., vol. 1. London: Macmillan, 1912.

Wines, W.B. "On Hegel's Idea of the Nature and Sanction of Law." *Journal of Speculative Philosophy* 18 (1884): 9–20.

Index

193